Logics of Hierarchy

LOGICS OF HIERARCHY

The Organization of Empires, States, and Military Occupations

Alexander Cooley

CORNELL UNIVERSITY PRESS

ITHACA AND LONDON

First published 2005 by Cornell University Press

Printed in the United States of America

Library of Congress Cataloging-in-Publication Data
Cooley, Alexander, 1972-
Logics of hierarchy : the organization of empires, states, and military occupations / Alexander Cooley.
p. cm.
Includes bibliographical references and index.
ISBN-13: 978-0-8014-4386-2 (cloth : alk. paper)
ISBN-10: 0-8014-4386-5
1. International relations. 2. Comparative organization. 3. Comparative government.
4. Imperialism. 5. Military occupation. I. Title.
JZ1310.C663 2005
302.3'5—dc22
2005013204

Cornell University Press strives to use environmentally responsible suppliers and materials to the fullest extent possible in the publishing of its books. Such materials include vegetable-based, low-VOC inks and acid-free papers that are recycled, totally chlorine-free, or partly composed of nonwood fibers. For further information, visit our website at www.cornellpress.cornell.edu.

Cloth printing   10   9   8   7   6   5   4   3   2   1

For John Kent Cooley

Contents

FIGURES AND TABLES

PREFACE

Although the study of hierarchy is making something of a comeback in the public sphere, as can be seen in a renewed interest with imperialism in world politics, its importance as an academic topic is still fraught with controversy. My research interest in the dynamics of empires and military occupations, in how hierarchical polities are organized and governed, has culminated in this book. But so too has the critical commentary I have received at academic seminars and conferences from colleagues who have questioned my seemingly dispassionate approach to these politically charged phenomena. I have repeatedly heard comments such as "What is the political purpose of such an investigation?" or "Why would you want to approach the study of empire in this calculating manner?" This book provides answers to such questions.

Above all, this book is motivated by widespread misconceptions about hierarchy in both the academy and the "real" policy world. For some reason, we have been taught—especially in the field of international relations—that hierarchical polities are relatively functional, ordered, and well-governed entities. In most classes and textbooks, political hierarchy is contrasted with the condition of "anarchy," or the absence of a central governing authority, and students are dutifully instructed to note that the self-interest of individual states usually trumps any rudimentary mechanisms of international organization or world governance. Not surprisingly, from such an analytical starting point the dynamics of hierarchy do not seem as intriguing as the origins of war and peace, the interaction of international markets and states, or the role of NGOs and new contemporary challenges to the sovereign authority of states.

Moreover, even when we do address the issue of hierarchy in international politics, we tend to spend very little time on its problematic nature: the types of control losses and authority slippages in hierarchical organizations and why the mere imposition of hierarchical governance does not always lead to the outcomes predicted by a dominant power. In truth, we have a caricatured understanding of the politics of hierarchy.

Such misconceptions are not limited just to academic discussions. The most recent U.S. military campaign in Iraq was predicated on the belief that the mere imposition of governance by an external power would automatically transform a political system, culture, and identity. Many believed that Iraqi democracy would be built "naturally" in the wake of Saddam Hussein's discredited and brutal regime. Yet the daily stream of gruesome images from post-Baathist Iraq suggests that American hierarchical rule has not been sufficient for maintaining political order or promoting institutional transformation in Iraq. Why not?

It is time to reexamine just how hierarchical political organizations such as states, empires, and military occupations operate and how they actually govern political peripheries. We must explicitly identify the different ways in which hierarchies are organized and explore what types of hierarchical organization are likely to lead to significant institutional transformation in a periphery and what types are likely to fail. The analytical tools required for such an investigation are readily available in the social sciences, yet they have yet to be brought to bear on the topic.

This book has been a long, drawn-out project. Hendrik Spruyt, Jack Snyder, Lisa Anderson, Rajan Menon, and Alexander Motyl—some of the most extraordinary scholars and public thinkers I know—gave me initial support and subsequent feedback that allowed this project to evolve beyond my original expectations. In addition, I am particularly grateful for the invaluable insights and help of peers and colleagues over the years, including Fiona Adamson, Karen Ballentine, Thomas Berger, Padma Desai, Daniel Deudney, Jonathan Hopkin, Patrick Jackson, Robert Jervis, Robert Legvold, Kimberly Marten, Martha Merill, Daniel Nexon, Jeffry Olson, James Ron, Adam Sheingate, Peter Sinnott, Robin Varghese, and Thomas Wood. Special thanks go to my colleagues at Barnard College, Columbia University's Harriman Institute, and Columbia's Department of Political Science for all their support over the years, as well as to the Social Science Research Council for a Title VIII fellowship during the 1997–98 academic year. Publication of this book was made possible, in part, with a grant from the Harriman

Institute. Stephanie Boyum read several versions of this manuscript in its infancy and provided extraordinarily helpful guidance, while Adelle Tilebalieva provided excellent research assistance. The external reviewers and editors at Cornell University Press were true partners in shaping the manuscript and improving the quality of the work. Jack Snyder and James Ron encouraged me to apply the theoretical schema to Yugoslavia, although they are in no way responsible for the case's shortcomings. But my greatest appreciation is reserved for Mark Blyth, who has seen this project evolve over the course of our long and immensely rewarding friendship.

Books are, no doubt, most difficult for those unlucky enough to be around the author. I am thankful to my parents—Eugenia and John Kent Cooley—for their incredible support over these years as well as to my friends and relatives in the United States, Greece, and elsewhere for tolerating my rants. Above all, I thank my life love Nicole Jacoby for showing the patience of a saint and always encouraging me to make headway on the project, even when it involved real sacrifices on her part. She is truly incomparable.

Finally, I thank my two greatest mentors, without whom I would have never entered this business. The first is James Kurth (now Emeritus) of Swarthmore College. All those lucky enough to have been introduced to the world of international politics by him would agree that he is a brilliant, eloquent, and profoundly influential teacher. The second is John Kent Cooley, my father, an insightful political correspondent, fearless critic, and seasoned observer of world affairs for many years. This book is dedicated to him.

Alexander Cooley
New York, New York

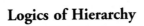

Logics of Hierarchy

UNDERSTANDING HIERARCHY IN

INTERNATIONAL POLITICS

A central motivation of the United States in its 2003 invasion of Iraq was to topple the regime of Saddam Hussein and fundamentally change the domestic political institutions and political culture of an oil-rich Middle Eastern country. Proponents of the campaign argued that American military power could and should be wielded in order to promote democratization, speculating that a "free" Iraq would serve as an important model of political transformation for the surrounding region. Summarizing this view, on November 6, 2003, United States President George W. Bush declared that American foreign policy, as embodied by events in Iraq, had adopted a "forward strategy for freedom."[1]

Although the overall military and strategic goals of the Iraq campaign were relatively clear (if controversial), the mechanisms through which the reconstruction and transformation of Iraq took place were not. Politicians and analysts of various political leanings criticized the American occupation of 2003–4 as disorganized, piecemeal, and lacking an overall strategy. The initial decision by the Pentagon-appointed Coalition Provisional Authority (CPA) to disband the old Baathist-operated institutions of the Iraqi state, most notably the Iraqi military, clashed with the practical requirements of stabilizing the country and establishing political order. The original plan to convene a national convention to draft a new Iraqi Constitution was postponed when it became clear

---

1. Dana Milbank and Mike Allen, "Bush Urges Commitment to Transform Mideast," *Washington Post,* November 7, 2003, A1.

that Iraq's ethnic and religious differences, not new political parties or Western political ideologies, endured as the basis for political affiliation. Dozens of American companies were assigned major reconstruction contracts amidst criticisms of noncompetitive bidding, cronyism and overcharging, but their overall project coordination was mismanaged and their exact relationship with the interim ministries and government agencies remained ill-defined. Throughout all of these political difficulties, the security situation in pockets of the country destabilized to the point where a permanent insurgency, not Coalition forces, controlled several cities. As the American occupation revealed, successful reconstruction was a far more challenging task than most policymakers had anticipated before the start of the military campaign.

From a historical perspective, the optimistic prewar assumptions of U.S. policymakers about governing Iraq were hardly atypical. Rulers of expanding states, empires, and military occupations consistently have assumed that the mere imposition of hierarchical rule would allow them to transform a periphery's domestic institutions according to their national values, ideologies, and preferences. Such ambitious plans to enact dramatic and fundamental change were often compromised by the practical realities of governance. Whether we look at imperial Japan's attempt to transform Manchuria (Manchukuo) into a neighboring utopia, Soviet efforts to transform the very social fabric and identities of its Eurasian satellites, France's campaign to impose its civilizing values in Western Africa, or current American efforts to promote its supposedly more enlightened and progressive form of empire at the beginning of the twenty-first century, successful instances of institutional transformation have been rare.

Although such organizational issues often lie at the heart of understanding the political governance of states, empires, and occupations, we rarely address them as objects of analysis or formulate empirical investigations around them. Scholars of empire and hierarchy, much like policymakers, often place excessive emphasis on the ideology or identity of a particular polity and ignore the common organizational issues and dilemmas that confront all hierarchical polities. What types of hierarchical organization are more likely to promote institutional change in a periphery, and what types will entrench preexisting political and social structures? What kinds of institutions do various types of hierarchical rule and governance mechanisms create within a periphery? When will actors entrusted with formal governing authority complete the tasks they are assigned as opposed to acting opportunistically in their own self-interest or colluding with peripheral actors? In short, how can we better understand the causal effects of hierarchical organization on the institutional formation and development of governed polities?

A LESSON FROM MANAGEMENT STUDIES: THE IMPORTANCE OF ORGANIZATIONAL FORMS

Political analysts rarely address questions about hierarchical organization, yet these same issues are the explicit focus of management scholars concerned with understanding the organizational properties and trade-offs associated with various types of economic organization. Management scholars examine the mechanisms and incentive structures through which hierarchical governance within corporations is exercised and the powerful causal effects they exert. Variation in the organization of firms accounts for important differences in firm behavior as well as the behavior of individual actors within them.

Perhaps the most widely recounted anecdote about the importance of corporate organization is the comparison of the contrasting interwar era fortunes of the American auto-manufacturing giants Ford Motor Company and General Motors. Both companies managed a number of divisional lines and products and both were making the transition from wartime production to producing commercial vehicles. Yet, during the 1920s and 1930s, General Motors grew at almost an exponential rate while Ford remained mired in a productivity slump and internal fighting.

In his pioneering study of the organizational evolution of the American firm, business historian Alfred Chandler advanced a simple explanation for the contrasting fortunes of these corporate giants.[2] The variation in corporate performance, he argued, was explained not by standard variables such as product quality or capital investments but by how each firm organized its production lines and administrative divisions. In the case of Ford, executive management retained its prewar unitary form of organization, in which subordinate divisions were divided according to function. Accordingly, each division—such as finance, marketing or engineering—was responsible for its particular functional responsibilities across all of the different cars and products the company produced. Chandler observed that this functional structure created severe inefficiencies by encouraging infighting and fierce

2. See Alfred D. Chandler Jr., *Strategy and Structure: Chapters in the History of the American Industrial Enterprise* (Cambridge: MIT Press, 1969).

competition among the divisions concerning the overall strategic decisions of the firm. Each division advanced its own preferences regarding the company's overall strategy and goals, thereby equating its own divisional interests with those of the firm. In the meantime, a weak core executive allowed this interdivisional conflict to persist, believing it could consolidate the core's wavering authority by arbitrating these factional disputes and brokering compromises among the self-interested divisions.[3] Like a weak monarch clinging to power by playing his various subordinates and councilors against one another, the central management office at Ford became embroiled in an organizational mess that crippled its ability to effectively govern.

The dysfunctional organization of Ford contrasted sharply with the contemporaneous organizational revolution initiated by Alfred Sloan at General Motors. Sloan's innovative reorganization eliminated the previous functional structure of the corporation and replaced it with a set of semiautonomous divisions, organized by geographic area and product. Under this new "multidivisional" structure, the executive core was freed from making routine everyday decisions and took on the primary responsibilities of setting general strategic goals and monitoring the performance of its various divisions. The reorganization proved so successful that by the onset of World War II, General Motors increased its market share from 12 percent to 50 percent, successfully diversified its product line and, like a dynamic empire, even expanded operations to overseas subsidiaries.[4] This form of corporate organization endured well into the postwar era.

Chandler's analysis of the contrasting fortunes of the organizationally dysfunctional Ford with the dynamic General Motors is still used to instruct students of business administration in the importance of form and structure in economic organizations. Is there a comparable lesson here for political analysts? If variation in hierarchical organization can have such profound effects on the incentive structures, behavior, and performance of corporate entities, should we not expect it also to have a significant causal impact on the structure and institution-building capacities of political entities?

An Organizational Theory of Political Hierarchy

This book uses these basic insights of management scholarship to develop a new organizational approach to the study of hierarchy in inter-

3. Gary Miller, *Managerial Dilemmas: The Political Economy of Hierarchy* (New York: Cambridge University Press, 1994), 98–100.

4. Chandler, *Strategy and Structure*, 373–74.

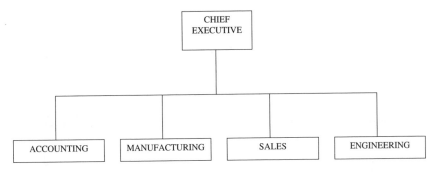

FIGURE 1.1
The Unitary Form (U-form) adapted from Oliver Williamson, *Markets and Hierarchies* (New York: Free Press, 1975), 134

national politics. I define hierarchy as a condition of relational power in which a dominant polity "possesses the right to make residual decisions while the other party—the subordinate member—lacks this right."[5] Drawing on the organizational distinctions developed by Alfred Chandler and, later, economist Oliver Williamson, I argue that hierarchies can be governed as either a unitary form (U-form) or a multidivisional form (M-form).[6] The U-form organizes its periphery according to distinct administrative functions (such as sales, manufacturing, and finance), which require integration and coordination by the center for the whole range of products produced by the firm (fig. 1.1). By contrast, the M-form governs its subordinate divisions according to product or geography, as each division is relatively autonomous and encapsulates a wide range of functions so that it can successfully produce its particular product (fig. 1.2). This distinction between functional governance and territorial governance is the central insight of the "firm-type model" outlined in this book.

Each of these forms of hierarchy represents a distinct type of political organization studied by political scientists. U-forms of political organization are associated most often with state-formation and functional modes of integration and political consolidation while M-forms characterize most types of modern imperial organization and overseas military occupations. In still other cases, polities such as socialist federations

5. This is the definition used by David Lake. See Lake, "Anarchy, Hierarchy and the Variety of International Relations," *International Organization* 50 (1996): 7.
6. In particular, see Oliver Williamson, *The Economic Institutions of Capitalism* (New York: Free Press, 1985); and Williamson, *Markets and Hierarchies: Analysis and Antitrust Implications* (New York: Free Press, 1975).

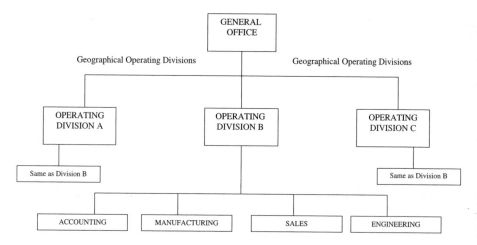

FIGURE 1.2
The Multidivisional Form (M-form) adapted from Oliver Williamson, *Markets and Hierarchies* (New York: Free Press, 1975), 138

(Soviet Union, Yugoslavia) have employed both modes of organization across different sectors of governance. Conceptualizing political governance in terms of U-forms and M-forms provides a common set of conceptual tools to examine the political dynamics of what are usually assumed to be disparate polities.

In terms of their causal governance effects, the U-form and M-form create varying types of political institutions in their peripheries— harmonizing institutions in U-forms and patrimonial institutions in M-forms—and encourage different forms of opportunism within their administration. Consequently, their organizational capacity to promote institutional change within a given periphery will also vary. Across a range of conceptual and practical issues relating to political governance, differences in organizational form will account for important variations in political behavior. This book develops a theory of organizational forms and political hierarchy and advances a number of testable propositions and insights regarding its conceptual and practical applications.

METHODOLOGICAL ASSUMPTIONS: COMPARING ECONOMIC AND POLITICAL ORGANIZATION

Drawing on a body of work originating in a different discipline, in this case managerial studies and organizational economics, inevitably begs the question of whether the analogy is apt and whether the economic and political spheres are actually comparable. In employing the firm-type model, I do not wish to imply that states, empires, and other polities ultimately share the same goals or values that a firm would have in a market setting. Obviously, as organizational entities, firms are driven by the overriding need to maximize profits within the competitive setting of the market. While states also face competitive pressures for survival within the international system, they pursue a number of additional goals and objectives. Nor in making the analogy to the organization of firms do I mean to imply that such analogies should be the only or "correct" way that scholars should think about the politics of hierarchy. Organizational theory is but one of a number of approaches that can be applied to the subject.

Rather, what is important for this project is that both economic firms and political hierarchies are forms of complex social organization that, when organized, administered, or delegated according to similar logics, will face common problems and challenges related to these logics. By applying the firm-type model to political settings, one can better understand how individual administrators, regardless of their exact functions or task assignments, will behave when faced with similar organizational pressures and imperatives. Accordingly, not only do functional and territorial hierarchical governance exhibit similarities across both economic and political contexts, but the logic of the argument should hold for a broad range of functions and issues that are managed by political organizations, including both security and economic affairs.

Finally, in presenting this study, I do not make any normative judgments regarding the merits or desirability of hierarchy over other types of political organization. The sad fact remains that, historically, a wide variety of political organizations—including states, empires, and military occupations—have been responsible for inflicting a tremendous amount of human suffering for their respective political causes. Studying the organization of these political hierarchies does not condone them any more than studying a particular political party would associate the analyst with that party's platform. But just as we should not necessarily take the word of a party elite as to how her organization operates internally, so too we should be skeptical of the governing ideologies and publicly stated claims of rulers of hierarchical polities. Whatever the officially stated purpose of a particular state or empire, in-depth study of its actual organization is necessary to accurately explain its political dynamics.

The Contributions of an Organizational Theory of Hierarchy

This organizational theory of international hierarchy is consistent with recent efforts in international relations to study vertical integration as a central political process in international politics. Drawing on a related literature in the economics of organization or the "new institutionalism," such institutional approaches have typically tried to determine the conditions under which states, in both the international economy and the security sphere, prefer to enter hierarchical governance arrangements instead of more traditional forms of statecraft.[7] Such approaches also fundamentally differ from more traditional approaches to international politics and international organization that focus on variables such as relative power distribution and identity-based processes and explore only limited certain instances of hierarchy, such as the behavior of hegemonic states or the dynamics of particular empires. In general, existing theories do not examine how the organization of hierarchy can, as a causal variable, independently affect the governance and behavior of political actors.

The organizational theory developed here offers both theoretical and practical contributions. Theoretically, employing an organizational approach to hierarchy allows us to unify the study of previously disparate political phenomena and engage with critical methodological issues in the social sciences, especially the relative merits of rationalist and social constructivist approaches. Practically, the firm-type theory offers important predictive power about the patterns of institutional formation under hierarchy and their organizational legacies.

Establishing and Unifying the Study of Hierarchy

First, the firm-type theory can both clarify and unify the study of hierarchy in international politics. Given that international hierarchy traverses many seemingly disparate topics usually studied in different

---

7. On institutional theories of hierarchy and security, see David Lake, *Entangling Relations: American Foreign Policy in Its Century* (Princeton: Princeton University Press, 1999); and Katja Weber, *Hierarchy amidst Anarchy: Transaction Costs and Institutional Choice* (Albany: State University of New York Press, 2000). On hierarchy and modern state formation, see Hendrik Spruyt, *The Sovereign State and Its Competitors* (Princeton: Princeton University Press, 1994). For applications to the international political economy, see Jeffry Frieden, "International Investment and Colonial Control: A New Interpretation," *International Organization* 48 (1994): 559–94; and Beth V. Yarbrough and Robert M. Yarbrough, *Cooperation and Governance in International Trade: The Strategic Organizational Approach* (Princeton: Princeton University Press, 1992).

subfields, the study of hierarchy has yet to emerge as an independent subject with its own robust literature. Traditionally, the study of international hierarchy has been split between the subfields of "comparative politics"—the study of political processes and institutions within countries—and that of international relations—the study of political relations between states and other international actors.[8] While comparativists usually study comparative state formation, totalitarian states, the colonial state apparatus, secessionism, and the organizational of multinational states, international relations theorists study topics such as international hegemony, imperial expansion, international monetary unions, and military occupations.[9] Not surprisingly, both comparativists and international relations theorists have studied the organization of empires and imperial rule, although often from very different analytical vantage points.[10]

Unfortunately, rigid adherence to these traditional subfield divisions has also prevented investigation of important connections among various empirical processes and real-world puzzles as they relate to hierarchical governance. Consequently, the common organizational processes and institutional problems identified by individual scholars have not been mutually recognized as part of the broader organizational problems inherent in the governance of transnational political entities. For example, ensuring that the administrators of peripheral polities faithfully execute the goals of the center was as much an enduring challenge for central authorities in communist multinational states as it was

8. By contrast, the subfield of American politics has developed a robust literature on the organization of institutions, delegation, and hierarchical processes. For an overview, see David Epstein and Sharyn O'Halloran, *Delegating Powers: A Transaction Costs Politics Approach to Policy Making under Separate Powers* (New York: Cambridge University Press, 1999).

9. On institutions and governance in communist multinational states, see Valerie Bunce, *Subversive Institutions: The Design and the Destruction of Socialism and the State* (New York: Cambridge University Press, 1999); and David Laitin, *Identity in Formation: The Russian-Speaking Populations in the Near Abroad* (Ithaca: Cornell University Press, 1998). On colonial governance, see Crawford Young, *The African Colonial State in Comparative Perspective* (New Haven: Yale University Press, 1994). On international hegemony, see G. John Ikenberry, *After Victory: Institutions, Strategic Restraint, and the Rebuilding of Order after Major Wars* (Princeton: Princeton University Press, 2001). On military occupation, see Peter Liberman, *Does Conquest Pay? The Exploitation of Occupied Industrial Societies* (Princeton: Princeton University Press, 1996). On monetary arrangements, see Benjamin Cohen, *The Future of Money* (Princeton: Princeton University Press, 2004).

10. For varied examples, see Hendrik Spruyt, *Ending Empire* (Ithaca: Cornell University Press, 2005); Niall Ferguson, *Empire: The Rise and Demise of the British World Order and Lessons for Global Power* (New York: Basic, 2003); Dominic Lieven, *Empire: The Russian Empire and Its Rivals* (New Haven: Yale University Press, 2001); David B. Abernethy, *The Dynamics of Global Dominance: European Overseas Empires 1415–1980* (New Haven: Yale University Press, 2000); Alexander Motyl, *Imperial Ends: The Decay, Collapse, and Revival of Empires* (New York: Columbia University Press, 2000); and Michael Doyle, *Empires* (Ithaca: Cornell University Press, 1986).

for modern imperial metropoles when dealing with their colonial governors. Even though central authorities in states and empires often adopted similar strategies for controlling their administrators, such as rotating administrators or periodically sending special envoys to monitor their loyalty to the center, the common organizational logic of these strategies has been ignored.

In sum, the firm-type model aids identification of a set of political processes and organizational forms that, to date, have remained separate and allows a more systematic study of empirical connections by introducing a common vocabulary and set of analytical concepts.

Contribution to the Social Sciences: The Rationalist-Constructivist Debate Revisited

The firm-type theory of hierarchy developed also seeks to make a theoretical contribution to the broader ongoing debate in the social sciences between rationalists and social constructivists. Rationalists believe that social behavior can be explained as a function of the cost-benefit analyses individuals make so as to instrumentally pursue their preestablished preferences while social constructivists maintain that social and ideational factors generate the meanings, motivations, and identities of actors in a manner that cannot be assumed a priori.[11] In the study of international politics, social constructivists tend to equate rationalism with materialism and argue that material factors, alone, are insufficient explanatory motives for the choices and actions of political actors.[12] Although constructivists are certainly correct to argue the importance of nonmaterial determinants of human behavior, they incorrectly assume that sociological approaches are the best suited or most effective means of explaining these factors.

The firm-type theory suggests that there are, indeed, strong rationalist logics and bases for behavior that can become deeply embedded in

---

11. This literature is vast. On rationality, see Jon Elster, ed., *Rational Choice* (Oxford: Blackwell, 1986). On social constructivism, see Peter L. Berger and Thomas Luckmann, *The Social Construction of Reality* (Garden City, N.Y.: Anchor Books, 1966). For a critical assessment of rational choice approaches in political science, see Donald Green and Ian Shapiro, *Pathologies of Rational Choice: A Critique of Applications in Political Science* (New Haven: Yale University Press, 1996). For contrasting views on rationality in the study of international politics, see Stephen Walt, "Rigor or Rigor Mortis: Rational Choice and Security Studies," *International Security* 23 (1999): 5–48; and Helen Milner, "Rationalizing Politics: The Emerging Synthesis of International, American, and Comparative Politics," *International Organization* 52 (1998): 759–86.

12. See, especially, Alexander Wendt, *Social Theory of International Politics* (New York: Cambridge University Press, 1999).

nonmaterial settings. There is nothing "material" about organizing a firm or polity according to functional or territorial principles, yet, once adopted, these different hierarchical forms tend to structure the behavior of administrators logically and predictably and do so across varying cultural, historical, and geographical settings. Moreover, by exploring how common pathologies arise out of similar types of organizational design, the firm-type model suggests that not all informal rules or behaviors require formal sociological reasoning or an understanding of actors' identities. Rejecting purely materialist approaches does not invalidate alternative rationalist approaches.

Second, the firm-type model seeks to highlight how rationalist logics and incentive structures tend to encourage similar behavior across many nominally different types of polities and political orders. A key claim of recent constructivist scholarship is that political orders, especially hierarchies such as empires and states, cannot be understood without reference to the prevailing norms, ideas, and self-understandings that sustain these orders.[13] Social constructivists generally dismiss rationalist attempts to generalize about the formation and governance of institutions. For example, Rodney Bruce Hall argues that political identities impart meaning and legitimacy to prevailing modes of political organization. He asserts that the authority of each type of these political forms derives from social factors that necessarily differ across polities: "this authority is constructed from the prevailing collective self-identifications and self-understandings, and from the principles that legitimate these. Importantly, these institutional forms are not fundamental. They are not theoretically or ontologically primitive. They are not enduring. These forms change with the prevailing conceptions of legitimate social order and with the collective identities consistent with this order."[14]

The claim here, then, is that different "self-identifications" and "self-understandings" should account for clear and observable variation in political behavior across different types of hierarchical units and that political forms have no inherent qualities or identifiable characteristics

13. For recent indicative works, see Mlada Bukovansky, *Legitimacy and Power Politics: The American and French Revolutions in International Political Culture* (Princeton: Princeton University Press, 2002); Daniel Philpott, *Revolutions in Sovereignty: How Ideas Shaped Modern International Relations* (Princeton: Princeton University Press, 2001); and Christian Reus-Smit, *The Moral Purpose of the State: Culture, Social Identity, and Institutional Rationality in International Relations* (Princeton: Princeton University Press, 1999).

14. Rodney Bruce Hall, *National Collective Identity: Social Constructs and International Systems* (New York: Columbia University Press, 1999), 44.

when they are divorced from their social contexts. Indeed, it is almost an accepted wisdom that the identities and purpose of polities such as states or empires must be understood in detail in order to appreciate their political dynamics.

The problem with such reasoning is that by defining every political actor, polity, or institution as distinct or unique, social constructivists lack a mechanism for explaining the astonishingly similar types of organizational behavior evident across many different types of supposedly different polities, cultures, and historical eras. By showing how similar types of organization and hierarchical processes created similar political trade-offs, pathologies, and outcomes for administrative actors, across various supposedly ideationally "different" polities, the firm-type model explains both similarities and differences across polities all within a relatively simple theoretical framework. As a result, the nonmaterial— but still rationalist—logic of organizational design offers a potentially important addition to the broader debate among rationalists and social constructivists in the social sciences.

The Predictive Advantages of the Theory

Finally, beyond its theoretical contributions, the firm-type theory developed here generates predictions about the relative capacity of organizational forms to enact institutional change as well as their more downstream consequences. The firm-type model can generate predictions about which type of hierarchical organization is more likely to successfully transform the institutions of a peripheral or governed polity. In general, functional or U-form governance will be much more likely to initiate and sustain institutional transformation within a periphery than territorial or M-form governance. By contrast, the M-form is much more likely to preserve and even entrench existing peripheral institutions and is far more susceptible to control problems, cooptation, and patrimonial-types of bargains than the U-form. Chapter 6 discusses the peculiar M-form adopted by U.S. occupation authorities in Iraq, which did not yield the institutional change anticipated by many policymakers. This institutional stagnation is likely to persist for the medium- and even long-term regardless of future American efforts to promote democratic change.

The firm-type model also generates predictions about which forms of hierarchical organization and institutionalized practices are likely to endure after the collapse of an original hierarchy. A primary focus of much postcolonial or postimperial scholarship has been to show how the legacies of empires and larger states continue to structure political development of newly emergent states. The firm-type model suggests that M-form legacies and institutions are more likely to endure after the collapse of a hierarchy than U-form institutions. These predictive insights are particularly relevant in terms of charting the organizational legacies of recently collapsed polities such as the Soviet Union and the state-formation of their successor states. Typically, post-Soviet states are expected to exhibit strong M-form legacies well into their independence while shunning their U-form legacies. This predictive power helps reinterpret important trends in the organization of security and economy in postimperial states more broadly without having to examine the particular ideologies or identities of these postcolonial polities.

The Plan of This Book

Given the analytical task at hand, this book is organized differently than is typical for most studies of international politics, in which a strict differentiation between "theoretical" chapters and case studies is maintained. The following chapters are organized according to analytical theme—such as hierarchical "forms," "governance," or "legacies"—and are designed to unpack, elaborate on, and apply the organizational approach, as well as the relevant managerial studies literature, to these different facets of hierarchy. Thus, the book is designed not only to demonstrate the analytical and empirical advantages of the organizational approach but also to explore the broad array of hierarchical political phenomena that can be explained or fruitfully reinterpreted with these analytical tools.

Chapter 2 expands on the organizational distinctions introduced here and places this organizational theory of hierarchy within the prevailing literature on hierarchy. It analyzes the U-form and M-form in greater detail, identifies the political analogies to these forms, and discusses the theoretical "value-added" of conceptualizing political hierarchy in organizational terms in greater depth.

Chapter 3 examines the governance effects of these organizational forms and, in particular, the contrasting types of political institutions they engender in any given periphery. As Douglass North suggests, organizations and institutions are not equivalent entities. Although both structure human interactions, organizations are the formal settings, structures, and bodies in which individuals with a common purpose are grouped. Institutions are the framework of constraints under which individuals within an organization operate. Whereas organizations define the actual structures or "players" of a social interaction, institutions "define the way the game is played."[15]

Accordingly, the chapter draws on the organizational literature to identify the varying characteristics of the U-form and the M-form that shape their governance capacities: relative governance costs, informational flow patterns, and opportunism type. First, U-forms generally incur higher governance costs than M-forms. Second, M-forms exhibit comparatively greater informational asymmetries between the periphery and core than the U-form counterpart. Third, M-forms and U-forms differ in the types of opportunism that they engender in their peripheries. Functional divisions in U-forms seek greater influence within the overall political organization as they pursue their own parochial interests in the name of the organization's greater good, a practice commonly referred to as departmentalism. Opportunism in M-forms is characterized by acute agency problems and shirking as M-form divisional leaders use their delegated positions and state resources to pursue their own interests as opposed to those of the center.

As a result, these different organizational characteristics create very different types of political institutions within each governed periphery. U-forms are more likely to actually harmonize their peripheries along functional lines and make them resemble the institutions of the core. Conversely, M-form governance is more likely to create patrimonial political institutions, allowing peripheries to retain their distinct institutional characteristics in parallel with new official administrative structures. All things being equal, U-form governance is more likely than M-form governance to successfully promote institutional transformation and change in a periphery.

Having defined the different organizational forms, identified their political equivalents, and developed a theory of hierarchical governance and institutional formation, chapter 4 presents a more systematic empirical illustration of the firm-type model's predictions in the setting of Soviet Central Asia. The chapter examines trends in four sectoral cases in both the security and economic spheres.

Two main criteria justify the selection of the region as the main empirical focus of this study. First, Soviet Central Asia demonstrates significant variance on the independent variable as outlined in this

---

15. Douglass North, *Institutions, Institutional Change, and Economic Performance* (New York: Cambridge University Press, 1990), 4–5. Some institutional scholars have criticized this distinction. See Kiren Aziz Chaudhry, *The Price of Wealth: Economies and Institutions in the Middle East* (Ithaca: Cornell University Press, 1997), 9–11.

study—namely, hierarchical form.[16] Unlike either a case of pure state-formation (U-form) or imperial governance (M-form), Soviet planners implemented both forms of governance within the areas of security and economy, thereby also allowing us to control for issue-area. In security, the Soviet armed forces were strictly organized in a U-form fashion, with Moscow deliberately deterritorializing military districting and recruitment policies in an attempt to integrate the institutions of the military into the Soviet state while internal policing functions were administered primarily in M-form fashion at the republican and local levels. Similarly, while most heavy industry was organized as a classic U-form and subordinated under the union-wide industrial ministries located in Moscow, agricultural production was arranged in a more territorially based M-form fashion. For both security and economy, Soviet forms of governance varied, which allows observation of the political effects of each hierarchical form independent of other factors (such as ideology, identity, or nationality) that remained constant throughout the Central Asian region. Moreover, the density and penetration of the Soviet totalitarian state and its administrative apparatus make it an especially appropriate social science "laboratory" for testing predictions about the varying causal effects of different forms of hierarchical governance.

Each of these organizational forms produced very different types of institutions. The U-forms harmonized these Central Asian functions with the overall structure of the Soviet state and its goals, although this type of integration encouraged departmentalism on the part of Soviet ministries and a lack of regional state-building. By contrast, M-form rule produced patrimonial institutions in the areas of agriculture and policing and precipitated severe principal-agent problems between the Soviet center and Central Asian republican administrators. Within the same ideational and cultural setting, these various organizational forms produced strikingly different types of political institutions. The sectoral approach to institutional development and the attention to both issues of security and political economy in a common theoretical framework make this case interpretation a unique one within the scholarly literature on the Soviet and post-Soviet region.

The second main reason for examining Soviet Central Asia as an empirical setting is rooted in the widespread perception that identity and ideology were the determinants of political behavior in the Soviet

---

16. On the logic of case selection and the importance of demonstrating variance in qualitative research, see Gary King, Robert Keohane, and Sidney Verba, *Designing Social Inquiry: Scientific Inference in Qualitative Research* (Princeton: Princeton University Press, 1994).

Union, both in terms of individual behavior (and the impact of communist ideology) and in the broader relationships between Moscow and the individual republics. For example, some commentators in acts of retrospective reasoning have argued that the collapse of Soviet system was inevitable because of the particular ideological tenets embodied in Marxist-Leninism.[17] Indeed, Soviet-era analysts who focused primarily on the identity of the Central Asian republics predicted a clash between their Islamic values and Soviet communist doctrine in the region, even arguing that these regional identities constituted a significant threat to future security and even viability of the Soviet state.[18] As it turned out, the "Muslim" Central Asian states were relatively quiet during the Soviet national upheavals of the late 1980s and were the last of the republics to demand independence.[19] Clearly, in a case where identity-based variables are so prevalent, the justification for an organizational approach would be strengthened considerably if it could explain variations in patterns of political institutionalization and postimperial trajectories within the same region that purely ideational theories failed to account for.[20] Moreover, if the firm-type theory provides some analytical purchase in the Soviet setting, greater confidence in the merits of its applicability to other cases of less ideologically dominated hierarchies is warranted.

While chapters 2 and 3 explore the varying effects of different hierarchies on the development of political institutions, and chapter 4 offers an empirical application, chapter 5 explores the second dependent variable of the project—the varying political trajectories taken by new states after a hierarchy collapses. New states or polities that arise from the wreckage of larger multinational states or empires do not automatically develop all the functional requisites of mature states. The firm-type model has relatively straightforward hypotheses about political trajectories after the collapse of a hierarchy: institutions or functions previously governed as U-forms will tend to exhibit path-divergence in the independence era, as they will collapse or be fundamentally reconfigured by an internal or external organization; by contrast, functions previously

17. Martin Malia, *The Soviet Tragedy: A History of Socialism in Russia, 1917–1991* (New York: Free Press, 1995).
18. For examples, see Michael Rywkin, *Moscow's Muslim Challenge: Soviet Central Asia* (Armonk, N.Y.: M. E. Sharpe, 1990); and Alexandre A. Bennigsen and S. Enders Wimbush, *Muslim National Communism in the Soviet Union: A Revolutionary Strategy for the Colonial World* (Chicago: University of Chicago Press, 1979).
19. On the nationalist upheavals, see especially Mark Beissinger, *Nationalist Mobilization and the Collapse of the Soviet State* (New York: Cambridge University Press, 2002).
20. For an important exception that does examine variations in patterns of Soviet and post-Soviet state-building and identity formation, see Laitin, *Identity in Formation*.

governed as M-forms should exhibit path-dependence and remain relatively intact in the posthierarchy period, as they retain their patrimonial political ties to the new state. This endogenous theory of posthierarchical extrication contrasts significantly with prevailing accounts that emphasize the importance of nationalism and other forms of identity in the postimperial era.[21]

The firm-type model's predictions about posthierarchy trajectories also have important implications for how external actors impact posthierarchical states. Rather than promote institutional change and transition, external inflows of capital and other resources from international financial institutions, private lenders, and nongovernmental organizations to postimperial states are likely only to perpetuate M-form type patronage practices, *even if they are intended to reform these domestic institutions or have attached macroeconomic conditions.* By contrast, external actors and capital flows are much more likely to reform or change sectors previously governed as U-forms. Thus, the firm-type model can predict which sectors international actors such as the World Bank and the International Monetary Fund will transform and in which sectors external actors will merely feed internal rent-seeking and further entrench patrimonial governance.

The latter part of chapter 5 revisits the Central Asian case and empirically explores these various paths of extrication in the post-Soviet era. Central Asian sectors previously governed as U-forms, such as heavy industry and the armed forces, collapsed dramatically, while M-form governed sectors, such as policing and agriculture, emerged with their Soviet-era institutions relatively intact and even strengthened, often expanding their organizational scope and jurisdiction. For example, in the realm of security, the M-form governed internal security and police forces made the transition to independent statehood relatively unreformed, thereby appropriating the vast majority of security functions in these independent states from the organizationally weaker national armed forces. The post-Soviet Central Asian case also shows how external flows of aid and assistance designed to promote the institutional transformation of the region, unwittingly perpetuated Soviet-era legacies. Despite claims by Central Asian elites that they would adopt new national identities and foreign-policy orientations, their state-building

21. See especially Rawi Abdelal, *National Purpose in the World Economy: The Post-Soviet States in Comparative Perspective* (Ithaca: Cornell University Press, 2001); and Mark Beissinger and Crawford Young, eds., *Beyond State Crisis? Postcolonial Africa and Post-Soviet Eurasia in Comparative Perspective* (Baltimore: Johns Hopkins University Press, 2002).

trajectories were determined by the sectoral institutional legacies of their previous organizational forms, not by new forms of national identity.

A hallmark of any useful theory is whether it gains greater analytical purchase on a wide range of important topics and debates. Chapter 6 demonstrates how the firm-type model can contribute to a range of debates within the field of political science. Three particular issues have been selected to include hierarchy-related issues within international political economy and international security.

The first case examines how the firm-type model might contribute to understanding the origins of the breakup of Yugoslavia. I highlight how, in the late Yugoslav-era, the sudden reorganization of crucial economic and security sectors from M-forms to U-forms created the structural conditions for disintegration along republican-administrative lines. This account contrasts with prevailing institutionalist approaches that argue that Yugoslavia's federal structure, by itself, was the underlying cause of the country's collapse. In the second case, I explore how distinguishing between U-forms and M-forms might inform and recast the current debate about how Japanese colonial legacies contributed to Korean economic development. I conclude by exploring how the firm-type model might improve our understanding of the organizational strategy being employed by the United States to govern occupied Iraq to promote institutional change. Instructively, the organization of the formal Iraqi occupation differed significantly from the U.S. post–World War II occupations of Germany and Japan. In particular, I focus on the incentive structures generated by the U.S. Defense Department's delegation of reconstruction projects to individual for-profit contractors and examine the types of opportunism that these contracting forms encouraged during the occupation.

Chapter 7 summarizes the main points of the study and applies the firm-type model to current debates on the governance of globalization. It shows how the behavior and governance of emerging actors in the international system, usually studied by constructivists as new forms of ideational-motivated actors, can be fruitfully identified and explained by the firm-type model. The first case uses the firm-type model to analytically distinguish between the different types of deterritorialized monetary arrangements currently proliferating, including currency unions, currency boards, and dollarized countries. The next case explores how the M-form organizational status of many contemporary colonies and dependencies allows them to operate as tax havens. The final cases demonstrate how the firm-type model can explain the organizational goals and behavior of even nonstate political actors, such as international credit-rating agencies and nongovernmental organizations. Although globalization theorists often present nonstate actors as members of normatively driven "networks"—and many nonstate actors like to publicly represent themselves in this fashion—a closer examination reveals that even they have hierarchical structures that exert important and predictable consequences on their organizational behavior. While globalization may be creating new types of nonstate actors and novel forms of global governance, an organizational approach to these forms and actors explains many aspects of their behavior ignored by prevailing accounts of global governance.

FORMS OF HIERARCHY

THE U-FORM AND M-FORM

There are an array of forms associated with functional and territorial modes of hierarchical organization. Applying the U-form and M-form to various political actors and processes in international politics allows the drawing of connections among political organizations usually considered disparate. In both the security and the economic spheres, a common set of organizational forms structure and order hierarchical interactions. Chapter 3 will explore the organizational characteristics and causal effects of these organizational forms, but this chapter is concerned with identifying these organizational forms, applying them to various political settings, and demonstrating the conceptual advantages of thinking about political organization in these organizational terms versus using prevailing theories of hierarchy, especially power-based and identity-based approaches.

ORGANIZATIONAL FORMS IN MANAGEMENT STUDIES

The usual distinction made by the institutional literature in economics, in particular transaction-costs approaches, is between the contractual setting of the market and the hierarchical setting of the firm. Institutional economists such as Ronald Coase, Oliver Williamson, and Douglass North have examined the conditions under which economic agents bypass the market and organize their activity within the firm.[1]

---

1. Douglass North, *Institutions, Institutional Change and Economic Performance* (New York: Cambridge University Press, 1990); Oliver Williamson, *The Economic Institutions of Capitalism*

Although the capitalist firm is often referred to as a uniformly hierarchical entity, firms themselves vary in their organizational structure. Beyond making decisions over what to produce, for whom and at what price, firms must also decide how to organize their various product lines and activities and how to optimally delegate multiple levels of managerial and administrative functions. The principle by which hierarchies are structured is an organizational form, and management scholars have identified several variants within the modern firm, such as networks, holding companies, and franchises.[2] The enduring distinction among firms, however, remains whether to organize subordinate divisions by function or by product.

Business historian Alfred Chandler first identified and formally distinguished between these two ideal types of firms—the unitary form and the multidivisional form.[3] For Chandler, and later Oliver Williamson, the unitary form (U-form) is the most centralized or integrated type of firm and was the predominant form of early industrial organization (see fig. 1.1).[4] The U-form organizes the firm along functional lines as each operating division corresponds to a different function of the firm's operations. Functions such as sales, engineering, manufacturing, and finance all maintain separate divisions that are directly subordinated to the central chief executive. The major operating and strategic decisions of the firm are formulated by the chief executive and transmitted to the managers of each functional division. In turn, division managers must maintain extensive horizontal ties with each other, as well as the executive, as they continuously coordinate and sequence their activities during the planning and production processes. Within this organizational structure, an expansion of the firm adds increasing levels of management within the overall structure of these functionally differentiated divisions.[5]

Now consider the structural characteristics of the multidivisional firm (M-form, see fig. 1.2). Unlike the U-form, subordinate operating

(New York: Free Press, 1985); Oliver Williamson, *Markets and Hierarchies: Analysis and Antitrust Implications* (New York: Free Press, 1975); and Ronald Coase, "The Nature of the Firm," *Economica* 4 (1937): 386–405. For a synthesis, see Thrainn Eggertsson, *Economic Behavior and Institutions* (New York: Cambridge University Press, 1990).

2. For a theoretical overview of various institutional forms and related governance issues, see Masahiko Aoki, *Toward a Comparative Institutional Analysis* (Cambridge: MIT Press, 2001).

3. Alfred D. Chandler Jr., and S. Salisbury, *Pierre du Pont and the Making of the Modern Corporation* (New York: Harper & Row, 1971); and Alfred D. Chandler Jr., *Strategy and Structure: Chapters in the History of the American Industrial Enterprise* (Cambridge: MIT Press, 1969).

4. See Williamson, *The Economic Institutions of Capitalism*; and Williamson, *Markets and Hierarchies*.

5. Williamson, *Markets and Hierarchies*, 133.

divisions do not correspond to the separate functions of the firm; instead, the subdivisions are differentiated by product or geography and are responsible for a wide range of functions.[6] Within each of these quasi-autonomous operating divisions, the array of different functions is subordinate to the decision-making authority of the division head or manager. Under this schema, the divisional heads are responsible for the routine functions of finance, accounting, and manufacturing in their respective divisions and have little or no contact with their counterparts in other divisions. Furthermore, each division operates as a financially autonomous unit, usually through the creation of an internal capital market. Thus, the U-form structure eventually emerges in the subdivisional hierarchy, but it is responsible only for the operating activities of that particular division.

This decomposition also results in a decentralized decision-making structure in the M-form. Everyday operating decisions are removed from the chief executive or functional heads and assigned to the essentially self-contained hierarchy of the subdivision or quasi-firm. Routine management and accounting take place within the subsidiary itself as opposed to a separate functional division directly under the control of the chief executive. In multinational subsidiaries, for example, each product or geographical subsidiary has an extensive managerial structure that is responsible for the various functional tasks of that division. While exerting nominal control, the chief executive is restricted to broad strategic planning and decisions pertaining to the allocation and distribution of resources among its operating divisions. Introduced by corporations such as General Motors and DuPont in the 1920s, the M-form rapidly diffused through American industry and was adopted overseas.[7] By the 1970s, surveys indicated that the M-form had become the dominant organizational structure throughout the industrialized world, prompting theorists such as Chandler and Williamson to highlight and praise its organizational advantages.[8]

6. Ibid., 136.

7. Chandler, *Strategy and Structure*. Also see Chandler, *The Visible Hand: The Managerial Revolution in American Business* (Cambridge: Harvard University Press, 1977).

8. For examples, see John Cable and Manfred Dirrheimer, "Hierarchies and Markets: An Empirical Test of the Multidivisional Hypothesis in West Germany," *International Journal of Industrial Organization* 1 (1983): 43–62; and John Cable and Hirohiko Yasuki, "Internal Organisation, Business Groups and Corporate Performance: An Empirical Test of the Multidivisional Hypothesis in Japan," *International Journal of Industrial Organization* 3 (1985): 401–20. See also Williamson, *Economic Institutions of Capitalism*; Williamson, *Markets and Hierarchies*; and Chandler, *Strategy and Structure*.

POLITICAL APPLICATIONS: M-FORM and U-FORM HIERARCHICAL GOVERNANCE

As with the U-form and M-form organization of firms, transnational political hierarchies vary depending on whether political cores organize their peripheries according to function or territory. Typically, U-form governance denotes the process usually referred to as "state-formation" whereas M-form governance describes most cases of modern imperial control and overseas occupation. Consequently, these two types of hierarchy traditionally have been studied as distinct processes by different subfields within the political science—comparativists and international relations theorists. Accordingly, the firm-type theory allows the study of hierarchy across the political science discipline to be unified and also develops previously unidentified theoretical and empirical connections.

Hierarchy Organized by Function: U-form Governance

The U-form structure is analogous to the administrative structure of a modern centralized state, where the functional divisions are usually ministries, state organs, and their respective bureaucracies. Like the functional divisions of firms, state ministries are responsible for implementing general policies within their particular functional areas. A pyramidal hierarchy staffs each ministry, subordinating political agents to increasing levels of authority. Ministers, like division mangers, are ultimately accountable to the chief executive or president of the state within their particular function or set of policy domains.[9]

When a periphery is completely incorporated into the functional divisions or administrative organs of the core, it ceases to operate as a distinct political or juridical entity and, instead, is subsumed within the agencies and governing divisions of the core. The various functions of the periphery, such as foreign affairs, internal security, education, culture, and transportation, are administered directly by the corresponding separate ministries within the core state (fig. 2.1). For example, educational policy in the subordinate unit under the U-form is governed by the core's Ministry of Education rather than by a special educational division within the periphery.

This organizational form—hierarchical governance by functional integration—best represents what scholars typically refer to as "state-

9. Michael Laver and Kenneth A. Shepsle, eds., *Cabinet Ministers and Parliamentary Government* (New York: Cambridge University Press, 1994).

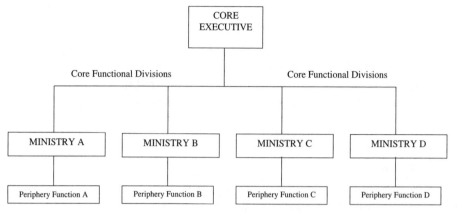

FIGURE 2.1
U-form Peripheral Administration (State Formation)

formation."[10] Peripheries that are highly integrated into the functional divisions of core states lose their juridical status as distinct political units and become an integral and organizationally nondistinct part of the core state. The operational divisions and institutions of the core subsume peripheral political institutions, such as the legislature, the judiciary, and the military. Bureaucracies with functional specializations assume responsibility for overseeing and standardizing those functions within various peripheries.[11] Finally, citizens of functionally integrated territories lose their previous jurisdictional affiliation and adopt the rights, such as the right to participate in the political process, and obligations, such as the obligation of military conscription, associated with core citizenship.[12] This type of integration can transpire through a number of different mechanisms, including military conquest, voluntary union, and the emulation of other successful institutional forms.

Formal or juridical U-form integration does not necessarily mean that a political periphery, in practice, will be treated always in a fully egalitarian manner as the rest of the core polity. Functional political integration may obscure or consolidate uneven patterns of development, unequal divisions of labor, and socioeconomic disparities within inte-

10. For different explanations of state-formation in the modern international system, see Thomas Erstman, *Birth of the Leviathan* (New York: Cambridge University Press, 1997); Hendrik Spruyt, *The Sovereign State and Its Competitors* (Princeton: Princeton University Press, 1994); and Charles Tilly, *Capital, Coercion and the Formation of European States: AD 990–1990* (Cambridge, Mass.: Blackwell, 1990).
11. Spruyt, *Sovereign State and Its Competitors*.
12. Reinhard Bendix, *Kings or People: Power and the Mandate to Rule* (Berkeley: University of California Press, 1978).

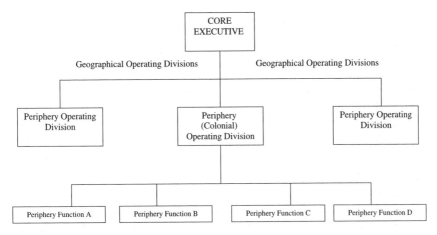

FIGURE 2.2
M-form Peripheral Administration (Modern Empires and Occupied States)

grated peripheries.[13] In many cases, U-form peripheries protest on the grounds that they are actually treated differently than other peripheries or discriminated against. For example, Hawaiians claim they are "last among equals" within the American political system, while Basques maintain they contribute a disproportionately high share of tax revenues to the Spanish state. Similarly, representatives of the Japanese prefecture of Okinawa complain that the small island, one of forty-seven prefectures of the Japanese state, bears a disproportionate national security burden by hosting 75 percent of all American military installations.[14] Regardless of the empirical validity of these specific claims, such appeals invoke the sense of juridical equality created by U-form organization and the functional integration of peripheries.

Hierarchy Organized by Territory: M-form Governance

Core polities can also govern territorial peripheries through the M-form, thereby differentiating various peripheries from one another. This form characterized most relationships between metropoles and their peripheries in modern European empires and most modern military occupations (fig. 2.2).

13. See, especially, Michael Hechter, *Internal Colonialism: The Celtic Fringe in British National Development, 1536–1966* (Berkeley: University of California Press, 1975).
14. See Chalmers Johnson, ed., *Okinawa: Cold War Island* (Cardiff, Calif.: Japan Policy Research Institute, 1999).

Colonized peripheries were not annexed and incorporated into the functional divisions or ministries of the core but were designated as separate and subordinate territorial divisions. Indeed, the joint public-private charter companies that founded a number of overseas colonies—such as the British and Dutch East India companies, the British South Africa Company, or the Royal Niger Company—were actual autonomous profit-making entities contracted by the state to govern designated peripheries.[15] Like the executives of M-form corporations, imperial metropoles formulated broad policies and strategies that pertained to the periphery and implemented their decisions through an administrative apparatus that was responsible for the full array of tasks necessary for the routine operation of the colonial state. The divisional heads of colonies were colonial governors, either from the metropole or drawn from indigenous power structures, who exercised wide-ranging powers over everyday operational issues.

Like the distinct divisions of an M-form, colonial divisions had little systematic contact with each other. Interperipheral relations were mediated by the core, which determined the particular responsibilities and obligations of each peripheral division.[16] As with Alexander Motyl's imperial analogy, M-form organization made empires resemble the "hub and spokes of the wheel," with the imperial core radiating out to its unconnected peripheries.[17] The colonial subdivisions were autonomous and maintained few contacts with the core over routine operating issues. While full authority ultimately resided within the metropole, the modern colonial state—like the subdivision of the M-form firm— remained organizationally distinct.

The autonomy afforded by the M-form also created a distinct political differentiation between the metropolitan core and the periphery. As with the M-form firm, imperial peripheries as a general rule were also fiscally autonomous and had to raise revenue internally to fully finance their everyday operations.[18] Furthermore, indigenous residents of

15. See David B. Abernethy, *The Dynamics of Global Dominance: European Overseas Empires, 1415–1980* (New Haven: Yale University Press, 2000); and James D. Tracy, ed., *The Political Economy of Merchant Empires: State Power and World Trade, 1350–1750* (New York: Cambridge University Press, 1997).

16. Unlike in the U-form, M-form contracts with divisional units were unequal and differentiated. On empires and the inequality of contracts, see Charles Tilly, "How Empires End," in *After Empire: Multiethnic Societies and Nation-Building*, ed. Karen Barkey and Mark Von Hagen, 1–11 (Boulder, Colo.: Westview, 1997); and Daniel Nexon, "Contending Sovereignties: Religion and the Fate of Empires in Early Modern Europe," Ph.D. diss., Columbia University, 2003.

17. Alexander Motyl, *Imperial Ends: The Decay, Collapse, and Revival of Empires* (New York: Columbia University Press, 2001), 13–15.

18. On the fiscal autonomy of the colonial state, see Crawford Young, *The African Colonial State in Comparative Perspective* (New Haven: Yale University Press, 1995), 124–33.

M-form peripheries were not afforded the rights of core citizenship—although some powers, such as France, made this choice possible in theory—despite the fact that all were subject to taxation by the colonial state and frequently were forced into military service for the metropole.

Of course, the issue of whether a certain periphery should be governed as a U-form or M-form can itself be politically contentious. In some cases, where M-forms were governed by a distinct bureaucratic faction in the core—such as the U.S. Navy in Micronesia or the Portuguese military in colonial Africa—this faction actively resisted and lobbied against changing to an organizational form that would require it to relinquish power to other agencies within the core polity.[19] In other cases, peripheries themselves have appealed that their status should be "upgraded" from that of an M-form to that of a U-form, thereby gaining access to the state institutions and political rights enjoyed by other core citizens. This was a common claim among home country settlers in Algeria, Ireland, Israel, Rhodesia, and Cyprus in their political struggles with their respective metropoles.[20]

The Special Case of Federal Systems

The organizational structures of the hierarchical U-forms and M-forms should be distinguished from those of a federal system. In their ideal form, federations are not hierarchies. Like a hierarchy, federations devolve political authority in multiple polities along territorial lines to subdivisions. Unlike hierarchies, however, federations lack a distinct "core" state or polity. Instead, federal unions are achieved through the integration of co-equal political states, all of which are bound together by the same contractual obligations, such as constitutional arrangements.[21] In terms of organizational theory, such an

19. On the United States in Micronesia, see Roger W. Gale, *The Americanization of Micronesia: A Study of the Consolidation of U.S. Role in the Pacific* (New York: Rowman & Littlefield, 1979). On the power of the Portuguese military in Africa, see Hendrik Spruyt, *Ending Empire* (Ithaca: Cornell University Press, 2005). Spruyt regards such bureaucratic intransigency as institutional "veto points" against disengagement.

20. See Ian Lustick, *Unsettled States, Disputed Lands: Britain and Ireland, France and Algeria, Israel and the West Bank-Gaza* (Ithaca: Cornell University Press, 1993).

21. Integration can be initiated by a number of factors. According to William Riker, federal governance is created when constituent governments combine their territories in the face of a threat (external or internal) and delegate political authority to this new federal level. See William H. Riker, *Federalism: Origins, Operation, Significance* (Boston: Little, Brown, 1964), chap. 1. Federations also have been established as institutional solutions to managing multiple ethnicities. See Valerie Bunce, *Subversive Institutions: The Design and the Destruction of Socialism and the State* (New York: Cambridge University Press, 1999); Rogers Brubaker, *Nationalism Reframed: Nationhood and the National Question in the New Europe* (New York: Cambridge University Press, 1996);

arrangement resembles what is known as a holding company, or an H-form.[22]

In its classic republican formulation, federalism explicitly rejects hierarchy as a political arrangement. Daniel Deudney has aptly described such forms of political union in the international system as "negarchical"—in contradistinction to the principles of both anarchy and hierarchy—where key state functions, such as security, are pooled through mechanisms of constitutional cobinding, as was the case with the American Federal Union.[23] Similarly, as European integration continues to expand over a range of functions, such as a common currency, social chapter, and even defense policy, such efforts subordinate national legislation and state sovereignty to European Union (EU) supranational institutions rather than a territorially distinct core polity.[24]

In reality, however, the ideal distinction between federalism and hierarchy is often blurred because distinct polities dominate or take over the governing institutions of a federal structure. Arguably, such "corrupted" forms of federalism historically have been more prevalent than ideal federations, and they certainly have not, over the long term, guaranteed political order. For example, the nominally federal systems of the Soviet Union, Yugoslavia, and Nigeria were all, in practice, administered as hierarchies by a distinct core polity.[25] While, in principle, federal systems of governance can be viewed as the organizational antithesis to hierarchy, more often than not they develop hierarchical characteristics and can be fruitfully analyzed by the firm-type model.

Organizational Form and Organizational Intensity

Within the U-form and M-form, core polities can differ in the degree to which they organize and penetrate a periphery. Totalitarian states are highly penetrative U-forms that exhibit "a functional structure, involving a core elite and state and functionally defined peripheral elites and societies."[26] As the core centrally governs a high number of peripheral

and Philip Roeder, "Soviet Federalism and Ethnic Mobilization," *World Politics* 43 (1991): 196–232. On federalism and the equality of contracts, see Nexon, "Contending Sovereignties."

22. On the H-form, see Williamson, *Markets and Hierarchies*, 143–44.

23. Daniel Deudney, "The Philadelphian System: Sovereignty, Arms Control, and Balance of Power in the American States Union, c. 1787–1861," *International Organization* 49 (1995): 191–228. Also see Deudney, *Bounding Power* (Princeton: Princeton University Press, forthcoming).

24. J. H. H. Weiler, *The Constitution of Europe* (New York: Cambridge University Press, 1999).

25. On the dynamics of socialist federations, see Bunce, *Subversive Institutions*.

26. Motyl, *Imperial Ends*, 49. On totalitarian states, also see Bunce, *Subversive Institutions*; and Giovanni Sartori, "Totalitarianism, Model Mania, and Learning from Error," *Journal of Theoretical Politics* 5 (1993): 5–22.

functions, it eliminates independent social or civic space outside the state. Conversely, U-form incorporation can take a more limited intensity, whereby the periphery and core remain juridically integrated, but the actual number of governing institutions and functional contacts are minimal. For instance, Spanish America was an administrative province of Castile that was functionally ruled by the mainland bureaucracy and lacked any institutionalized mechanisms of self-government at the regional level.[27] In practice, however, the remoteness of the territory precluded the Spanish state's various functional bureaucracies from effectively governing the colony.[28]

M-forms can also differ in their organizational intensity and bureaucratic scope. In certain older imperial forms, the peripheral administrative apparatus remained rudimentary and did little to extend the scope of its activities.[29] For example, the Roman Republic initially had to rely mainly on tax farming within its various territories to extract revenues.[30] Imperial expansion headed by mercantile companies such as the Dutch East India Company or the British South Africa Company initially featured a similar lack of social penetration. Certain modern military administrations, such as the Italian administration of North Africa, also exhibited these characteristics as the colonial apparatus was responsible mainly for maintaining political order in the periphery and did not actually organize political and social life to any notable extent.[31] Modern postconflict occupations of industrial powers, such as the United States in post–World War II Japan, also governed through preexisting bureaucracies and administrative agencies.[32]

In other instances, modern European empires employed an increasingly complex and deep bureaucratic apparatus within their peripheries. For instance, Crawford Young argues that owing to its late colonization, the African colonial state developed a uniquely intrusive and coercive

27. Mark Hanson, "Organizational Bureaucracy in Latin America and the Legacy of Spanish Colonialism," *Journal of Interamerican Studies and World Affairs* 16 (1974): 202–3.
28. See Henry Kaman, *Empire: How Spain Became a World Power, 1492–1763* (New York: Harper-Collins, 2003).
29. See S. N. Eisenstadt, *The Political Systems of Empire* (Glencoe, Ill.: Free Press, 1963), especially chap. 5.
30. Margaret Levi, *Of Rule and Revenue* (Berkeley: University of California Press, 1988), chap. 4.
31. Lisa Anderson, *The State and Social Transformation in Tunisia and Libya, 1830–1980* (Princeton: Princeton University Press, 1986).
32. On modern occupation and institutional cooptation, see Peter Liberman, *Does Conquest Pay? The Exploitation of Occupied Industrial Societies* (Princeton: Princeton University Press, 1996). On the occupation of Japan, see Eiji Takemae, *The Allied Occupation of Japan* (New York: Continuum, 2003); and John W. Dower, *Embracing Defeat: Japan in the Wake of World War II* (New York: W.W. Norton, 2000).

administrative order.[33] Timothy Mitchell proposes that the fundamental purpose of British rule in Egypt was to create a modernizing colonial state that attempted to reorder the very institutions of Egyptian society within a new colonial bureaucracy.[34] The M-form, then, more precisely reflects political forms in which cores actively sought to order and modernize peripheral societies, although the looser examples of military colonial rule still conform to the basic tenets of the M-form (i.e., differentiated, decentralized, and delegated rule).

The Origins of Organizational Forms

Finally, it should be noted that a systematic examination of why certain types of hierarchy are chosen over others, although an important topic in its own right, is beyond the scope of this project. Explanations for the origins of imperialism, federalism, and modern state-formation all combine a number of potential material and ideational variables. Material factors that may lead to the adoption of a particular form over another may include relative rates of development and modernization between the core and periphery, the interests of factions or groups within the core, geographic barriers and constraints, the presence of certain idiosyncratic or specific assets within a periphery, and competitive external pressures, including war and other forms of external security threats. Ideational factors that might affect decisions over whether to employ the U-form or M-form core-periphery include differences in ethnicity, religion, ideology, culture, race, as well as prevailing international norms. For example, these ideational variables readily explain why many European powers governed their modern colonial peripheries as subordinate M-forms rather than as integrated parts of the metropole. Certainly, notions of European superiority, religious mission, and racial identity all infused European decisions on how to organize modern colonial governance.[35]

The ideational argument, however, should not be stretched too far, as choices over organizational forms do not always correspond to identity affiliations or notions of "us and them." For example, while many former West Germans may continue to look down on former East Germans as

---

33. Young, *African Colonial State in Comparative Perspective.* However, this thesis has been challenged. See Jeffrey Herbst, *States and Power in Africa: Comparative Lessons in Authority and Control* (Princeton: Princeton University Press, 2000).
34. Timothy Mitchell, *Colonising Egypt* (Berkeley: University of California Press, 1988).
35. The literature on identity and imperialism is vast. For an overview, see Young, *African Colonial State in Comparative Perspective.*

"others," the administrative structures of the East were absorbed relatively quickly as a U-form into the functional divisions of the West as part of German reunification. Similarly, the organizational forms employed over a given periphery often have varied over time and have been subject to sudden change. For example, the Yugoslav Federation in 1989 functionally reintegrated Kosovo into its center as U-form despite that the province previously had been autonomously governed as an M-form under the terms of the 1974 Constitution.[36] As constructivists themselves maintain, ideational patterns often vary and change over time, but these shifts do not necessarily determine the adoption of organizational form. Moreover, degrees of national or ethnic heterogeneity also can have organizational consequences, as they may change the overall governance costs of a particular polity, depending on the bundle of rights and public goods conferred by the center.[37] Regardless of why one form is adopted over another in any given periphery, over time, the organizational forms outlined by the firm-type model will produce similar institutional tendencies and governance problems, irrespective of the types of identities present in the core and periphery.

PREVAILING THEORETICAL APPROACHES TO HIERARCHY

The firm-type typology is not the only way of conceptualizing variations in the structure and governance of transnational hierarchies. The organizational approach proposed here differs in key ways from the two approaches that dominate prevailing studies of hierarchy in international politics, namely, realist and constructivist theories. Each differentiates hierarchy from the international systemic condition of anarchy according to a different underlying principle—power and identity. Neither of these approaches satisfactorily explains the stark variation in political order and control that exist both within and across hierarchical polities, nor do they systematically explain the various organizational forms that political hierarchies take.

Realist Approaches and Power-based Theories of Hierarchy

Power-based theories such as realism examine international hierarchy in terms of the preponderance of power, especially military power, held

36. See James Ron, *Frontiers and Ghettos: State Violence in Serbia and Israel* (Berkeley: University of California Press, 2002), chap. 5.
37. See Alberto Alesina and Enrico Spolaore, *The Size of Nations* (Cambridge: MIT Press, 2003).

by dominant states in the international system. For example, theories of hegemonic cycles view international politics as the product of the rise and decline of dominant global powers, while the theory of hegemonic stability explains the rise of a liberal international economic system by the presence of an international hegemon that is willing to enforce the rules of the system's governance.[38] Likewise, analyses of U.S. unipolarity outline the incentives for aggressive expansion that a preponderance of systemic power offers a global hegemon.[39]

For some neorealists, such as Kenneth Waltz, pure organizational hierarchy in *international* politics tends to be rather exceptional given that the system is fundamentally anarchic and is comprised of states that compete for influence according to their various levels of military capabilities.[40] Waltz elegantly distinguishes the self-help dynamics of the anarchical international state system from the relatively well-ordered domain he sees as characterizing domestic politics. While the international system is made up of self-interested states competing in an anarchic order, the political systems found within states are hierarchically ordered and controlled by a state government.

Yet, not only is the anarchy/hierarchy dichotomy empirically problematic, as critics of Waltz have pointed out, but the assumption that hierarchy necessarily implies political control is also false, as current events in Iraq or Chechnya testify.[41] The often-mentioned fact that about five times more conflicts and battle deaths have occurred since 1945 as a result of civil wars than interstate wars suggests that hierarchy is neither correlated with peace nor internal control.[42] Nor can power-based theories accurately explain the various forms that hierarchies take. Given that realists view relational power as the determinant of unit behavior, it should follow that polities in similar positions of power vis-à-vis their peripheries should establish similar types of political orders. As David Lake has pointed out, the fact that after World War II the

38. Paul Kennedy, *The Rise and Fall of the Great Powers* (New York: Vintage Books, 1987); and Robert Gilpin, *War and Change in International Politics* (Princeton: Princeton University Press, 1983). Also see Charles Kindleberger, *The World in Depression* (Berkeley: University of California Press, 1986).

39. For overviews, see John Ikenberry, ed., *America Unrivalled: The Future of the Balance of Power* (Ithaca: Cornell University Press, 2002); and Ethan Kapstein and Michael Mastanduno, eds., *Unipolar Politics* (New York: Columbia University, 1999).

40. Kenneth Waltz, *Theory of International Politics* (New York: Random House, 1979). Indeed, for Waltz, complete international hierarchy would imply the establishment of world government.

41. Helen Milner, "The Assumption of Anarchy in International Relations Theory: A Critique," *Review of International Studies* 17 (1991): 67–86.

42. For data, see James Fearon and David Laitin, "Ethnicity, Insurgency and Civil War," *American Political Science Review* 97 (2003): 75–90.

United States established an alliance system with Western Europe while the Soviet Union established an informal empire cannot be explained purely by the relative distribution of military capabilities held by the two superpowers in their respective spheres of influence.[43]

Realist theories may explain broad trends in systems dynamics and the pursuit of international power, but they are less useful for understanding the various forms that hierarchy takes and they erroneously equate a preponderance of relative power with the concepts of control and/or stability.

Constructivism and Identity-based Theories of Hierarchy

Constructivist theorists of international politics have dealt with hierarchy more explicitly than realists. For constructivists, international relations are determined by the identities and norms held by political actors and the social environments that generate these understandings and beliefs.[44] According to constructivists, hierarchical political forms embody distinct identities and self-understandings, thereby leading to variations in the purpose and behavior of such polities within the international system.[45] Thus, while realists tend to conflate hierarchy with the concept of control, constructivists equate hierarchy with certain types of political and social order.

For constructivists, hierarchies are socially constructed political orders, produced by the identities, constitutions, and normative understandings held by a dominant polity. In his epic comparison of the Spanish, French, and British empires, Anthony Pagden argues that understandings of empire varied across European imperial powers and that these differing ideologies created divergent conceptions of political order within their respective imperial communities.[46] Alexander Wendt and Daniel Friedheim argue that informal empires are constructed through ideological diffusion, hegemonic processes, and propaganda disseminated by the dominant state and that this relationship fundamentally clashes with the norm of territorial sovereignty assumed by rationalist

---

43. David A. Lake, "Anarchy, Hierarchy and the Variety of International Relations," *International Organization* 50 (1996): 1–34.
44. Alexander Wendt, *Social Theory of International Politics* (New York: Cambridge University Press, 1999).
45. David Strang, "Contested Sovereignty: The Construction of Colonial Imperialism," in *State Sovereignty as Social Construct*, ed. Cynthia Weber and Thomas Biersteker, 22–49 (New York: Cambridge University Press, 1996).
46. Anthony Pagden, *Lords of All the World: Ideologies of Empire in Spain, Britain and France c. 1500–c. 1800* (New Haven: Yale University Press, 1995).

accounts of states' interests.[47] Ian Lustick explores how states that dominate or occupy territorial peripheries must pass through a series of psychological thresholds before a rational consideration of disengagement even becomes possible.[48] Others view hegemony itself as more of an ideological project, as opposed to a power-based one, with prevailing hegemons securing control and systemic acquiescence through the diffusion of certain norms and understandings about the international order and its organization.[49] Furthermore, just as international relations scholars maintain that an international imperial norm sustained the modern system of European empires, others argue that the collapse of that norm and a change in the understanding of colonial legitimacy initiated rapid decolonization in the post–World War II period.[50]

The major problem with such ideational theories is that they cannot account for variation in forms of political organization because they view each individual form of hierarchy as unique or historically distinct. For example, all imperial metropoles faced the problem of retaining the political loyalty of their peripheral governors. This control issue was prevalent in ideationally diverse empires such as the Roman, Ottoman, Spanish, and Soviet empires, yet ideational theories have no theoretical basis from which to explain the similar strategies and techniques these empires employed to deal with such common organizational dilemmas. How does one account for like patterns in organizational behavior and informal rules when the purposes, sources of legitimacy, and social identities of all these empires were so dramatically different? Just as power-based theories cannot account for variance among hierarchical forms, constructivist theories cannot account for their similarities.

Theories of Empire and Imperialism

Finally, it is worth noting briefly that historians and social scientists undertaking comparative imperial studies also have employed various

47. Alexander Wendt and Daniel Friedheim, "Hierarchy under Anarchy: Informal Empire and the East German State," *International Organization* 49 (1995): 689–721.

48. Lustick, *Unsettled States, Disputed Lands.*

49. John G. Ruggie, "International Regimes, Transactions, and Change: Embedded Liberalism in the Postwar Economic Order." *International Organization* 36 (1982): 379–415; and Robert Wade, "U.S. Hegemony and the World Bank: The Fight over People and Ideas," *Review of International Political Economy* 9 (2002): 215–43.

50. On constructivism and decolonization, see Neta C. Crawford, *Argument and Change in World Politics: Ethics, Decolonization and Humanitarian Intervention* (New York: Cambridge University Press, 2002); and Peter Jackson, "Weight of Ideas in Decolonization: Normative Change in International Relations," in *Ideas and Foreign Policy: Beliefs, Institutions, and Political Change,* ed. Judith Goldstein and Robert O. Keohane, 111–38 (Ithaca: Cornell University Press, 1993).

criteria to distinguish among empires. Distinctions have been on the basis of temporality (ancient imperialism vs. modern imperialism), geography (contiguous vs. maritime empires), and ideational factors, such as imperial ideologies and legitimacy.[51]

Perhaps the most influential theory of imperial governance remains the distinction between direct and indirect rule as first formulated by the revisionist historians John Gallagher and Ronald Robinson.[52] Gallagher and Robinson observed that certain metropoles ruled their peripheries indirectly, with the assistance of domestic collaborationists within peripheral societies, while other metropoles occupied and administered their territories directly. Accordingly, many political historians explain the difference between British and French imperialism in these terms, with the pragmatic British having relied on indirect rule to further their global commercial interests while France favored direct rule because of its "civilizing mission" and national imperial ideals.[53] Is this distinction tantamount to the M-form and U-form?

While initially helpful, the direct/indirect rule distinction has conceptual limitations. First, the type of agents (Western or local) that administered imperial peripheries did not necessarily correspond to the juridical status of a particular periphery. In most empires other than France and Britain, the governing apparatus employed a mix of rulers drawn from both the metropole and the periphery, thereby rendering the direct/indirect distinction less applicable. For example, the Japanese bureaucracy in its colonies of Korea and Taiwan made a point of including both Japanese bureaucrats and domestic collaborators.[54]

51. For issues of temporality, see Gary B. Miles, "Roman and Modern Imperialism: A Reassessment," *Comparative Studies in History and Development* 32 (1990): 629–59. Regarding geography, see Dominic Lieven, *Empire: The Russian Empire and Its Rivals* (New Haven: Yale University Press, 2001); and Lieven, "The Dilemmas of Empire 1850–1910: Power, Territory, Identity," *Journal of Contemporary History* 34 (1999): 163–200. See Pagden, *Lords of All the World*, on ideational factors. On empire and legitimacy, see Ronald Grigor Suny, "The Empire Strikes Out: Imperial Russia, 'National Identity,' and Theories of Empire," in *A State of Nations: Empire and Nation-Making in the Age of Lenin and Stalin* (New York: Oxford University Press, 2001), 23–66; and Suny, "Ambiguous Categories: States, Empires and Nations," *Post-Soviet Affairs* 11 (1995): 185–96.

52. Ronald Robinson, "The Non-European Foundations of European Imperialism: Sketch for a Theory of Collaboration," in *Studies in the Theory of Imperialism*, ed. Robert Owen and Bob Sutcliffe, 117–41 (London: Longman, 1972); and Ronald Robinson and John Gallagher, *Africa and the Victorians* (Garden City, N.Y.: Doubleday/Anchor, 1968). Also see the discussion in Michael Doyle, *Empires* (Ithaca: Cornell University Press, 1986), chaps. 8–9.

53. See Alice Conklin, *Mission to Civilize: The Republican Idea of Empire in France and West Africa* (Palo Alto: Stanford University Press, 2000).

54. For details, see W. G. Beasley, *Japanese Imperialism, 1894–1945* (Oxford: Clarendon, 1987); and Ramon H. Myers and Mark R. Peattie, *The Japanese Colonial Empire, 1895–1945* (Princeton: Princeton University Press, 1984).

Second, as the next chapter will show, these distinctions often were of little practical significance as direct rule produced the same agency problems, control loss issues, and center-periphery tensions as indirect rule. The principal conceptual weakness with the direct/indirect distinction, however, is that by ascribing a particular type of rule, ideology, or imperial organization to a specific country, it becomes difficult to explain the variation in governance structures across different peripheries of the same metropole and/or the different organizational forms employed by the same metropole across different sectors within a single periphery. The firm-type typology captures this variation.

THEORETICAL VALUE-ADDED CONTRIBUTIONS OF THE FIRM-TYPE MODEL

The firm-model offers three distinct analytical advantages over prevailing distinctions made about empires and other international hierarchies. First, the firm-type model reveals how core powers have employed both forms of organization across their various peripheries; second, the firm-type model allows variations in the governance of different sectors within the same periphery to be distinguished; and, third, the firm-type model identifies and specifies single-sector hierarchies in both the security and economic realms.

Explaining Variation across Peripheries

First, the firm-type model distinguishes variations in the different peripheries of core imperial powers. Regardless of their national identities or ideologies, core powers have chosen to simultaneously implement U-forms in certain peripheries while retaining the M-form in others. Such distinctions have been made by nearly all recent great powers and even medium-sized states that have deployed both organizational forms in their hierarchical governance. Although the labels for these administrative distinctions differ across countries (i.e., American "unincorporated territories" vs. British "crown dependencies"), the organizational principles of territorial versus functional governance remain similar throughout.

Table 2.1 provides examples of how different core powers routinely adopted both U-forms and M-forms in their governance of various peripheries. Although the table illustrates these variations, in most cases

TABLE 2.1
Examples of U-form and M-form Governance, 2004 (Unless Other Year Specified)

Core Power	U-form Periphery	M-form Periphery
Australia	Tasmania	Solomon Islands (2003)
China	Guangdong	Hong Kong, Macau
	Tibet	
France	Reúnion Corsica	New Caledonia
		Tunisia (1952)
Germany	East Germany (1990–)	Denmark (1943)
Indonesia	Java	East Timor (1975–98)
Israel	East Jerusalem	Gaza, the West Bank
Italy	Sicily	Eritrea (1920)
Japan	Okinawa	Taiwan (1920)
Portugal	Azores	Angola (1974)
Russia	Steppe (1900)	Turkestan (1900)
	Chechnya	Tajikistan (1993)
Serbia and	Bosnia (1992)	Kosovo (1985)
Montenegro	Kosovo (1989)	
Spain	Mallorca	Ceuta
		Melilla
		Western Sahara (1975)
Turkey	Southeastern Anatolia	Northern Cyprus
United Kingdom	Isle of Wight	Jersey
	Northern Ireland	Guernsey
		Ireland (1920)
United States	Hawaii	Guam
		American Samoa
		Iraq (2003)

it controls for geography by showing how major international and regional powers have employed both forms of governance over proximate peripheries, often with inhabitants of similar national identities or political affiliation. For example, the Israeli annexation of East Jerusalem after the 1967 war integrated both the territory and most of its Arab inhabitants into the Israeli state while Israel's formal occupation of Gaza and the West Bank (M-forms) did not confer the same legal status and integrative administration on these territories and their inhabitants. Similarly, while Hong Kong reverted to Chinese sovereignty in 1997, it has retained an M-form organizational status as a "special administrative province" within China, thereby allowing it to retain certain territorial features such as its currency board (Hong Kong dollar) and special commerce laws.

Explaining Variation across Sectors within the Same Periphery

While the firm-type model permits examination of variation in administrative techniques across different types of peripheries, perhaps its greatest analytical "value-added" component is its ability to show how both functional and territorial techniques can be employed across different sectors within the same periphery.

The ability to isolate the governance of individual sectors and compare such with that of others is especially critical for understanding the political dynamics of contiguous empires or multinational states such as the Byzantine, Ottoman, Habsburg, Russian, and Soviet empires, where political cores simultaneously employed both hierarchical forms in their administrative structures. As figure 2.3 indicates, and as chapter 4 will show, the Soviet center in the 1970s and 1980s employed both organizational forms in its governance of the Central Asian republics by governing the armed forces and heavy industry as U-forms while administering functions such as agriculture, education, and policing as M-forms. Thus, in certain sectors Soviet rule could be viewed as an "empire" while in others it was more akin to an integrated state. Understanding the different logics of organization allows us to differentiate among hierarchical forms in different sectors within the same state.

Not surprisingly, peripheries employing such mixed forms, especially in more recent eras, are likely to generate intense internal debate and discord regarding their exact political status. For example, French settlers and their metropolitan allies claimed Algeria was an integral part of the French Republic, not just a colonial periphery, and, consequently,

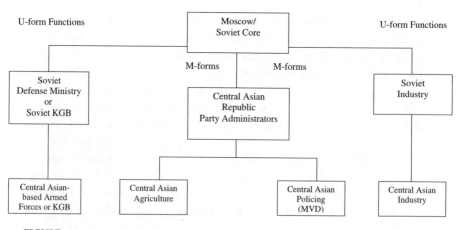

FIGURE 2.3
Hierarchical Governance in Soviet Central Asia

several U-form techniques used in governing Algeria were absent in neighboring colonies such as Tunisia or Morocco. Algeria was exempt from the usual colonial requirement of fiscal self-sufficiency and the territory received revenue transfers from Paris as if it were a regular French province.[55] French settlers were allowed to vote in the French legislative assembly, where they formed a powerful political force within France's multiparty electoral system and effectively resisted decolonization for decades.[56] Similarly, James Ron has shown how state security forces in Serbia and Israel employed mixed forms of organization over state violence within their contiguous territories, thereby precipitating different forms of policing and military actions within their cores (Montenegro and the West Bank) and frontiers (Bosnia and Southern Lebanon).[57] Such variations in the organization of security activities within the contiguous peripheries of the states led to administrative inconsistency and institutional confusion regarding the exact mandates of security services within these different peripheries.

Explaining Single-sector Hierarchies

The firm-type model also allows precise description of the type of hierarchical governance within any single sector or issue area, such as within the realm of security or economy. Single-sector hierarchies are becoming increasingly important in that core powers can control important functions or territories without having to necessarily resort to formal annexation or territorial conquest. As states and transnational actors extend their influence and governance structures worldwide, hierarchy is often established and maintained in a particular sector (military, economic) while the rest of the polities remain organizationally separate.

For example, although the extensive overseas network of United States military installations has been described as an "empire," U.S. basing and security policy actually features both single-sector U-form as well as more classically imperial M-form elements.[58] In order to maintain its global basing network, the United States must integrate both functional

---

55. Young, *African Colonial State in Comparative Perspective*, 125.
56. See Miles Kahler, *Decolonization in Britain and France: The Domestic Consequences of International Relations* (Princeton: Princeton University Press, 1984).
57. Ron, *Frontiers and Ghettos*.
58. See Chalmers Johnson, *The Sorrows of Empire: Militarism, Secrecy and the End of the Republic* (New York: Metropolitan, 2004); and C. T. Sandars, *America's Overseas Garrisons: The Leasehold Empire* (New York: Oxford University Press, 2000).

and geographic organizational tasks.[59] On the one hand, U.S. military operations are conducted on a functional basis from a variety of installations that are owned, leased, or simply maintained by the U.S. military, but these do not necessarily require a permanent territorial presence or governance agreement. For example, the special forces units of the United States currently conducting antiterrorist operations in the Philippines are doing so on a purely U-form or functional basis, given the provision in the Philippine constitution that explicitly prohibits the stationing of foreign military forces in the country. On the other hand, other military bases and overseas installations are governed as discrete territories or M-form type jurisdictions. For example, the United States military exclusively administered the Japanese island of Okinawa until its reversion in 1972, as well as a network of Pacific islands such as Guam and Midway. Similarly, the British RAF bases of Dhekalia and Akrotiri in Cyprus are fully sovereign British territory that is administered by a governor appointed by the United Kingdom's Ministry of Defense. Thus, within the hierarchy of overseas military installations and security institutions, both M-form and single-sector U-forms can prevail.

Similar distinctions can be made in the realm of economic policy, as both hierarchical forms historically have been employed to manage monetary policies and currencies across territories.[60] Dollarization is a specifically U-form type of hierarchy that replaces a country's monetary governance with the institutions of the country whose currency it adopts (regardless of whether the currency is the dollar or not).[61] Countries and their markets can remain juridically distinct but can be critically linked with important political implications through monetary integration. For example, Eric Helleiner observes that support for dollarization in Latin America has varied historically, as policymakers in the United States favored dollarization as an instrument to promote economic integration

59. For discussions of the organization of the basing hierarchy, see James Blaker, *United States Overseas Basing: The Anatomy of the Dilemma* (Westport, Conn.: Praeger, 1990); and Robert Harkavy, *Bases Abroad: The Global Foreign Military Presence* (New York: Oxford University Press, 1989).

60. For a historical overview of international monetary arrangements, see Eric Helleiner, *Making of National Money: Territorial Currencies in Historical Perspective* (Ithaca: Cornell University Press, 2003). Chapter 7 discusses in greater length the variety of hierarchical monetary orders in the contemporary international system.

61. For analytical overviews, see Benjamin Cohen, *The Future of Money* (Princeton: Princeton University Press, 2004), especially 33–66. Also see John Williamson, "Dollarization Does Not Make Sense Everywhere," in *The Dollarization Debate*, ed. Dominick Salvatore, James W. Dean, and Thomas D. Willett, 172–76 (New York: Oxford: 2003).

with Cuba, Puerto Rico, and Panama at the turn of the century while they supported national territorial currencies after World War II.[62]

Monetary integration also can take place through the formation of a currency board, which can be fruitfully analyzed as an M-form. In a currency board, a country effectively agrees to relinquish an autonomous national bank and peg its circulating territorial currency to the value of an external or anchor currency that remains freely exchangeable. The currency board was widely employed by the British in its colonial peripheries but has been revived more recently as a monetary arrangement in countries such as Argentina (1991–2002, dollar), Lithuania (1994, dollar), and Bulgaria (1997 Euro).[63] In the economy, as in military sectors, an organizational understanding of hierarchy allows observation of deep hierarchical processes in certain sectors, even when the two polities involved are otherwise legally independent or distinct.

In sum, the principle conceptual advantage of analyzing transnational hierarchies by their organizational form is that one can identify important differences in governance both across and within individual hierarchical peripheries and sectors. Thus, while noting the contrasts between certain imperial ideologies and governing philosophies, such as those between the British and French empires, is important, the firm-type model captures institutional variation that broad generalizations based on ideational variables such as national character, religion, and ideology cannot.

Transnational hierarchies vary according to their organizational form. This chapter has outlined a firm-type typology that shows how firms and polities can govern their peripheries according to either function or territory. Pure U-form governance is analogous to state-formation and consolidation as the core administers the periphery in an undifferentiated manner. Pure-M form governance, as with the case of most modern European empires, delegates authority to geographically specified units, which, in turn, are responsible for the formulation, execution, and administration of peripheral governance. Hierarchies also can employ a mix of both forms or use them selectively to govern a more limited number of sectors or issues across polities. Having established the distinction between organizational forms, we are now ready to investigate

---

62. See Eric Helleiner, "Dollarization Diplomacy: US Policy towards Latin America Coming Full Circle." *Review of International Political Economy* 19 (2003): 406–29.
63. Helleiner, *Making of National Money*, 174–79. For a complete contemporary list, see Cohen, *Future of Money*, 63.

their political consequences. The next chapter explores the varying kinds of political institutions that each of these types of governance produces and examines the particular control losses and problems engendered by each.

THE GOVERNANCE OF HIERARCHY

PATHS OF INSTITUTIONAL FORMATION

Having defined the concepts of organizational form and applied them to political settings, this chapter examines the causal effects of the U-form and M-form on the governance and institutional formation of a periphery. Each of these organizational forms is characterized by a relatively different set of governance costs, information flow patterns, and opportunism types. Accordingly, these characteristics tend to create harmonizing political institutions in a U-form periphery and patrimonial institutions in an M-form periphery. All else being equal, the harmonizing tendencies of the U-form are more likely to produce real institutional change within peripheries than the patrimonial dynamics engendered by the M-form.

The organizational theory of governance advanced in this chapter differs significantly from most prevailing ideational accounts of hierarchical governance that emphasize social factors in the institutional development of hierarchical polities. Ideational variables such as imperial purpose, national identity, and religious affiliation are usually understood to produce distinct types of political institutions, orders, and political development in hierarchical polities.[1] By contrast, the theory

---

1. For representative examples, see Rawi Abdelal, *National Purpose in the World Economy: Post-Soviet States in Comparative Perspective* (Ithaca: Cornell University Press, 2001); Rodney Bruce Hall, *National Collective Identity: Social Constructs and International Systems* (New York: Columbia University Press, 1999); Ronald Grigor Suny, "The Empire Strikes Out: Imperial Russia, 'National Identity,' and Theories of Empire," in *A State of Nations: Empire and Nation-Making in the Age of Lenin and Stalin* (New York: Oxford University Press, 2001); and Anthony Pagden, *Lords of All the World: Ideologies of Empire in Spain, Britain and France c. 1500–c. 1800* (New Haven: Yale University Press, 1995).

advanced in this chapter maintains that regardless of intentions, governing ideologies or norms or particular identities, organizational forms determine variations in the development of political institutions. Organizational form is a more powerful explanatory variable for understanding the governance of hierarchy than ideational factors, even in cases of empires and states heavily infused with a governing ideology. After summarizing the organizational literature on the attributes of U-form and M-form governance, this chapter presents an organizational theory of hierarchical governance.

U-FORM AND M-FORM ORGANIZATIONAL CHARACTERISTICS

The question of which hierarchical form is organizationally "superior" has been debated extensively among scholars and analysts of industrial organization.[2] According to his often-cited "M-form" hypothesis, Oliver Williamson, building on Alfred Chandler's observations, argues that the M-form is the more efficient organizational form.[3] Although Williamson's hypothesis has found qualified cross-national empirical support, critics have challenged both the theoretical logic and empirical validity of the M-form hypothesis.[4] Rather than make definitive judgments about the inherent economic superiority of these organizational forms, this section examines their contrasting organizational attributes in order to develop a theory of the political consequences of each type of governance. Specifically, the literature suggests that three factors—governance costs, informational asymmetries, and opportunism—will vary across each organizational form. These fundamental characteristics provide the analytical basis from which the institutional consequences of these different types of hierarchical governance can be deduced.

2. For examples, see Barry Harris, *Organization: The Effect of Large Corporations* (Ann Arbor: University of Michigan Press, 1983); and H. O. Armour and D. J. Teece, "Organizational Structure and Economic Performance," *Bell Journal of Economics* 9 (1978): 106–22.

3. Oliver Williamson, *The Economic Institutions of Capitalism* (New York: Free Press, 1985); Williamson, *Markets and Hierarchies: Analysis and Antitrust Implications* (New York: Free Press, 1975), 173; and Alfred D. Chandler Jr., *Strategy and Structure: Chapters in the History of the American Industrial Enterprise* (Cambridge: MIT Press, 1969).

4. For dissenting views or qualifications of the argument, see Anindya Sen, "The Structure of Firms," *Journal of Economic Behavior and Organization* 20 (1993): 119–30; Robert E. Hoskisson, Charles W. L. Hill, and Hicheon Kim, "The Multidivisional Structure: Organizational Fossil or Source of Value?" *Journal of Management* 19 (1993): 269–98; N. M. Kay, "Markets, False Hierarchies and the Evolution of the Modern Corporation," *Journal of Economic Behavior and Organization* 17 (1992): 315–33; C. A. Bartlett and S. Ghoshall, "Beyond the M-form: Towards a Managerial Theory of the Firm," *Strategic Management Journal* 14 (1993): 23–46; and Gregory Dow, "The Function of Authority in Transaction Costs Economics," *Journal of Economic Behavior and Organization* 8 (1987): 13–38.

Governance Costs

First, organizational forms vary in their relative governance costs. Typically, governance costs will be higher in U-forms than in M-forms.

As Chandler observes in his analysis of the U-form, coordinating decisions and routine operations in U-forms between the different functional divisions tends to be costly, especially as the number of managers and personnel in the firm increases.[5] Under such conditions, the chief executive must cope with ever-increasing amounts of information about the subdivisions while continuing to coordinate and allocate resources throughout the organizational structure of the firm. Similarly, information flows within each division become increasingly complex during periods of expansion as each of the functional divisions must interact with new layers of bureaucracy. Differentiating functional responsibilities and jurisdictional boundaries also becomes increasingly unclear during firm expansion, making it difficult for the core to identify and assess the efforts of each department.[6] As Chandler observes in his study of the evolution of DuPont and General Motors, such coordination problems inhibit the executive from accurately identifying the profit contribution of each functional division to each product or business, thereby leading to the internalization of efficiency losses.[7] Both Williamson and Chandler attribute the general organizational shift of large firms away from the U-form to the high governances costs incurred by the organizational structure.[8]

In contrast to the U-form, the M-form's governance costs are relatively low and resolve several of the U-form's efficiency losses. First, the center can identify efficient divisions more clearly by comparing their activity and performance to that of other divisions. Poorly performing divisions can be eliminated or have their divisional management replaced.[9] Second, the decoupling of routine activities at the divisional level from issues of overall strategy relieves the center of the excessive costs associated with its coordination responsibilities under the U-form. Furthermore, subdivisions under the M-form can adapt themselves to specific local conditions and environmental idiosyncrasies and develop

---

5. Alfred Chandler, *The Visible Hand: The Managerial Revolution in American Business* (Cambridge: Harvard University Press, 1977); and Williamson, *Economic Institutions of Capitalism*, 279–85.
6. Sen, "Structure of Firms," 122–23.
7. Chandler, *Strategy and Structure*.
8. Chandler, *Strategy and Structure*; and Williamson, *Economic Institutions of Capitalism*. However, this view has been challenged. See Neil Fligstein, "The Spread of the Multidivisional Form among Large Firms, 1919–1979," *American Sociological Review* 50 (1985): 377–91.
9. In this respect, Williamson views the diversified M-form structure as operating in a manner similar to an internal capital market, correcting for external market failure. Williamson, *Markets and Hierarchies*, 143–48.

routine decision-making procedures for local tasks, such as recruitment, operations evaluations, and production problem solving. For these reasons, both Chandler and Williamson argue that, solely on the grounds of efficiency, the M-form is the superior organizational form.[10] According to Williamson's M-form hypothesis, "The organization and operation of the large enterprise along the lines of the M-form firm favors goal pursuit and least cost behavior more nearly associated with the neoclassical profit maximization hypothesis than does the U-form organizational alternative."[11]

Informational Flows: Architectures and Asymmetries

The second attribute by which the U-form and M-form vary is in the informational asymmetries they engender between the core and peripheral operating divisions. Informational flows follow the organizational architecture of the various divisions. U-forms feature strong horizontal interactions at the core level but exhibit weaker horizontal ties at the subordinate level. At the core level in U-forms, different functional divisions must coordinate their activities across various product lines in accordance with the overall strategic objectives set by the core. As the number of products increase, so do the interactions among the functional divisions. However, at the peripheral level, functional divisions have little or no communication with one another. Since all activities within the division are directed and coordinated by the divisional head, the lower levels of divisions operate as self-contained pyramids, transmitting information about their activities vertically through the various levels of divisional management and bureaucracy (fig. 3.1). Information, then, is processed and transmitted by functional divisions both to lower levels (vertically) and to the core executive (horizontally). In organizational terms, information is "hierarchically decomposed" down through the functional divisions.[12]

The exact opposite holds for the informational flows and asymmetries within the M-form. Interactions among the operating divisions are severely curtailed or nonexistent as the core delegates a range of functional powers and jurisdictional authority to each divisional manager. As quasi-autonomous entities operating on the basis of product or geogra-

10. This is true provided that a hierarchy has a greater number of functions than it does territorial or product divisions.
11. Williamson, *Markets and Hierarchies*, 134.
12. On organizational architecture and various modes of information-processing, see Masahiko Aoki, *Towards a Comparative Institutional Analysis* (Cambridge: MIT Press, 2001), 95–128.

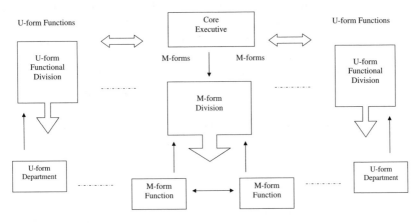

FIGURE 3.1
Information Flow Architecture in U-forms and M-forms

phy, M-form divisions have very little occasion to coordinate or interact with one another as overriding directives or strategic decisions flow
directly from the core executive to each divisional manager. However, at
the peripheral level, the range of functional divisions evident in the U-
form at the core reemerges within each autonomous M-form subdivision. Peripheral level interactions and informational flows between each
functional unit are stronger and mediated by the divisional head. In
organizational terms, information in M-forms is "encapsulated" within
the subdivisions, thereby increasing the informational symmetries
between the core and the subdivisions.[13]

Opportunism: Departmentalism and Agency Problems

Finally, hierarchical forms can be distinguished according to the type
of opportunism they engender within their divisions. Although there
is a tendency to conflate hierarchy with control, the very act of delegation brings a measure of control loss or opportunistic behavior to
all forms of hierarchy. In any hierarchy or organization with even a

---

13. On information encapsulation, see Aoki, *Towards a Comparative Institutional Analysis*, 102–9.

minimal amount of delegation, combinations of individual preferences must precipitate intransitivity in group choice or some degree of inefficiency.[14]

In general terms, Williamson defines opportunism as "self-interest seeking with guile," but this definition refers to several types of distinct behavior including evasion, shirking, contractual violation, moral hazard, adverse selection, divisionalism, and rent-seeking.[15] The management literature suggests that different types of opportunism characterize core-divisional relations in the U-form and M-form. The U-form is likely to engender departmentalism or divisional competition ("tribal conflict") among its functional divisions, whereas the M-form precipitates principal-agent problems between the division and the core executive.

Departmentalism in the U-form

Both Chandler and Williamson view the departmentalism engendered by the U-form as the organizational form's principal deficiency. As a firm's expansion overwhelms the information-processing and coordinating capacities of functional divisions, divisional managers are likely to give primary importance to achieving their operational subgoals instead of pursuing the overall best interests of the firm.[16] As Williamson observes, "The ability of the management [in large U-forms] to handle the volume and complexity of the demands placed upon it became strained and even collapsed. Unable meaningfully to identify with or contribute to the realization of global goals, managers in each of the functional parts attended to what they perceived to be operational subgoals instead."[17] In other words, departmentalism initially arises as a coping mechanism in response to the coordination and control-loss problems faced by functional divisions. Divisional managers make operational choices in the interest of self-preservation, but the core will find such opportunistic behavior difficult to disentangle from the routine functional decisions and divisional operations.

Such departmentalism may be exacerbated by the institutionalization of self-interested actions within the subdivision over time. In both firms

14. This is the so-called Sen paradox. For a discussion, see Gary Miller, *Managerial Dilemmas* (New York: Cambridge University Press, 1994), 88.
15. Quote from Williamson, *Markets and Hierarchies*, 6. For an analytical overview, see Kenneth H. Wathne and Jan Heide, "Opportunism in Interfirm Relationships: Forms, Outcomes, and Solutions," *Journal of Marketing* 64 (2000): 36–51.
16. Williamson, *Markets and Hierarchies*, 134; and Chandler, *Strategy and Structure*, 156.
17. Williamson, *Markets and Hierarchies*, 134.

and political hierarchies, functional organization inevitably leads to divisional infighting and jurisdictional competition as long-standing subdivisions adopt many of the traits that characterize mature bureaucracies. Individual functional divisions or "tribes" directly compete over budget and company resources, and each vies for a greater role in setting the overall strategy and direction of the company in a manner that also advances its divisional interests.[18] So-called tribal warfare in large organizations is an inevitable consequence brought by the devolution of everyday operating procedures and enforcement.[19] As described in chapter 1, the classic corporate case of departmental conflict involved the tensions between various divisions at the Ford Motor Company while it reorganized its operations in the interwar years. Each of the company's functional divisions advanced its own preferences about the strategies and product lines to pursue to maximize overall profits. Such interdivisional fighting and jurisdictional competition has also been noted by theorists of organizational competition and bureaucracy.[20]

Agency Problems in the M-form

Williamson champions the adoption of the M-form as a cure for the departmentalism of the U-form. As critics of Williamson's approach have pointed out, however, the M-form is also susceptible to a different type of opportunism—principal-agent problems. Theoretically, there is little reason to assume that divisional managers will act in the interests of the firm as opposed to their own individual interests. As critics observe, Williamson "assumes away" the potential agency problems created between the center and division managers.[21] Corporate managers seek to increase their own power, influence, status, and income and not merely the profits of the firm. They actively seek out and perpetuate arrangements (formal or informal) that will maximize this more complex utility function.[22]

18. For discussions, see Harry Leibenstein, *Inside the Firm: The Inefficiencies of Hierarchy* (Cambridge: Harvard University Press, 1987).

19. Miller, *Managerial Dilemmas*, 93.

20. Graham Allison, *Essence of Decision* (Boston: Brown & Little, 1971). Also see James Q. Wilson, *Bureaucracy* (New York: Basic Books, 1989).

21. Robert E. Hoskisson, Charles W. L. Hill, and Hicheon Kim, "The Multidivisional Structure: Organizational Fossil or Source of Value?" *Journal of Management* 19 (1993): 275–76.

22. These are the classic insights of the agency literature. For overviews, see Michael C. Jensen, *Foundations of Organizational Strategy* (Cambridge: Harvard University Press, 1998); and John W. Pratt and Richard J. Zeckhauser, *Principals and Agents: The Structure of Business* (Boston: Harvard Business School Press, 1985).

As in any organizational arrangement that relies on extensive delegation, core executives face the twin problems of hidden information and hidden action on the part of their managerial counterparts. While, in theory, the executive should be able to identify the activities of various divisions, in practice, vast informational asymmetries inhibit the center from performing accurate audits of subdivision activity and managerial performance. This is particularly evident in situations where divisions are located a great distance from the core and capacities for monitoring are underdeveloped. As agents, divisional managers have incentives to conceal information used for auditing purposes or to manipulate it in such a manner that presents upbeat characterizations of the division's activities. They will use the firm's assets and resources to advance their own individual goals. This is especially true when the very existence of the division is at stake and division managers understand that corporate management prefers to maintain a large array of diversified and performing operations.[23] Finally, divisional managers will be more susceptible to pursuing short-run profit maximization at the expense of long-term considerations, especially when their career prospects are dependent on such quantifiable measures.[24]

As Chandler himself observed of the decentralization of the Sears Company during the 1970s, local retailers accepted bribes on behalf of stores and used the reputation of the company to further their own profit-maximizing interests, not the interests of the firm.[25] Decentralization alleviated much of the departmentalism at the core only to create a series of acute agency problems at the retail level where the central executive could no longer control the self-interested behavior of franchise owners and their employees.

Debates about the inherent superiority of one organizational form remain inconclusive as each form incurs some type of cost relative to the other. Nevertheless, as table 3.1 summarizes, organizational studies suggest that hierarchical forms vary on three key dimensions: governance costs, information flow patterns, and opportunism type. In turn, these organizational characteristics provide the basis for assessing the political consequences of M-form and U-form governance.

23. Robert E. Hoskisson and Thomas A. Turk, "Corporate Restructuring: Governance and Control Limits of the Internal Capital Market," *Academy of Management Review* 15 (1990): 459–77. This phenomena is often referred to as "empire-building."

24. B. D. Baysinger and R. E. Hoskisson, "Diversification, Strategy, and R&D Intensity in Multiproduct Firms," *Academy of Management Journal* 32 (1989): 310–32; and C. W. L. Hill et al., "Are Acquisitions a Poison Pill for Innovation?" *Academy of Management Executive* 5 (1991): 22–34.

25. As discussed in Miller, *Managerial Dilemmas*, 91–93.

TABLE 3.1
Summary of Differing Attributes of U-form and M-form Governance

Organizational Attribute	U-form	M-form
Organizing Principle	Function	Territory
Governance Costs	High	Low
Information Flows	Low core-subdivision asymmetries; Divisional decomposition	High core-subdivision asymmetries; Divisional encapsulation
Opportunism Type	Departmentalism; Conflation of divisional goals and needs with those of overall organization	Principal-Agent Problems; Hidden self-interested action

POLITICAL APPLICATIONS: HIERARCHICAL GOVERNANCE AND INSTITUTIONAL FORMATION

The insights from the organizational literature provide the means for explicitly mapping the political consequences of U-form and M-form governance. Different combinations of these three characteristics produce distinct types of peripheral institutional development under each type of hierarchy (figs. 3.2 and 3.3). U-form governance—with its high governance costs, low informational asymmetries, and departmentalism—produces harmonizing political institutions, while M-form governance—with its low governance costs, high informational asymmetries, and agency problems—creates patrimonial institutions. *Regardless of the intentions of the core or its governing ideology and norms,* the U-form is more likely to actually transform peripheral institutions while M-form integration is likely to foster some form of modified institutional persistence.

U-form: Harmonizing Political Institutions

In political hierarchies, U-form governance promotes harmonizing institutional formation within peripheries. Through the mechanisms of standardization, focal points, and nondiscrimination, U-form governance can effectively bring peripheral institutions into line with core requirements and, when necessary, transform or change preexisting peripheral institutions, although the costs of doing so are relatively high. Furthermore, the main type of U-form opportunism—departmentalism—further encourages the deterritorialization of peripheral institutions and authority patterns.

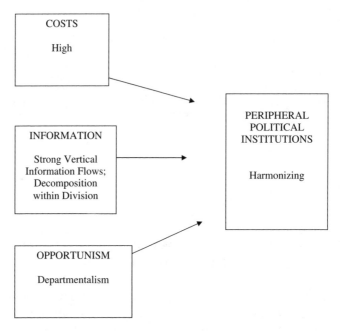

FIGURE 3.2
Political Institutions under U-form Governance

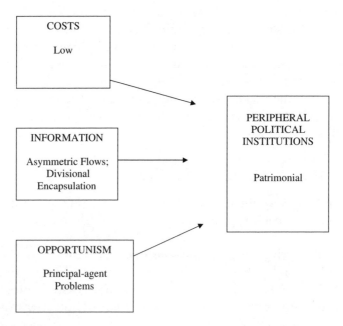

FIGURE 3.3
Political Institutions under M-form Governance

Hypothesis 1: U-form governance will promote the harmonization of peripheral institutions in line with those of the core's functional divisions.

Corollary 1a: U-form governance is more likely to transform or change a periphery's institutions than M-form governance.

Mechanisms of Harmonization

Harmonization is the process by which institutions and governing practices in a periphery are brought into accord with institutions in the core. Through functional governance and information flows within departments, three mechanisms can promote this institutional convergence between core and periphery. First, U-form governance forces particular sectors and organizations within various peripheries to standardize their operations in accordance with the requirements of the functional division. Once governed by the core's functional divisions, peripheral institutions will adopt the rules, patterns, and procedures of the core's functional divisions, which must remain the same for any given function across all peripheries. For example, Hendrik Spruyt has shown how functional governance in early modern states, as opposed to the nonhierarchically organized towns of the Hanseatic League, forced state peripheries and localities to standardize weights, measures, and commercial law.[26] In turn, this standardization greatly reduced the transaction costs of economic activity within state boundaries, increased long-distance trade and activity, and made the state an attractive organizational form to emulate.[27] Functional standardization can also promote actual changes in the social preferences and allegiances of peripheral inhabitants. For example, Eugen Weber's examination of the formation of the French nation reveals how the centralized French state eventually altered its many provincial forms of social affiliation through a process of central bureaucratic expansion (especially within the educational sector), functional reorganization, and assimilation.[28]

Second, the presence of a constitution or other central governing principle can align the preferences and calibrate the activities of various functional divisions. By delineating a set of universal principles or

---

26. Hendrik Spruyt, *The Sovereign State and Its Competitors* (Princeton: Princeton University Press, 1994).

27. Ibid. On the dynamics of "institutional isomorphism," see Paul DiMaggio and Walter Powell, "The Iron Cage Revisited: Institutional Isomorphism and Collective Rationality in Organizational Fields," in *The New Institutionalism in Organizational Analysis,* ed. DiMaggio and Powell, 63–82 (Chicago: University of Chicago Press, 1991).

28. Eugen Weber, *Peasants into Frenchman* (Palo Alto: Stanford University Press, 1976).

expectations, constitutions serve as focal points for coordinating subsequent institutional development and setting formal boundaries for acceptable forms of future state-building.[29] As Douglass North and Barry Weingast have shown, the adoption of constitutional principles after the Glorious Revolution curtailed the English monarchy's ability to arbitrarily alter rules without parliamentary consent and limited its ability to give preferential economic treatment to certain segments of the population.[30] Focal points offer an endogenous mechanism through which various actors and divisional factions in a political U-form can coordinate expectations and behavior.[31]

Finally, U-form governance promotes institutional harmonization through the use of nondiscriminatory contracting. By granting the same legal status to a periphery as to the core, U-forms reduce the distributional issues or asymmetrical group payoffs that might promote territorial and administrative particularism within a governance function. For example, theorists have shown how national conscription in modern European states played a key role in breaking down local identities among Europe's citizenry and forging new allegiances to the nation-state.[32] In Margaret Levi's formulation, more universalistic and nondiscriminatory national laws of conscription are more likely to generate widespread citizens' consent, independent of regime type.[33] Similarly, nondiscriminatory systems of taxation are more likely to generate compliance and loyalty to the state.[34]

Departmentalism and Divisional Interests

While functional integration is more likely to harmonize patterns of institutional formation and state-building, it will also encourage departmentalism among functional divisions. A negative consequence of U-form governance is that each division tends to adopt its own positions and jurisdictional concerns when formulating policy. State agencies and

29. See Douglass C. North and Barry R. Weingast, "Constitutions and Commitment: The Evolution of Institutions Governing Public Choice in Seventeenth Century England," *Journal of Economic History* 49 (1989): 803–32.

30. Ibid.

31. Judith Goldstein and Robert Keohane, eds., *Ideas and Foreign Policy: Beliefs, Institutions and Political Change* (Ithaca: Cornell University Press, 1993).

32. Barry Posen, "Nationalism, the Mass Army, and Military Power," *International Security* 18 (1993): 80–124. Also see Margaret Levi, *Consent, Dissent, and Patriotism* (Cambridge: Cambridge University Press, 1997); and Charles Tilly, *Capital, Coercion and the Formation of European States: AD 990–1990* (Cambridge, Mass.: Blackwell, 1990).

33. Levi, *Consent, Dissent, and Patriotism*, chap. 4. Although Levi does note that democratic regimes are more likely to uphold such universalistic standards of conscription and service.

34. Margaret Levi, *Of Rule and Revenue* (Berkeley: University of California Press, 1988).

ministries, in turn, tend to conflate their own organizational interests with that of the state at large. According to Michael Laver and Kenneth Shepsle, departmentalism among cabinet ministers in parliamentary governments effectively precludes collective deliberation or decision making, as ministers tend to act only on policy matters that relate to their individual authority and discretion.[35] As a result, the agenda control of individual ministers effectively constrains the policy set to which a cabinet can commit.[36] In its extreme, departmentalism equates the goals and interests of a particular functional division with that of the overall organization or polity.

Departmentalism need not be confined to a particular formal cabinet or ministerial position in mature democracies. Jack Snyder has shown that in certain states that are "cartelized" or lack well-institutionalized processes of democratic deliberation, political factions or interest groups can "hijack" the state and make it adopt policies, such as military expansion, that serve their own immediate departmental needs but that ultimately damage the overall national interest.[37] Even within democracies, militaries and competing military organizations, especially in times of crisis or political uncertainty, demonstrate organizational competition and departmentalist tendencies.[38]

Of course, the very proliferation of departmentalism cuts against or even openly conflicts with the preservation of peripheral territorial institutions. In Yugoslavia, for example, the Yugoslav Federal Army (JNA) saw itself not only as providing defense against external threat but, given its disproportionate influence within federal politics, as the ultimate guardian of the unity and territorial integrity of the Yugoslav state.[39] The Portuguese military viewed its administration of Portugal's five African colonies and East Timor as inseparable from the political hegemony it exercised at home, even as its ongoing colonial rule drained one-third

---

35. Michael Laver and Kenneth Shepsle, *Making and Breaking Governments: Cabinets and Legislatures in Parliamentary Democracies* (New York: Cambridge University Press, 1995); and Laver and Shepsle, eds., *Cabinet Ministers and Parliamentary Government* (New York: Cambridge University Press, 1994). But see John Huber, "The Vote of Confidence in Parliamentary Democracies," *American Political Science Review* 90 (1996): 269–82.

36. John M. Carey, "Parchment, Equilibria, and Institutions," *Comparative Political Studies* 33 (2000): 743–44.

37. Jack Snyder, *Myths of Empire: Domestic Politics and International Ambition* (Ithaca: Cornell University Press, 1993).

38. Deborah Avant, *Political Institutions and Military Change: Lessons from Peripheral Wars* (Ithaca: Cornell University Press, 1994); and Graham Allison, *Essence of Decision* (Boston: Brown & Little, 1971).

39. See James Gow, *Legitimacy and the Military: The Yugoslav Crisis* (New York: St. Martin's Press, 1992). This case is discussed further in chapter 6.

to one-half of the Portuguese annual national budget in the 1960s and 1970s.[40] Similarly, the Soviet military integrated the militaries of its East European satellites according to its own functional defense needs, not the dictates or preferences of the East European states or their governing communist parties.[41]

Summary of U-form Governance

Through mechanisms such as standardization, the provision of focal points, and nondiscriminatory contracting, the U-form harmonizes peripheral institutions with those of the core. While such a pattern of state-building is effective, it is also costly. Incorporating a political periphery within the full array of core functional institutions and bureaucracies is expensive and, as detailed previously, presents significant coordination and logistical challenges. Such integration may also impose unacceptable political costs on the core. For example, complete U-form annexation grants the full array of citizenship entitlements to a periphery's inhabitants, including rights of institutionalized representation and political participation, and these may threaten the political balance within the core.[42] In short, the U-form and its institutional harmonization make it an effective organizational form for promoting institutional transformation within a periphery. Nonetheless, its economic and potential political costs will temper its frequency of use.

M-form: Patrimonial Institutional Development

By contrast, peripheral subdivisions in M-forms are likely to produce patrimonial political institutions. In patrimonial political systems, rulers typically use traditional or personal modes of authority to dispense particularistic political favors (as opposed to public goods) to societal clients

---

40. Crawford Young, *The African Colonial State in Comparative Perspective* (New Haven: Yale University Press, 1995), 191. On the institutionalization of the Portuguese military's interests, see Spruyt, *Ending Empire*.

41. Condoleezza Rice, *The Soviet Union and the Czechoslovak Military, 1948–1973: Uncertain Allegiance* (Princeton: Princeton University Press, 1984). Rice also points out that this tight functional integration and resulting departmentalism effectively made the Soviet military a "domestic" constituent within Czechoslovak internal politics.

42. Consider, for example, contemporary debates within Israel about the advantages and disadvantages of annexing the West Bank and/or Gaza and/or debates in the United States concerning granting statehood to Puerto Rico. For a discussion, see Ian Lustick, *Unsettled States, Disputed Lands: Britain and Ireland, France and Algeria, Israel and West Bank-Gaza* (Ithaca: Cornell University Press, 1993).

in exchange for their political support.[43] Usually, patrimonial systems embed this "unofficial" traditional hierarchy within a parallel hierarchy that is officially or legally responsible for the organization of political, economic, and social activity.[44]

Regardless of national ideologies, policy intentions, and particular geopolitical concerns, M-form organization tends to institutionalize patrimonial institutions in peripheries, thus allowing imperial administrators to simultaneously maintain political order through collaborative arrangements while they opportunistically pursue their individual political ambitions. Maintaining political order and legitimacy usually necessitates the use of existing authority structures to serve new administrative goals and functions.[45] Whether a colonial administration's goal was to increase revenues through the collection of taxes, mobilize the indigenous labor force, or quell potential political opposition, colonial rulers required the services of social intermediaries and interlocutors to help them implement their policies. As long as colonial administrators could maintain political hegemony and extract revenues, the center did not overtly concern itself with the patrimonial nature of the institutions that characterized the colonial state.

Hypothesis 2: M-form governance will promote patrimonial institutions within the periphery, regardless of the core's intentions or governing ideology.

Corollary 2a: M-form governance is less likely to transform or change a periphery's institutions than U-form governance.

Low Governance Costs and High Informational Asymmetries

In general, M-form peripheries were less costly for cores to govern than U-forms. With only a few modern exceptions (French Algeria, Portuguese Africa), modern colonial states operated as financially self-sufficient entities. In early colonial expeditions to the Americas and Asia, charter companies raised money for their expeditions with the guarantee from the metropole that they could accumulate a percentage of

---

43. On the dynamics of patrimonial systems, see Thomas M. Callaghy, *The State-Society Struggle: Zaire in Comparative Perspective* (New York: Columbia University Press, 1984); S. N. Eisenstadt and L. Roniger, *Patrons, Clients and Friends: Interpersonal Relations and the Structure of Trust in Society* (New York: Cambridge University Press, 1984); and Ernest Gellner and John Waterbury, *Patrons and Clients in Mediterranean Societies* (London: Duckworth, 1977).

44. S. N. Eisenstadt, *The Political Systems of Empires* (Glencoe, Ill.: Free Press, 1963), 9.

45. Although as Michael Doyle points out, this applied more to peripheries with an existing patrimonial structure than to those with a tribal social structure. See Doyle, *Empires* (Ithaca: Cornell University Press, 1986), 198–208.

profits drawn from these territories. Such contractual forms of colonial exploration were a low-cost way for metropoles to expand their global authority.[46] Without having to expend national blood or treasure, the autonomous financing of M-form peripheries allowed core powers to simultaneously support the governance of multiple peripheries at a relatively low cost. Thus the drive for financial autonomy within each operating division usually culminated in a series of repressive taxes, such as the head taxes, that were tremendous burdens to colonized populations.[47]

Second, the high informational asymmetries between the core and periphery, coupled with the M-form's autonomous governance structure, further encouraged the cooption of preexisting peripheral social and political authority patterns into the formal and informal power structures of the colonial state.[48] Rather than expend resources to completely reorder domestic social life according to core national ideologies or identities, modern European colonial elites used domestic elites as collaborators and governed through traditional institutions whenever they could to ensure political stability. As studies of British colonialism in Africa have shown, the growth of the colonial state was predicated on sustaining the support of indigenous elites who functioned as symbolic rapporteurs between the colonial apparatus and the subjugated society.[49] While it is true that colonial states sometimes ruptured traditional social structures, especially in tribal or undifferentiated peripheries, the incentive structure of the M-form encouraged colonial governors to manipulate strategically, but not wholly uproot, existing authority patterns.

Principal-Agent Problems in M-forms

Perhaps the most striking aspect and ubiquitous characteristic of M-form rule is the set of acute agency problems it engenders. Across all modern empires, metropoles experienced great difficulty in monitoring and controlling the actions of their peripheral administrators. The vast distances, communications problems, and informational asymmetries

46. See David B. Abernethy, *The Dynamics of Global Dominance: European Overseas Empires 1415–1980* (New Haven: Yale University, 2000); and Janice Thomson, *Mercenaries, Pirates, & Sovereigns* (Princeton: Princeton University Press, 1994).
47. See Young, *African Colonial State in Comparative Perspective,* 126–28.
48. See Doyle, *Empires,* 141–231.
49. Jeffrey Herbst, *States and Power in Africa* (Princeton: Princeton University Press, 2000); and David Laitin, *Hegemony and Culture: Politics and Change amongst the Yoruba* (Chicago: University of Chicago Press, 1986).

inherent in these transnational M-form arrangements ensured that colonial administrators had great leverage to pursue their own preferences.

Every Western metropole confronted major problems controlling its M-form rulers, and cases of systematic corruption and fraud on behalf of colonial administrators were ubiquitous. In perhaps the most famous corruption case of the British empire, Warren Hastings—the former director of the British East India Company—was tried in the House of Lords on charges including embezzlement, extortion, fraud, and "applying [the company's] money to purposes totally improper and unauthorized [and with] enormous extravagances and bribery in various contracts with a view to enrich his dependants and favorites."[50] Although the House of Lords eventually acquitted Hastings, the case brought public scrutiny to the operations and murky financial practices of chartered companies and initiated an administrative overhaul in the company. Similarly, cases of endemic corruption within the Dutch East India Company helped to precipitate its bankruptcy in 1776, while Janice Thomson's comparative research on colonial charter companies suggests that European metropoles' inability to control or properly account for their commercial activities played a critical role in their demise.[51]

It is important to recognize that agency problems plagued all imperial powers that employed M-form organization, not just those that relied on external contractors or charter companies for their peripheral governance. For example, in France—a colonial power that favored "direct" rule and an official policy of "civilizing" and pursuing social transformation in its peripheries—there is substantial evidence of these severe M-form agency problems. For instance, William Cohen's analysis of French colonial administration shows that French colonial agents routinely ignored official directives and policies in order to pursue personal profit. French central authorities found it impossible to adequately monitor the activities of governors who deliberately delayed reporting to superiors, misinformed inspectors about local decisions and projects, and even cut off communications such as telegraphs in an effort to maintain their secrecy. As long as administrative agents could avoid situations that would require more direct metropolitan intervention, such as local

---

50. Quoted in Niall Ferguson, *Empire* (New York: Basic Books, 2003), 55.
51. See Julia Adams, "Principals and Agents, Colonialists and Company Men: The Decay of Colonial Control in the Dutch East Indies," *American Sociological Review* 61 (1996): 12–28. Also see Thomson, *Mercenaries, Pirates, & Sovereigns*, 59–68, and 97–105.

rebellions or insufficient revenue collection, the metropole could not constrain, in practical terms, the actions of administrators.[52]

Indeed, from a historical perspective, even earlier forms of identity-based empires characterized by strong identities and ideological imperatives (or universal empires) were severely hampered by agency problems. As S. N. Eisenstadt observed, imperial bureaucracies in early-modern political systems tended to use the resources of rulers, "to acquire entirely independent and uncontrollable power and status positions, to monopolize these positions, and to minimize any effective control over itself and over the scope of activities of the various autonomous regulative mechanisms."[53] The Byzantine bureaucracy was plagued by self-interested and unrestrained actions on the parts of civil servants and tax collectors.[54] Similarly, the Spanish metropole, despite its powerful ideology of empire and religious fervor, found it nearly impossible to maintain the political loyalty of its viceroys, magistrates, and administrators, as they cut individual deals on the side with Creoles and local political agents.[55] In both the Roman and Ottoman empires, acute control problems were exacerbated by the high transaction costs of monitoring distant peripheries with limited capabilities.[56] In fact, the moral or ideological "decay" that many historians saw as contributing to the withering away of these polities could just as easily be explained as the sum of opportunistic actions taken by peripheral administrative agents.

Regardless of how individual cases are interpreted, the combined histories of identity-based empires suggest that they faced principal-agent problems similar to those of their modern counterparts. More significantly, the projection of a common or universal identity into the periphery was insufficient to control the opportunistic behavior of administrative agents. Political order within M-form peripheries could not be achieved through ideational means alone.

52. William Cohen, *Rulers of Empire: The French Colonial Service in Africa* (Stanford, Calif.: Hoover Institution Press, 1971), particularly 57–73. Also see Young, *African Colonial State in Comparative Perspective*, 122.

53. Eisenstadt, *Political Systems of Empires*, 171.

54. Warren Treadgold, *A History of the Byzantine State and Society* (Palo Alto: Stanford University Press, 1997).

55. Mark Hanson, "Organizational Bureaucracy in Latin America and the Legacy of Spanish Colonialism," *Journal of Interamerican Studies and World Affairs* 16 (1974): 199–219; and John Leddy Phelan, "Authority and Flexibility in the Spanish Imperial Bureaucracy," *Administrative Science Quarterly* 5 (1960): 47–65.

56. Halil Incalek, *The Ottoman Empire: The Classical Age, 1300–1600* (London: Weidenfeld and Nicolson, 1973).

Mitigating Principal-Agent Problems

Of course, core polities in both modern and early-modern M-form empires implemented a number of monitoring techniques that attempted to reduce these principal-agent problems. Interestingly, many of these techniques are similar to the strategies of control employed by modern M-form corporations. Metropoles can adopt a policy of rotating administrators, like the rotation of middle managers, to prevent them from being "captured" by agents in the periphery, as was the case with the Ottoman empire, the Roman empire, and even the U.S. Pacific Naval command.[57] Second, cores can install agents with similar organizational allegiances, cultures, and preferences by establishing extensive screening and selection procedures for potential administrators.[58] For example, the British favored installing administrators from England's elite "public schools" in the hope that the preferences of its governors would be aligned with those of the Home Office. Third, cores can deliberately create multiple channels of overlapping jurisdictional authority, thus allowing various agents to monitor each other. This was a favored technique of Spanish administrators in America.[59] Fourth, the core can periodically send inspectors to distant territories where agency problems are most acute. Periodic inspection was a routine feature of early and modern empires, not unlike the functions of internal auditing units in modern corporations, though inspectors themselves were bribed with payments once they reached the periphery. Finally, the center can reward compliance by offering agents in the periphery possibilities for promotion into the political or diplomatic ranks of the core, what David Laitin has referred to as "most favored lord" status.[60]

The efficacy of these different mechanisms varied. Although a comprehensive evaluation of their usefulness is beyond the immediate scope of this study, some organizational studies suggest that attempts to align incentives between the core and periphery are more effective than improving the core's monitoring techniques or even its enforcement capabilities.[61] That is, unless the basic structural incongruity of

57. Karen Barkey, *Bandits and Bureaucrats: The Ottoman Route to State Consolidation* (Ithaca: Cornell University Press, 1994).

58. David Kreps, "Corporate Culture and Economic Theory," in Perspectives on Positive Political Economy, ed. James Alt and Kenneth Shepsle, 90–143 (New York: Cambridge University Press, 1990).

59. Phelan, "Authority and Flexibility," 47–65.

60. David Laitin, *Identity in Formation: The Russian-Speaking Populations in the Near Abroad* (Ithaca: Cornell University Press, 1998).

61. For good discussions, see Miller, *Managerial Dilemmas*, and Kreps, "Corporate Culture and Economic Theory."

preferences generated by M-form governance can be overcome, agency problems will inevitably persist.

M-form Theoretical Reprise

It would be imprudent and historically inaccurate to label every modern colonial or imperial arrangement as a patrimonial bargain of uniform dynamics. Clearly, the firm-type model cannot capture all the nuances or exceptional cases within such a broad historical domain. What is more apparent according to recent studies of imperial political history is that colonial powers used a variety of techniques to pursue clientelistic arrangements through preexisting indigenous hierarchies.[62] Although the exact strategies and methods varied somewhat across metropoles and peripheries, M-form governance imposed certain structural parameters on both the actions of colonial administrators and peripheral indigenous authority figures. Collective resistance to foreign rule and colonial control was neither as absolute nor as exclusively predicated on ideational dimensions as is commonly thought. In fact, understanding imperial governance as a partial function of these nested agency problems can aid the systematic identification and exploration of important evolutions within the control systems, power structures, and monitoring techniques established by different imperial powers. Such studies of incentive structures would complement most prevailing ideational analyses of colonialism and, more broadly, integrate colonial studies with the political science literature on institutions.[63]

Finally, a further application of the firm-type model's predictions might include an examination of the subset of cases in which the core suffered control losses resulting from both U-form and M-form types of opportunism. This occurred when representatives from a distinct functional branch of the core state—usually the military—were granted exclusive control over a political periphery. In this case, the usual agency problems inherent in M-form delegation were compounded by the departmentalist impulses of maintaining control for that division's more narrow purposes. A cursory glance at the post–World War II record of administration by the Portuguese army in Africa or the U.S. Naval command in Pacific territories such as Guam and Micronesia suggests

62. For an overview, see Colin Newbury, *Patrons, Clients, and Empire: Chieftaincy and Over-rule in Asia, Africa, and the Pacific* (Oxford: Oxford University Press, 2003); and Newbury, "Patrons, Clients, and Empire: The Subordination of Indigenous Hierarchies in Asia and Africa," *Journal of World History* 11 (2000): 227–63.
63. In this regard, David Laitin's study of British control techniques and governance strategies in Yorubaland remains significant. See Laitin, *Hegemony and Culture*.

that these ruling departments were able to administer these peripheries in a relatively unconstrained manner given their prominent institutional standing and veto power within the core.[64]

To summarize, hierarchical governance under the U-form and M-form creates very different institutional effects. These organizational forms differ fundamentally in their governance costs, informational asymmetries, and opportunism types, and these varying characteristics generate different political institutions within their peripheries. Regardless of the governing ideologies of identities inherent in the core, U-form governance will produce patterns of state-building that harmonize its institutions with those of the core and is more likely to actually transform the periphery. By contrast, M-form governance tends to produce patrimonial institutions in its political peripheries and lacks the capacity of the U-form to enact fundamental institutional change. Given the organizational logics associated with these hierarchical forms and their governance, the next chapter examines and illustrates these organizational processes and effects in the case of the Soviet governance of Central Asia.

64. On veto points and domestic factions, see Spruyt, *Ending Empire.*

AN EMPIRICAL ILLUSTRATION

SOVIET CENTRAL ASIA

Conceptual distinctions among different forms of hierarchy, their characteristics, and predictions about their causal effects on patterns of governance and institutional formation have been set forth. This chapter presents four sectoral cases—two in security and two in economy—in Soviet Central Asia as empirical illustrations of these conceptual claims. Applying the firm-type model to the Soviet case allows us to chart how these two distinct governance logics generated very different types of political institutions and state-building within the same political setting. Thus, the sectoral approach offered here captures internal variation in the development of the Soviet polity, a matter other approaches that treat Soviet policy and institutional development as uniform cannot account accurately.

First, the methodological justification for selecting the Soviet case is described, and this chapter is located within broader debates about institutional approaches to Soviet politics. Next, I show how Soviet administrators employed both U-forms and M-forms in their governance of the Central Asian periphery across security (policing and defense) and economic (industry and agriculture) sectors, thereby governing some sectors as an M-form empire and others as a U-form integrated state. Last, I examine how each of these organizational forms produced contrasting modes of political development, thereby creating harmonizing institutions in some sectors and patrimonial institutions in others.

CRITERIA AND LOGIC OF CASE SELECTION

Two important criteria served to qualify Soviet Central Asia as the empirical focus of this study. As an empirical setting, the case exhibits significant variance on the independent variable within different issue areas as Soviet planners simultaneously employed both U-form and M-form techniques in their administration of the region's security and economy. Moreover, the Soviet case is commonly studied as a case where ideology and identity constitute important sources of political behavior. Accordingly, the organizational approach is intended to explain variation that ideational approaches to Soviet governance cannot.[1]

The other reason for selecting Central Asia as a focal case relates to the methodological debate within postcommunist and Central Asian studies regarding comparative theoretical frameworks and social scientific inquiry. As Valerie Bunce points out, scholars should be wary of comparing geographic regions and political systems that differ so fundamentally that they will render comparison theoretically meaningless.[2] Olga Dmitrieva eloquently advances the case against broad theoretical comparison when she explicitly rejects that Soviet Central Asia in any way resembled the colonies of other European powers:

> the system of relationships in the ethnic peripheries demands insight studies, in as much as the periphery displayed a curious mixture of preindustrial feudal relations with a strong Moslem heritage, interwoven with an administrative command business network and bureaucratic system . . . it resulted in a quite unusual system of relationships which could scarcely be found anywhere else. Therefore, studies of the ethnic periphery, including Central Asia, can hardly be done in the framework and terminology applicable to other Third World countries.[3]

The point is an important one, but like the general debate about theory and comparison in post-Soviet politics, it focuses too narrowly on the issue of whether transitology should be the appropriate frame of

---

1. For an important exception that does examine variations in patterns of state-building and identity formation, see David Laitin, *Identity in Formation: The Russian-Speaking Populations in the Near Abroad* (Ithaca: Cornell University Press, 1998).

2. For a fascinating debate on the role of transitology in post-Soviet studies, see Terry Lynn Karl and Philippe Schmitter, "The Conceptual Travels of Transitologists: How Far to the East Should They Attempt to Go?" *Slavic Review* 53 (1994): 173–85; and Valerie Bunce, "Should Transitologists Be Grounded?" *Slavic Review* 54 (1995): 111–27.

3. Oksana Olga Dmitrieva, *Regional Development: The USSR and After* (London: UCL Press, 1996), ix.

comparison between the post-Soviet region and the developing world. Rather than assume that a particular region is incomparable to others, the challenge for any comparative and theoretical framework is to show, preferably deductively, how the administration of one region conceptually relates to a broader universe of cases. In fact, recent studies of the political economy of Soviet institutions rest on strong analytical assumptions about the dynamics and incentive systems embodied in complex hierarchical organizations.[4] Following recent studies that compare the Soviet system to other imperial orders, the firm-type model places the Soviet case within a broader spectrum of theoretical and comparative theory.[5] In short, the organizational approach explains variations in Soviet governance effects and sectoral patterns of political institutionalization that other theories cannot.

M-FORM AND U-FORM ORGANIZATION IN SOVIET CENTRAL ASIA

Background to Soviet Rule

Soviet rule in Central Asia can be traced to the collapse of the Russian empire and the Civil War of 1918–21, although the area of Turkestan had been a colony of imperial Russia from 1865 to 1918. The Red Army had particular difficulty neutralizing the pan-Turkic and pan-Islamic resistance elements in the region that fermented the Basmachi Revolt, a rebellion that was only quelled in the late 1920s.[6] Wishing to fragment regional political identities and accelerate the region's integration, Moscow adopted classic "divide-and-rule" policies that created distinct nationalities from Central Asia's various tribal and clan-based groups. Through a number of reshufflings and boundary redrawings, the region

---

4. Some recent contributions have already demonstrated the theoretical fruitfulness of applying economic concepts of organization to the study of Soviet hierarchies. See Steven Solnick, *Stealing the State: Control and Collapse in Soviet Institutions* (Cambridge: Harvard University Press, 1998); and Randall Stone, *Satellites and Commissars: Strategy and Conflict in the Politics of Soviet-bloc Trade* (Princeton: Princeton University Press, 1996).

5. Alexander Motyl, *Imperial Ends: The Decay, Collapse, and Revival of Empires* (New York: Columbia University Press, 2001); Karen Dawisha and Bruce Parrott, eds., *The End of Empire? The Disintegration of the USSR in Comparative Perspective* (Armonk, N.Y.: M. E. Sharpe, 1996); Karen Barkey and Mark von Hagen, eds., *After Empire. Multiethnic Societies and Nation-Building: The Soviet Union and the Russian, Ottoman, and Habsburg Empires* (Boulder, Colo.: Westview Press, 1997); and Hendrik Spruyt, *Ending Empire* (Ithaca: Cornell University Press, 2005).

6. Martha B. Olcott, "The Basmachi or Freemen's Revolt in Turkestan 1918–24," *Soviet Studies* 33 (1981): 352–69.

was cartographically carved to create a number of republic administrative units, each with a distinct titular Soviet nationality and sizable national minorities.[7] By 1936, the boundaries of the five constituent republics of the region were institutionalized—Kazakhstan, Kyrgyzstan, Tajikistan, Turkmenistan, and Uzbekistan—and state-building was well underway. Unsanctioned Islamic activity and independent social movements were banned, republican communist party branches were established and Moscow charged a selected cadre of administrators with maintaining political order and promoting loyalty to the Soviet system.[8]

The Organization of Soviet Hierarchy

Officially, the Soviet system was committed to integrating each of the fifteen individual republics on an equal basis. The doctrine of "equalization" formed the ideological basis for peripheral political, economic, and social development, although Central Asian scholars have debated at length over whether these commitments represented the true intentions of Soviet policy toward the region.[9] Equalization was made a priority in all Soviet constitutions, such as Article 19 of the 1977 Soviet Constitution, which stated: "The government promotes the strengthening of the social homogeneity of society, the obliteration of class differences, of existing differences between city and country, between mental and physical work, and the all-sided development and convergence of all nations and nationalities of the USSR."[10] To support integration, the center promoted ideological homogenization through a nationalities policy that privileged and promoted titular Soviet nation-

7. On the political aims of Soviet nationalities policy, see Mark Beissinger, *Nationalist Mobilization and the Collapse of the Soviet State* (New York: Cambridge University Press, 2002); Laitin, *Identity in Formation;* and Philip Roeder, "Soviet Federalism and Ethnic Mobilization," *World Politics* 43 (1991): 196–232.
8. On Soviet strategies and Central Asian administration, see Pauline Jones Luong, *Institutional Change and Political Continuity in Post-Soviet Central Asia: Power, Perceptions, and Pacts* (New York: Cambridge University Press, 2002), especially chap. 2. Also see Steven L. Burg, "Muslim Cadres and Soviet Political Development: Reflections from a Comparative Perspective," *World Politics* 37 (1984): 24–47; and Geoffrey Wheeler, *The Modern History of Soviet Central Asia* (Westport, Conn.: Greenwood Press, 1974).
9. For representative works in this debate, see William Fierman, *Soviet Central Asia: The Failed Transformation* (Boulder, Colo.: Westview Press, 1991); and Nazif Shahrani, "Muslim Central Asia: Soviet Developmental Legacies and Future Challenges," in *Central Asia and the Caucasus after the Soviet Union,* ed. Mohiaddin Mesbahi, 56–71 (Gainesville: University of Florida Press, 1993).
10. As quoted in Ellen Jones and Robert Grupp, "Modernisation and Ethnic Equalisation in the USSR," *Soviet Studies* 36 (1984), 159, ft. 3.

TABLE 4.1
Indicators of Republican Inequality and Dependence in the Soviet Union

Republic	Per Capita GDP (current rubles, 1990)	Per Capita GDP as % of Russia	Transfers from Union Budget as % of Total Government Revenue
Baltic States			
Estonia	5,039	119.3	0.0
Latvia	4,542	107.5	0.0
Lithuania	3,561	84.3	0.0
Western Republics			
Belarus	3,902	92.4	16.3
Moldova	2,920	69.1	0.0
Russia	4,224	100	NA
Ukraine	3,177	75.2	5.9
Caucasus			
Armenia	2,915	69.0	17.1
Azerbaijan	2,056	48.7	0.0
Georgia	2,731	64.7	0.0
Central Asia			
Kazakhstan	2,706	64.1	23.1
Kyrgyzstan	1,893	44.8	35.5
Tajikistan	1,341	31.7	46.6
Turkmenistan	2,002	47.4	21.7
Uzbekistan	1,579	37.4	42.9

Source: World Bank, *Statistical Handbook: States of the Former USSR* (Washington, D.C.: 1992), 4–5, 14–15.

alities in each republic.[11] In addition, Moscow attempted to increase regional investment and enhance peripheral social welfare by subsidizing republican budgets with federal budget transfers. The Central Asian republics disproportionately benefited from these transfers and were highly dependent on them for their fiscal solvency, ranging in 1990 from 23.1 percent of Kazakhstan's republican budget to 46.6 percent of Tajikistan's (table 4.1).[12]

The question of whether to govern by function or by territory consistently preoccupied central authorities in Moscow, as it employed both forms in governing its fifteen republics. The most centralized functions were administered exclusively at the unionwide level through a series of vertically integrated hierarchies that linked ministries with administrative branches in peripheral republics, oblasts, and rayons. Such unionwide administration represented the typical U-form and was employed

11. On Soviet nationalities policy, see Laitin, *Identity in Formation*; Rogers Brubaker, *Nationalism Reframed* (New York: Cambridge University Press, 1996); and Alexander J. Motyl, *Sovietology, Rationality, Nationality: Coming to Grips with Nationalism in the USSR* (New York: Columbia University Press, 1990).
12. World Bank, *Statistical Handbook: States of the Former USSR, 1992* (Washington, D.C.: World Bank, 1992).

most frequently in those areas with issues or functions deemed critical to the Soviet state, such as defense, internal security, the energy sector, and heavy industry.

At the other extreme, certain functions were delegated to individual republics and bureaucratic organs under republican party control. These functions typified the M-form, as the Soviet center gave general guidelines and strategic directives but placed the management, oversight, and routine policy decisions in the hands of the territorial republics. This was true of much social policy, most notably education, as well as lighter industry and agriculture. Finally, certain functions within the Soviet polity were administered as a mix of U-forms and M-forms, according to a "dual-subordination" structure. In this case, administrative units at the republican and local levels were responsible to both vertical directives from unionwide agencies and horizontal directives emanating from republican-level bodies, which further coordinated and supervised their governance.[13]

Thus, the Soviet administration of Central Asia, as with all its peripheral republics, featured both U-form and M-form organization, thereby promoting state formation in some issue areas and imperial-style rule over others. Such modes of organization also varied within different types of state functions. In the realm of security, the Soviets employed both pure U-forms and mixed U- and M-forms. The armed forces and defense-related functions were organized in a pure U-form as command structures, installations, and military units were vertically integrated into the unionwide command under the auspices of the Ministry of Defense. In the realm of internal security, state security and surveillance (KGB) was organized as a U-form; however, internal policing functions were governed as mixed M-forms and evolved into M-forms. Organizational form also varied in the area of economy. Industry, particularly heavy industry, was administered as a U-form, as the Soviet state vertically integrated the Central Asian republics into its functional ministries, bureaucracies, and unionwide economic agencies. Nonetheless, the administration and oversight of agriculture was delegated to regional and territorially defined local planning authorities and units. The following discussion of four sectoral cases—defense (U-form), internal security (U-form and M-form), industry (U-form), and agriculture (M-form)—present an overview of these varying organizational forms within the Central Asian periphery.

---

13. On the organization of these vertical and horizontal links, see Merle Fainsod, *How Russia Is Ruled* (Cambridge: Harvard University Press, 1962).

Case 1: Defense and the Armed Forces as a U-form

Defense was the primary issue area that was governed as a U-form. Aside from a brief period during World War II when the center promoted republican armies, the Soviet military was the most centralized of all the institutions of the Soviet state. Beyond its security functions, the centralization of the armed forces was also designed to be a vehicle for socialization, state-building, and multiethnic integration.[14] This was particularly important in Central Asia, a region in which many identity-based Islamic and nationalist movements resisted Soviet rule during the interwar years.

As with all activities deemed central to the survival of the state, defense policy formulation was intimately tied with the preferences and directives of the Communist Party. The 1950s brought a wide-reaching reorganization of the structure of the armed forces that endured until the Soviet collapse.[15] After 1953, the Soviet Defense hierarchy was subordinated to two different structures of administration and operational command, both of which retained the unionwide functional form. Administratively, underneath the Ministry of Defense were the five major services of the armed forces—Ground Forces, Strategic Rocket Forces (established in 1959), Air Forces, National Air Defense Troops, and the Navy—each with a distinct set of functional tasks. Each of these five major services was headed by a Deputy Minister of Defense, who was appointed directly by the Ministry of Defense in consultation with the Politburo. In turn, the Ground Forces and Air Forces were each responsible for managing ground force units and frontal aviation units in both the union's internal military districts and the various groups of forces stationed abroad.[16] At the operational level, the Strategic Rocket Forces and Navy exercised direct authority over their respective activities, whereas ground and air forces were divided into sixteen military districts, none of which were congruent with republican jurisdictional lines. In Central Asia, the military district of Turkestan coordinated operational activities in Uzbekistan and Turkmenistan while the "Central Asia" district—established in 1969 to cope with growing Sino-Soviet border tensions—supervised unit operations in Kazakhstan, Kyrgyzstan, and Tajikistan.

14. See Ellen Jones, *Red Army and Society: A Sociology of the Soviet Military* (Boston: Allen & Unwin, 1985).

15. On the organization and bureaucratic agencies of the Soviet military, see William Odom, *The Collapse of the Soviet Military* (New Haven: Yale University Press, 1998); Albert Seaton and Joan Seaton, *The Soviet Army: 1918 to the Present* (New York: New American Library, 1987); and Harriet Fast Scott and William F. Scott, *The Armed Forces of the USSR* (Boulder, Colo.: Westview, 1979).

16. See Scott and Scott, *The Armed Forces of the USSR*, 131–53.

Consistent with the overall aims of creating a centralized and multinational Soviet force, Soviet planners integrated Central Asia into this overall U-form by "deterritorializing" the region's military assets and resources. First, Soviet Defense planners deliberately assigned conscripts to military districts outside of their native republics. For instance, an ethnic Uzbek would rarely serve in Uzbekistan and instead would be assigned to a post in the western republics, the Russian federation, or overseas. The other practical rationale of this policy, an extension of imperial Russian practice, was to prevent soldiers from developing social ties with local civilians and minimize any reluctance to use force against these local populations.[17] In addition, the relocation of Central Asian conscripts to other regions, particularly sparsely populated eastern Siberia, provided the state with the added benefit of easing the labor surplus in its rapidly expanding Muslim populations.[18] Setting aside the issue of whether such recruitment and deployment policies ameliorated or exacerbated ethnic tensions within the armed forces, military service represented the primary opportunity for institutionalized interethnic interaction in Soviet social and political life.[19] Thus, the organization of Soviet armed forces in Central Asia followed an almost pure U-form structure that, as described by Robert Barylski, was "unified, multinational, extraterritorial, and hierarchical."[20]

Case 2: Internal Security—The KGB (U-form) and MVD (Mixed Form)

While many aspects of internal security were also organized as U-forms, important aspects, especially policing functions, were organized as mixed forms and M-forms. In terms of internal security concerns, the Central Asian republics' loyalty to the center remained a constant concern among authorities in Moscow.[21] Aware of the social uprisings and Islamic upheavals during the interwar era, Moscow always maintained a close vigilance on the internal security of the region through a tight U-form hierarchy that reported directly to Moscow. While Moscow

17. Jones, *Red Army and Society,* 194–95.
18. Ellen Jones, "Manning the Soviet Military," *International Security* 7 (1982): 130.
19. See S. Enders Wimbush and Alex Alexiev, *The Ethnic Factor in the Soviet Armed Forces* (Santa Monica, Calif.: RAND Corp., 1982); Teresa Rakowska-Harmstone, "Nationalities and the Soviet Military," in *The Nationalities Factor in Soviet Politics and Society,* ed. Lubomyr Hajda and Mark Beissenger (Boulder, Colo.: Westview Press, 1990); and Jones, *Red Army and Society.*
20. Robert V. Barylski, "The Soviet Military Before and After the August Coup: Departization and Decentralization," *Armed Forces & Society* 19 (1992): 27.
21. For a discussion, see Teresa Rakowska-Harmstone, *Russia and Nationalism in Central Asia: The Case of Tadzhikistan* (Baltimore: Johns Hopkins University Press, 1970), 118–22.

afforded latitude to Central Asian republican and local party branches over local policing, state security was consistently governed in a rigidly centralized manner. The original Soviet internal security agency—the Ministry of Internal Affairs—underwent a number of consolidations and reorganization during the Stalin era and the first years of Nikita Khrushchev's tenure. The functional scope of the internal security apparatus was finally institutionalized in March of 1954 when the Committee for State Security (KGB) emerged from the Ministry of Internal Affairs. The KGB assumed control over security police and internal surveillance, border guards and patrols, foreign intelligence activities, and internal security troops, while the new Ministry of Internal Affairs (MVD) maintained jurisdiction over routine policing matters and militia affairs.

At the union level, a state committee under the USSR Council of Ministers coordinated KGB activity and formally appointed its chairmen and most of its deputy chairmen. Directly underneath the unionwide organization rested the KGB offices in each of the fourteen peripheral republics as well as two separate divisions responsible for operations in Moscow and Leningrad.[22] The central KGB committee retained exclusive authority to determine personnel appointments and policy direction within these republican branches. The vertical chain extended down to local levels, including areas, districts, and cities. Finally, the KGB also maintained an extensive network of representatives in particularly sensitive state institutions, enterprises, and departments, as well as special divisions for monitoring the activities of the armed forces.[23]

The U-form of KGB organization reflected the particular importance assigned by the Party to state security activities. As Amy Knight's study of the KGB observed, "the high degree of centralization in the KGB is reflected in the fact that regional KGB branches are not subordinated to the local Soviets but only to the KGB hierarchy. Thus they differ from branches of most union-republic ministerial agencies, such as the MVD, which are subject to dual subordination."[24] Suspicions of potential Central Asian disloyalty led to a policy of selecting KGB republican chairmen of Russian origin who had no preexisting ties to the region. Between 1954 and 1986, Russian chairmen staffed thirty-two of the

22. Outside its two largest cities, Russia had no republican KGB regional agency.
23. On the KGB surveillance of the military, see Amy Knight, *The KGB: Police and Politics in the Soviet Union* (Boston: Unwin Hymann, 1988), 249–75.
24. Knight, *The KGB*, 121.

thirty-four chairmanships of republican-level KGB posts (although deputies, for symbolic reasons, were native), a percentage likewise characteristic of Moldova and Azerbaijan but not of Armenia, Georgia, and the European-based republics.[25] As with the armed forces, internal security was a high-priority, U-form governed sector.

After the 1954 split with the KGB, Soviet policing (MVD) was formally subject to a system of mixed subordination, one functional and the other territorial. Functionally, the unionwide MVD determined main directives and policies, supervised the activities of republican MVD branches, and compiled and analyzed statistics on law enforcement. Territorially, a number of local governmental bodies (oblast, district, and city) administered operations but were ultimately responsible to their respective republican-level ministries and Party organizations.[26] Thus, unlike the KGB, which retained a segmented structure and reported only along a vertical chain of command, MVD activities were governed through a complex two-tiered system that horizontally linked territorial Party committees with MVD organs at each level of administration.

As with other republics, the decentralizing policies of Leonid Brezhnev greatly empowered the Central Asian republican-level party apparatus. During this period, republican control over MVD activities was so great that the functional divisions effectively lost much of their power. This was particularly true in the predominantly rural areas of the region, where local militia cadres drew recruits from the native population, forged ties with local elites, and routinely ignored directives from the center. As Louise Shelley observes, the density of horizontal ties between militia members and Central Asian republican administrators during the Brezhnev era "actually placed many of these republics outside of the control of the central militia apparatus altogether."[27] In other words, the mixed-form operational structure of internal policing steadily gave way to a predominantly M-form structure.

Economy: The Structure of Soviet Governance

In economic governance, organizational form also varied according to sector. Soviet industry, especially heavy industry and defense-related

---

25. Calculated from data in table 5.9 of Knight, *The KGB*, 167.
26. On the organization of Soviet policing, see Mark Galeotti, "Perestroika, Perestrelka, Pereborka: Policing Russia in a Time of Change," *Europe-Asia Studies* 45 (1993): 769–86.
27. Louise Shelley, *Policing Soviet Society: The Evolution of State Control* (London: Routledge, 1996), 125.

production, was predominantly governed as a U-form while agriculture evolved into an M-form, although both experienced bouts of organizational reshuffling.

Soviet economic planning hierarchy and its administration was coordinated through a labyrinth of unionwide ministries, economic bodies, and central organs responsible for the necessary array of different functional tasks, such as GosPlan (planning organ), GosKomstat (statistical and accounting organ), GosPromishelnost (industrial organ), and GosStroitel (construction organ). Unionwide economic divisions were linked via GosPlan and were ultimately responsible to the highest authorities of the Soviet state and the Communist Party.[28] While the republican-level economic divisions also played important roles in other economic sectors, heavy industry was exclusively the policy domain of these unionwide branches. As has been argued by several scholars of the Soviet economy, such a system was highly effective in mobilizing inputs necessary for vertical integration in industry (extensive growth); however, it proved to be largely inefficient as the economic system increased in complexity and interdependence.[29]

Case 3: Industry as a U-form

While the history of Soviet industrial organization in Central Asia cannot be summarized adequately here, some general historical trends can be identified. Although the Soviets did promote industrialization in the region under the U-form structure, Central Asia's raw material extraction also played an important role in the region's economic composition. The structural "backwardness" of the region at the time of Soviet state-formation, especially in comparison to other areas such as the Baltic republics or Russia, was a major factor. The region's initial heavy industrialization under the first two five-year plans was aimed at modernizing the processing facilities and infrastructure for the extraction of raw materials, most notably in the cotton sector. It was only during World War II that many of the heavier industries were relocated

28. On central planning and the structure of the Soviet economy, see Paul Gregory and Robert Stuart, *Soviet and Post-Soviet Economic Structure and Performance* (New York: HarperCollins, 1994); and Janos Kornai, *The Socialist System: The Political Economy of Communism* (Princeton: Princeton University Press, 1992).
29. For discussions, see Gregory and Stuart, *Soviet and Post-Soviet Economic Structure and Performance*, 229–68; A. V. Banerjee and M. Spagat, "Productivity Paralysis and the Complexity Problem: Why Do Centrally Planned Economies Become Prematurely Gray?," *Journal of Comparative Economics* 15 (1991): 646–60; and Richard Ericson, "The Classical Soviet-type Economy: Nature of the System and Implications for Reform," *Journal of Economic Perspectives* 5 (1991): 11–27.

to the region from European Russia, with over 100 being placed in Uzbekistan alone.[30] Despite heavy real-capital investments, growth rates for industrial output in Central Asia exceeded the USSR average level only in the 1980s, although Kyrgyzstan and Uzbekistan individually did so in the 1970s.[31] All this activity was organized under the U-form.

The general pattern of U-form administration over heavy industry was interrupted between 1957 and 1965 when First Secretary Nikita Khrushchev introduced a new system of M-form territorial economic administration known as *sovnarkhozy*.[32] For the only time in Soviet history, national regions were given the authority to formulate and implement regional industrial policy independently of the central economic organs. In Central Asia, the individual republican economic boards were consolidated into a unified regional organ that aimed to deepen regional integration and unify the Central Asian economies. Regional planners introduced a number of industrial enterprises in the areas of agroindustry, machine-building, construction, chemical industry, and hydrocarbon processing. No sooner had real signs of industrial diversification emerged, however, than the decentralization experiment was ended abruptly by Leonid Brezhnev and the five-year plan of 1966–70. The era was denounced as localism, industrial control was recentralized, and vertical integration was promoted once again in regional planning.[33]

After the abandonment of the *sovnarkhoz*, most heavy industry reverted to the U-form and Central Asia's industrial structure was made up of pure U-form heavy industries (chemicals, hydrocarbons, metals, machine-building) and a number of regionally based (mixed form and M-form) light industries such as cotton processing and agribusiness. As table 4.2 indicates, in 1980 the percentage of unionwide controlled industries (as a total of industrial production) ranged from 29 percent in Kyrgyzstan and Uzbekistan to 36.6 percent in Turkmenistan, a considerably high figure given the republics' constant local-territorial production needs (M-form sectors) in areas such as electricity generation (16–40 percent of total republican industry), food processing (5–7 percent) and agribusiness (2–5 percent).[34] Each republic also tended to

30. Boris Rumer, *Soviet Central Asia: 'A Tragic Experiment'* (Boston: Unwin Hyman, 1990), 54–55.
31. Dmitrieva, *Regional Development*, 43.
32. See Alec Nove, *An Economic History of the USSR, 1917–1991* (New York: Penguin Books, 1992), 331–78.
33. Rumer, *Soviet Central Asia*, 57.
34. Constant needs are calculated for the year 1990 from data presented in Ichiro Iwasaki, "Industrial Structure and Regional Development in Central Asia," *Central Asian Survey* 19 (2000): 161–62.

TABLE 4.2
Organization of Industry in Soviet Central Asia

Republic	1980 % of Industry Controlled by Union (U-form)	1980 % of Industry Controlled by Republic (M-form)	1989 % of Industry Controlled by Union (U-form)	1989 % of Industry Controlled by Republic (M-form)
Kazakhstan	31	69	46	54
Kyrgyzstan	29	71	33	67
Tajikistan	NA	NA	31	69
Turkmenistan	36.6	63.4	36.0	64.0
Uzbekistan	29	71	33	67

Sources: Statistical Agency of the Kazakh SSR, *Narodnoe Khoziaistvo v 1980 Gody* (Alma-Ata: 1981); Statistical Agency of the Kyrgyz SSR, *Narodnoe Khoziaistvo v 1980 Gody* (Frunze: 1981); Statistical Agency of the Turkmen SSR, *Narodnoe Khoziaistvo v 1980 Gody* (Ashghabat: 1981); Statistical Agency of the Uzbek SSR, *Narodnoe Khoziaistvo v 1980 Gody* (Tashkent: 1981); and Stanislav Zhukov, "Economic Development in the States of Central Asia," in *Central Asia in Transition: Dilemmas of Independence*, ed. Boris Rumer, 114–15 (Armonk, N.Y.: M. E. Sharpe, 1996).

have a particular, specialized U-form sector that dominated its industrial profile, such as hydrocarbon extraction in Turkmenistan, ferrous metallurgy and chemicals in Kazakhstan, machine-building (much of it defense-related) in Kyrgyzstan, and nonferrous metal industry (mostly aluminum smelting) in Tajikistan. Moreover, as table 4.3 shows, categorized by number of employees, the ten largest regional enterprises in the region in 1990 (and sixteen of the top twenty-five overall) were all in U-form sectors.

The segmented nature of U-form economic industrialization in Central Asia also demonstrated a significant ethnic component. Given the vast scale of most of these projects, the indigenous workforce lacked the skills, experience, and credibility to be entrusted with the operations of these new industrial complexes. Consequently, the center imported workers and managers from Russia to staff these industries, which led to Central Asia's well-documented ethnic divisions along economic sectors. On this topic, Nancy Lubin found that in 1967 ethnic Uzbeks comprised just 39 percent of men and 21 percent of women employed in the republic's industry.[35] The ethnic division was even more pronounced within heavy industry as Russians staffed large complexes while Uzbeks were concentrated mainly in light and agricultural industries. For instance, in 1975 Uzbeks accounted for just 5.5 percent of the Uzbek

35. Nancy Lubin, *Labour and Nationality in Soviet Central Asia: An Uneasy Compromise* (Princeton: Princeton University Press, 1984), 85.

TABLE 4.3
Twenty-five Largest Industrial Enterprises in Soviet Central Asia, 1991

Enterprise	Location (Oblast, Republic)	Sector	U-form or M-form	No. of Workers
Karagandaugoli P.O.	Karagandinskaya, KA	Fuel Industry	U	74,670
Karagandinskii metallurgicheskii kombinet	Karagandinskaya, KA	Ferrous Metallurgy	U	28,195
Sokolovsko-sarbayskoe gorno-metallurgicheskow P.O.	Kustanayskaya, KA	Ferrous Metallurgy	U	22,783
Pavlodarskii traktorni zavod	Pavlodarskaya, KA	Machine-building (tractors)	U	20,114
Dzhezkazgantsvetmet gorno-metallurgicheskoe P.O.	Dzhezkazganskaya, KA	Nonferrous Metallurgy	U	16,715
Kaztsvetmetmash P.O. (Metallugiya Konzern)	Alma-Atinskaya, KA	Machine-building	U	16,603
Almalykskii gorno-metallurgichekii kombinat	Tashkentskaya, UZ	Ferrous Metallurgy	U	14,509
Ala-Too P.O.	Chuyskaya, KY	Machine-building (torpedos)	U	13,780
Ekibastuzugoli P.O.	Pavlodarskaya, KA	Fuel Industry	U	13,650
Kyrgyzkomur Konzem	Oshkaya, KY	Fuel Industry	U	13,231
Namanganskoe P.O.	Namanganskaya, UZ	Light Industry	M	12,880
Khlopchatobumazhnoe P.O. (Uzbeklegprom Association)	Bukharskaya, UZ	Light Industry	M	12,607
Margilanskii shelkobyi kombinat (Uzbeklegprom Association)	Ferganskaya, UZ	Light Industry	M	11,507
Karatau P.O. (Kazfosfor Association)	Dzhamvulskaya, KA	Chemical Industry	U	11,517
Khudzhandskii shelovyi kombinat (Tadzhiklegprom Konzern)	Khudzhandskaya, TA	Light Industry	M	11,081
Ferganskoe khlopchatobumazhnoe P.O.	Ferganskaya, UZ	Light Industry	M	11,022
Tashkentskii Trakotrhyi zavod	Tashkentskaya, UZ	Machine-building (tractors)	U	10,846
Kyrgyzenergo	Chuyskaya, KY	Electricity	M	10,596
Balkhashmedi P.O.	Dzhezkazganskaya, KA	Ferrous Metallurgy	U	10,524
Karagandaenergo P.O.	Karagandinskaya, KA	Electricity	M	10,288
Leninogorskii polimetallicheskii kombinat	Vostochno-Kazakhstanskaya, KA	Nonferrous Metallurgy	U	10,256
Tadzhiskii aliuminievyi zavod	Dushanbe, TA	Nonferrous Metallurgy	U	9,981
Oshkoe Khlopchatbumazhnoe P.O.	Oshkaya, KY	Light Industry	M	9,821
Foton P.O.	Tashkentskaya, UZ	Machine-building	U	9,438
Juzhkazergo P.O.	Chimkentskaya, KA	Electricity	M	9,426

Adapted from: Ichiro Iwasaki, "Industrial Structure and Regional Development in Central Asia: A Microdata Analysis," *Central Asian Survey* 19 (2000): 170 (table 4); and *Viznes Karta-92: Promyshlenostii,* vols. 26–29 (Moscow: NIK, 1992).

Chemical Machinery Plant's workforce and, in 1978, just 3.5 percent of the Chirchik Agricultural Machinery Plant's workforce. By contrast, in 1979 the titular nationality accounted for 59 percent of the labor force of the Kokand Furniture Factory and 85 percent of the Andizhan Sewing factory, both M-form operations.[36] In addition, Lubin also found that Russians exclusively staffed administrative positions within the strategic sectors of Uzbekistan's economic bureaucracy.[37] These same patterns typify the ethnic composition of the region's workforce at large.

Case 4: Agriculture and M-form Governance

Whereas industry was administered predominantly as a U-form organization, agriculture in Central Asia was primarily an M-form. While official proclamations did not distinguish between organizing industry and organizing agriculture, over time, the M-form became the de facto form of governance.[38] The central economic organs formulated general plans and broad output targets, but the oversight of routine agricultural activity was almost exclusively undertaken at the republican and local levels. Of course, there were sound physical reasons to do so. As Peter Rutland argues, "the territorial structure of party organs above PPO level was well suited to agricultural supervision, since agriculture by definition is tied to the land, and thus a spatially defined management structure was appropriate—more so, for example, than for industry."[39]

The decentralizing trend was started by the radical reorganization enacted by Khrushchev, who abolished the unionwide Ministry of Agriculture in 1961 and replaced it with a series of territorial-network administrative units. Despite recentralization and the ministry's resurrection in 1965, republican party influence in agricultural production, unlike in industry, persisted. To complement the territorially based operating units, Brezhnev introduced a set of republican-level associations to coordinate agribusiness activities, construction, and agromachinery repair. Other new horizontal networks included the formation of interfarm associations and agroindustrial complexes in the 1960s, which were designed to coordinate local functions and integrate various levels of production.[40]

36. Ibid., 87.
37. Ibid., 84.
38. This argument stands in contrast to recent descriptions of the Soviet economic system as an exclusive U-form by scholars comparing the organization of the Chinese and Soviet economies. See Eric Maskin, Yingyi Qian, and Chenggang Xu, "Incentives, Information and Organizational Form," *Review of Economic Studies* 67 (2000): 359–78; and Yingyi Qian and Chenggang Xu, "Why China's Economic Reforms Differ: The M-form Hierarchy and Entry/Expansion of the Non-State Sector," *Economics of Transition* 1 (1993): 135–70. However, these authors' arguments about industry hold: while Chinese industry usually was governed territorially, Soviet industry was governed functionally.
39. Peter Rutland, *The Politics of Economic Stagnation in the Soviet Union: The Role of Local Political Agents in Economic Management* (New York: Cambridge University Press, 1993), 144.
40. Ibid., 144–47.

Several new unionwide ministries were also introduced in the 1970s to improve performance in specific sectors such as Machine Building for Animal Husbandry and Fodder Industries (1973); Fruit and Vegetable Industry (1980); and Mineral Fertilizer (1980). But this de jure increase in unionwide organizations merely exacerbated the coordination problems inherent in the agricultural sector and underscored the de facto responsibilities of regional and oblast party-level officials.[41] Despite official proclamations regarding the chain of economic authority, regional party organs were held accountable for agricultural output and performance in their territories in a manner that dramatically distinguished them from their industrial counterparts. For example, a striking political consequence of the party's heavy intervention in the sector was that an increasing proportion of obkom first secretaries in the 1980s and regional party elites had a background in agriculture.[42]

Making Organizational Sense of Soviet Central Asia

In short, the Soviet center—as with its other peripheries—employed a mix of U-form and M-form governance across different sectors in Central Asia (fig. 4.1). In some sectors, such as heavy industry and defense, Central Asia was vertically integrated into and ruled by the functional ministries and unionwide organs of the centralized Soviet state. These functional departments were multileveled hierarchies that extended from the unionwide ministries through a series of functional organs right through to the local levels in each republic. In other areas, such as agriculture and internal policing, M-form organization prevailed. In these cases, republican- and oblast-level bureaucracies were responsible for the implementation and monitoring of policy and retained a significant amount of de facto authority and autonomy from Moscow. Consequently, the popular and scholarly debate over whether

41. Mikhail Gorbachev's final major agricultural reform (1985) was the consolidation of many of these unionwide ministries into the superministry Gosagroprom. In practice, however, Gosagroprom's mandate was simply too large in size and scope to enact structural changes effectively and exerted very little influence before the collapse of the union. See Rolf H. W. Theen, "Hierarchical Reform in the Soviet Economy: The Case of Agriculture," in *Reorganization and Reform in the Soviet Economy*, ed. Susan Linz and William Moskoff, 73–87 (Armonk, N.Y.: M. E. Sharpe, 1988).
42. Rutland, *Politics of Economic Stagnation*, chap. 10. Also see Grey Hodnett, *Leadership in the Soviet National Republics: A Quantitative Study of Recruitment Policy* (Oakville, Ont.: Mosaic Press, 1978), especially chap. 7.

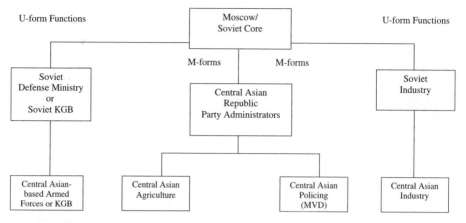

FIGURE 4.1
Hierarchical Governance in Soviet Central Asia

the Soviet Union was indeed a state or an empire depends on what set of Soviet functions is examined.[43]

Consequences of Governance: Varying Patterns of Institutional Development

Over time, these two forms of organization in Central Asia produced divergent types of political institutions coexisting within the same region. U-form sectors in Central Asia, most notably defense and heavy industry, were harmonized with the functional divisions of the Soviet state and its branch ministries, thus maintaining few interactions with republican-level party structures and networks. Consequently, U-form administrators and staffers maintained their political loyalty to their functional department rather than to their territorial location or home republic. Conversely, M-form sectors—such as agriculture or policing—developed patrimonial institutions and retained considerable de facto autonomy from the center. Within these M-form sectors, acute agency problems characterized center-periphery relations as republican administrators used their delegated power and resources to pursue their self-interests and consolidate their social and clientelist ties. This was

43. For well-reasoned discussions of the analytical distinction between state and empire as applied to the Soviet case, see Beissinger, *Nationalist Mobilization and the Collapse of the Soviet State*, Motyl, *Imperial Ends*; and Laitin, *Identity in Formation*.

particularly evident in agricultural areas where collusion between collective farm managers, workers, and republican elites cemented the patrimonial bargain.

Officially and ideologically, the Soviet state did not recognize or condone such differences in institutional formation. Republican cadre corruption was regularly denounced as localism and viewed as antithetical to the official aims of the Soviet state. Even so, Moscow's denouncements and periodic purges of Central Asian administrators did little to change the incentive structures created by the M-form structure. Despite the ubiquity of Soviet ideology and Communist Party dominance, the formation of political institutions in the Central Asian periphery varied according to the organizational form employed by the center.

U-forms and Harmonized State-building

The use of the U-form to integrate Central Asia into the Soviet state was most common in priority areas such as security and heavy industry. In the U-form governed sectors of defense, internal security, energy, and heavy industry, Central Asia was deterritorialized and integrated into the various functional divisions of the Soviet state, although not always on an equal basis. Although U-form sectors were vertically integrated into the overall unionwide system, they lacked interaction and coherent integration with republican-level parties or bureaucracies. In general, this process of functional integration was costly, strikingly inefficient, and encouraged departmentalism within each U-form division.

The Harmonization of Security Institutions

In defense, the armed forces within Central Asia were fully integrated within the Soviet-wide system of organization and administration. As a result, unionwide hierarchies determined the organizational goals of military districts and commands, as well as the personnel rotations and career moves of security forces. Communications and interactions between security U-forms and local Party cadres within the same republic were minimal, and the administrative divisions of the Turkestan Military District and the Central Asian Military District served the overall interests of the Soviet military, not the particular needs of the region.[44] Furthermore, Slavs dominated the general officer corps of the Soviet military and that Central Asian opportunity for advancement within the military hierarchy was quite limited. In 1986, for instance,

---

44. Rakowska-Harmstone, *Russia and Nationalism in Central Asia*, 147–48.

ethnic Slavs headed 86 percent of leading posts (74 percent Russian) in the Soviet military, while 89.7 percent of the officer corps was Russian.[45] In addition, few Central Asian conscripts spoke fluent Russian to the extent required for efficient service. Consequently, Central Asian conscripts were more likely to be assigned to logistical and support services rather than actual combat units and tended to resist assimilation with other nationalities.[46] Thus, while U-form integration did harmonize the armed forces in Central Asia under Soviet command and organization, it did not necessarily promote the social equality of Central Asians as official Soviet doctrines intended.

Even in the face of conflicts and immediate threats to national security located in neighboring regions, the Central Asian republics themselves remained marginalized and organizationally sequestered in the military decision-making process. For example, the 1979 Soviet invasion of Afghanistan marked the most significant sustained involvement of the Central Asian military districts in combat operations since World War II.[47] The Turkestan military district served as the staging post for the initial foray of the Soviet 40th Army and continued to be the launching ground for subsequent air attacks against Afghan guerillas as well as the main training center for Soviet conscripts bound for Afghanistan. Despite the renewed importance of Central Asia in the Afghan campaign, the activities of the Central Asian and Turkestan military districts remained separated from republican-level institutions and Central Asian Party politics. For instance, in 1980 the commander of the Central Asian district and four of five of his deputies were Russian. Of the 35 known members of the district's high command, only two were Central Asians, while in the adjacent Turkestan Military district, all 33 staff members were Russian.[48] Moreover, newspapers accounts from the period indicate that the military districts received only limited support from local government and law enforcement officials in clamping down on regional conscription evasions.[49]

Similar patterns were evident in the structure and institutional development of the region's state security forces as well. Not only were the

---

45. Deborah Yarsike Ball, "Ethnic Conflict, Unit Performance, and the Soviet Armed Forces," *Armed Forces & Society* 20 (1994): 246.

46. Thomas S. Szayna, *The Ethnic Factor in the Soviet Armed Forces: The Muslim Dimension* (Santa Monica, Calif.: RAND, 1991), 28–29.

47. With the possible exception of border skirmishes with China in the 1960s.

48. Michael Rywkin, *Moscow's Muslim Challenge* (Armonk, N.Y.: M. E. Sharpe, 1990), 136.

49. Bruce R. Porter, "The Military Abroad: Internal Consequences of External Expansion," in *Soldiers and the Soviet State: Civil-Military Relations from Brezhnev to Gorbachev*, ed. Timothy Colton and Thane Gustafson (Princeton: Princeton University Press, 1990), 329–30.

KGB chairmen in Central Asia and Azerbaijan exclusively non-native, they also demonstrated significantly higher rates of turnover and served for limited periods before leaving again for posts outside the region. The same holds true of the KGB's regional border troops in Central Asia (and the Caucasus), where the turnover of district commanders—all Russian—was markedly more frequent than in any of the other seven regions. Moscow's historically grounded fears of localism and regional disloyalty were rekindled after the start of the Afghanistan campaign when Soviet authorities accused the United States of a concerted effort to use Islam on the Central Asian population as a means of "ideological sabotage."[50]

As the firm-type model predicts, the U-form organization in defense and internal security exacted high governance costs on the Soviet state. Attempts to vertically integrate these activities in Central Asia with the functionally based ministries in Moscow resulted in massive inefficiencies and escalating costs throughout the Soviet era. As a share of gross domestic product (GDP), defense spending officially accounted for around 25 percent, although the proportion was probably significantly higher and reached 40 percent in the Glasnost era by some estimates.[51] Departmentalist tendencies within the Soviet security hierarchies exacerbated these coordination problems and inefficiencies. The Soviet General Staff had no comparably powerful civilian body to formulate decisions about defense affairs, leading the military body to dominate all issues relating to the formulation and organization of defense policy.[52] In addition, the preponderant influence of Soviet defense planners on the overall formulation of state priorities and national domestic and foreign policy is well documented. As Edward Warner summarized:

[T]he Ministry of Defense appears to enjoy regular access to the most important Soviet policy-making forums, thus allowing it to present its case and, in some cases, directly participate in those decisions which have substantial impact on its institutional fortunes. Since this high degree of access is combined with the Ministry of Defense's strong predominance with regard to both information and expertise in the defense field . . .

50. Knight, *The KGB*, 162–65, 232–34, and 201.
51. The figure of 40 percent for the late 1980s is taken from Martin Malia's examination of intelligence estimates. See Malia, *The Soviet Tragedy: 1917–1991* (New York: Free Press, 1995), 372. On Soviet military budgets and military departmentalism, see Timothy J. Colton, *Commissars, Commanders, and Civilian Authority: The Structure of Soviet Military Politics* (Cambridge: Harvard University Press, 1979).
52. See Condoleezza Rice, "The Party, the Military, and Decision Authority in the Soviet Union," *World Politics* 40 (1987): 55–81.

the Soviet military is in an excellent position to wield enormous influence in those matters that concern it the most—budgetary allocations for defense, weapons development and production, military doctrine, arms control, and the exercise of military capabilities in support of Soviet foreign policy.[53]

Of course, the center was aware of these problems but could do little to alleviate them. Defense was the single greatest priority of the Soviet state and Party officials never seriously considered abandoning U-form organization, despite the ever-increasing share of the state budget and resources that defense efforts consumed. Practically, mitigating the departmentalism of the security sectors proved impossible.

The Harmonization of Industry

Similar patterns of institutional development characterized U-form industrial sectors in the region. Although industrial levels in Central Asia were below the union-level average, they were nonetheless significant in certain sectors and specific localities. These pockets of industrial development were promoted for the benefit of the overall Soviet economic structure, however, and not for the individual republics. Paradoxically, while the U-form vertically integrated Central Asian industrial production within the Soviet economic system, it did not contribute to cohesive regional development. Rather than encourage the increased equalization of Central Asia's regional economic structure, as Soviet ideology professed, U-form governance established sequestered islands or pockets of development that did not interact with republican-based institutions. Boris Rumer summarizes the organizational consequences of the post-*sovnarkhoz* reversion to U-form industrial administration:

Although industrial growth in Central Asia continued at a significant pace for some time after the end of the *sovnarkhoz* period, it bore an entirely different character. Branch ministries, not regional planning organs, determined where and what kind of plants were to be built, giving scant regard to the need for complex, integrated development. The central ministries increasingly tended to concentrate industrial production in areas with well-developed infrastructures, where capacity

53. Edward L. Warner III, *The Military in Contemporary Soviet Politics: An Institutional Analysis* (New York: Praeger, 1977), 55. Also see Jones, *Red Army and Society*, and Colton, *Commissars, Commanders, and Civilian Authority*. For a comparative discussion of military influences in domestic politics in communist states, see Valerie Bunce, *Subversive Institutions: The Design and the Destruction of Socialism and the State* (New York: Cambridge University Press, 1999).

could be expanded more quickly and at less expense. This policy meant, however, a concentration of industrial complexes in previously developed centers and persisting neglect of sparsely settled territories.[54]

These "oases" of industrial development and patterns of uneven vertical integration were prevalent throughout the region and included, as prominent examples, the Tashkent industrial area and the South Tajik Territorial Production Complex, the latter hosting the largest hydroelectric station and aluminum plants in the USSR.[55] In addition, the military industrial complex also had a web of installations scattered throughout the region, such as a torpedo-assembly plant in Kyrgyzstan, that were vertically linked to overall Soviet defense production but had no horizontal ties to any other regional economic institutions.[56]

These pockets of vertical integration also created dramatically uneven levels of economic development within the region. For example, Oksana Dmitrieva's comparison of Soviet developmental policies in the adjacent oblasts of Chardzhou (Turkmenistan) and Surkhandarya (Uzbekistan) found that Moscow's U-form promotion of chemical and hydrocarbons in the Chardzhou oblast resulted in an industrial output per capita of 1,402 rubles, higher than the republican average of 1,329. By contrast, the adjoining Uzbek province's figure, a heavily M-form agricultural area, was just 646 rubles per capita, about half of the republican average of 1,235. Similarly, the percentage of population classified as urbanized was 46.0 percent (republican average of 47.6) in the Turkmen oblast as opposed to just 19.7 percent in the Uzbek oblast (republican average of 44.5).[57] As with the armed forces, U-form organization harmonized Central Asia's institutions with those of the Soviet functional divisions but, in doing so, did not promote cohesive regional integration or development.

As in defense, promoting vertical integration in industry proved enormously costly for the Soviet state and widespread departmentalist tendencies characterized the vast functional hierarchies that linked local enterprises with industrial planners in Moscow. As scholars of the Soviet

54. Rumer, *Soviet Central Asia*, 57–58.
55. On the organizational logic and problems of territorial complexes, see David S. Kamerling, "The Role of Territorial Production Complexes in Soviet Economic Policy," *Soviet Economy in the 1980s: Problems and Prospects*, Part I, Collection of papers submitted to the Joint Economic Committee of the Congress of the United States (Washington, D.C.: U.S. Government Printing Office, 1983).
56. On Soviet industrial legacies, see Richard Pomfret, *The Economies of Central Asia* (Princeton: Princeton University Press, 1995).
57. Dmitrieva, *Regional Development Policy*, 103.

economic bureaucracy observed, monitoring functional units and divisions was nearly impossible given their poorly defined responsibilities and unclear overall contributions.[58] In classic U-form fashion, the inability to distinguish policymaking and allocative decisions from coordinative decisions created acute difficulties for the center in terms of identifying and assessing individual departmental responsibility.[59] These multilayered hierarchies lacked clear jurisdictional boundaries and promoted general administrative confusion, especially in an increasingly complex production structure where information was transferred up and down the multilevel hierarchy during the iterative planning process.[60] At times, dozens of different ministries with operating oversight for an economic sector could stake a claim on a particular project or resources.[61] Moreover, important members of the administrative hierarchy ended up spending most of their time in Moscow, lobbying for jurisdictional oversight for individual projects as well as negotiating and readjusting the overall plan.[62] Over time, the departmentalism and informational structure of the economic ministries shifted relative power to the ministries and away from both the enterprises and the center, prompting some analysts of the Soviet economy to hypothesize that the branch ministries were actually the "maximizing units" within the Soviet economy.[63]

Organizationally, little could be done by the center to sanction or curb ministerial departmentalism in the economy. GosPlan did occasionally send inspectors to visit ministries and compile data on activities it deemed antithetical to the national interest, but the ultimate responsibility to punish ministries actually lay with the Council of Ministers, not the central planning agency, and the central body rarely acted to curtail widespread departmentalist abuses. As a 1983 report by the economists in the Soviet Academy of Sciences observed:

> The consensus among Soviet economists is that the existing system of economic management has been characterized by a weakening of powers

58. See Paul R. Gregory, "Soviet Bureaucratic Behaviour: Khozyaistenikki and Apparatchiki," *Soviet Studies* 41 (1989): 511–25. On the problems of monitoring in the Soviet hierarchy in general, see Solnick, *Stealing the State*.
59. William J. Conyngham, *Industrial Management in the Soviet Union* (Stanford, Calif.: Hoover Institution Press, 1973), 220–24.
60. See Ericson, "The Classical Soviet-type Economy," 21–23.
61. See Rutland, *Politics of Economic Stagnation*, especially chaps. 2–3.
62. Conyngham, *Industrial Management in the Soviet Union*, 221.
63. See Alice C. Gorlin, "The Power of Soviet Industrial Ministries in the 1980s," *Soviet Studies* 37 (1985): 353–70; and David Granick, "The Ministry as the Maximizing Unit in Soviet Industry," *Journal of Comparative Economics* 4 (1980): 255–73.

of the State Planning Committee [GosPlan], representing the state interest, and by a parallel decline in the powers of the lower entities, i.e., the industrial corporations and enterprises. . . . In stark contrast, the functions of intermediate levels of management, the ministries and agencies, have grown out of all proportion, giving rise to departmentalism, to disproportions in the economy, to a growth of economic activity outside the formal economic structure.[64]

In sum, the use of the U-form in heavy industry promoted vertical integration in the Central Asian periphery in the interests of the Soviet system as a whole. While this harmonized peripheral institutions and empowered functional ministries, Soviet enterprises in Central Asia remained isolated pockets that were not integrated into the territorial governance structures of each republic.

M-forms and the Development of the Soviet Patrimonial State

In the M-form governed sectors, very different types of political institutions formed in the Central Asian periphery that were antithetical to official Soviet ideology and purpose. Rather than harmonized statebuilding, M-form rule in areas such as agriculture, law enforcement, and education created patrimonial institutions that penetrated every level of the Central Asian state. Regional ties based on clan and kinship overlapped with republican-level administrative networks. Furthermore, acute principal-agent problems characterized the behavior of both individuals and regions within Soviet Central Asia as corruption, fraud, and embezzlement became ubiquitous practices among administrators. This patrimonial form of political development culminated in the rule of Leonid Brezhnev, who tolerated massive regional corruption in exchange for political support.[65]

Sectoral Case: Agriculture and Patrimonial Development

In theory, collectivization was a cooperative agricultural undertaking that produced for the state, while state planners and administrators assumed responsibility for setting procurement prices and coordinating the systems of intermediary exchange necessary for the redistribution of the finished products within society.[66] However, as the firm-type theory

---

64. Quoted in Gorlin, "The Power of Soviet Industrial Ministries in the 1980s," 353.
65. For an overview, see John P. Willerton, *Patronage and Politics in the USSR* (New York: Cambridge University Press, 1992).
66. Kornai, *Socialist System*, 77.

predicts, the decentralization of agricultural administration afforded tremendous opportunities for shirking among administrative agents and agricultural producers as they used the resources and property of the Soviet state to promote their individual and group interests. Consequently, patrimonialism, not harmonized "Sovietization," characterized Central Asia's agricultural regions.

The M-form administration of agriculture placed the oversight of collective farms under the republics' Party bureaucracies. In turn, regional elites delegated responsibility for routine activities to farm directors who were appointed to their respective areas of origin. Thus, in addition to conducting their nominal managerial duties, farm directors were also concerned with moving up the regional Party hierarchy. While fulfilling plan targets and production outputs, farm directors formed rent-seeking coalitions with obkom administrators and diverted investments from the center into their pockets.

Opportunistic behavior was also rampant among the individual peasants of the farm, as it was permitted and even encouraged by managers. Given that farm directors had long-standing social or familial ties with peasants, directors also colluded with workers to engage in unofficial profit-seeking activities.[67] The most significant of these was the extensive private farming undertaken by peasants, frequently observed and denounced by outside observers who remained loyal to official Party doctrines.[68] In theory, the private plot was intended to serve as a supplementary source of family foodstuffs, but the evidence suggests that crops were grown for the demand of the informal market as opposed to personal consumption. Communal markets revolved around illegal bazaars, where farmers and traders would exchange items for cash and bartered goods. Farmers also produced for a unionwide "gray" market where intermediary "traders" purchased crops for prices above state levels and exported them to regions or even other republics where the scarce commodity could be sold for as much as three times its official value.[69] These practices were sustained through the acquiescence of local administrators who received shares of these unofficial activities.[70]

67. Grey Hodnett, "Technology and Social Change in Soviet Central Asia: The Politics of Cotton Growing," in *Soviet Politics and Society in the 1970s*, ed. Morton and Tokes, 60–117 (New York: Free Press, 1974).
68. Sergei Poliakov, *Everyday Islam: Religion and Tradition in Rural Central Asia*, ed. Martha Brill Olcott (Armonk, N.Y.: M. E. Sharpe, 1993).
69. Ibid., 28.
70. See "Private Property Tendencies in Central Asia and Kazakhstan," *Central Asian Review* 10 (1962): 147–56.

Measuring the full extent of unofficial economic production is difficult and the relevant data are scarce. One survey of private farming in Soviet Turkmenistan, based on official sources, estimated that the non-state economy employed 14 percent of the indigenous labor force compared with just 3 percent on state farms and 22.3 percent on collective farms.[71] When factoring in the illegal bazaar trading and inflated traders' prices, it seems likely that income generated from the nonofficial sector approached, if not exceeded, that derived from collective and state farms. Another survey in Uzbekistan found that as much as 66 percent of peasant income in the late Soviet era was derived from such illegal activities.[72]

Republican Administrators: Systematic Opportunism

Opportunistic behavior in agriculture was not only confined to actual producers; it extended to the highest ranks of the republican Communist Party cadres. Given the asymmetries of information between Moscow and republican bosses, regional elites were able to conceal a broad range of illicit activities from the center. As a number of scholars have argued, republican elites, especially in rural areas, used the revenues and resources of the state to promote their own regional patronage and kinship ties.[73]

The most publicized of these high-level corruption scandals was the "cotton affair" in Uzbekistan. In 1986 Moscow discovered that Uzbek officials at every level of republican administration had conspired to defraud the center through an elaborate network of systematic bribing and production quota falsification. According to the investigating Russian prosecutor, between 1978 and 1983 Moscow paid Uzbekistan more than one billion rubles for cotton that was never produced.[74]

Perhaps the most infamous of the elites implicated in the scandal was the hailed Uzbek cotton baron Akhmadzan Adylov, director of the Papskii cotton combine. Until his arrest in 1984, Adylov operated his own "sovereign mini-state," according to contemporary newspaper accounts.[75] The director was solely responsible for the organization and

71. Various International Donors, *A Study of the Soviet Economy*, vol. 2. (Paris: IMF, World Bank, OECD, and EBRD, 1991), 198.

72. Dmitrieva, *Regional Development*, 123.

73. For broader discussions, see Luong, *Institutional Change and Political Continuity*, chap. 3; Erika Weinthal, *State Making and Environmental Cooperation* (Cambridge: MIT Press, 2002), chap. 4; and Dmitrieva, *Regional Development*, 121–34.

74. James Critchlow, *Nationalism in Uzbekistan* (Boulder, Colo.: Westview Press, 1992), 41. For more on the cotton scandal, see Gregory Gleason, "Nationalism or Organized Crime? The Case of the 'Cotton Scandal' in the USSR," *Corruption and Reform* 5 (1990): 87–108.

75. Rumer, *Soviet Central Asia*, 151.

administration of a labor force of 30,000 and even controlled local law enforcement and the freedom of movement in and out of his territory. Throughout the Brezhnev era, Adylov's cotton enterprise received millions of rubles as investment funds from the center, of which half were pilfered for personal profit and used to bribe the Uzbek leadership.[76] This type of organized crime was replicated throughout the agricultural sectors of the other republics.

M-form organization allowed Central Asian elites to maintain their informal networks and patronage institutions while appropriating the assets of the Soviet state. Regional opportunism was exacerbated by the equalization funds distributed by the center to promote regional investment and social welfare. Ironically, rather than promote the integration of the republics or their "equalization," these funds were transferred and used by elites to consolidate their patrimonial base. Some have even argued that it was this abrupt termination of external subsidies after the Soviet collapse that contributed to the breakdown of these patrimonial institutions and precipitated the civil war in highly dependent Tajikistan.[77]

Opportunism and Patrimonial Bargains in Other M-form Sectors

The same patterns of opportunistic behavior and patrimonialism characterized policing and law enforcement. As a legally mixed form, local MVD policing staffs were accountable to regional party organs and their clients, not the purely vertical chain of command that characterized the U-form KGB and armed forces. Law enforcement within the republics was tied to local political networks and regional Party officials held significant sway over local procurators, judges, and police investigators.[78] Nick Lampert outlined the basic structural problems and principal-agent dilemmas in law enforcement faced by the center:

On the one hand, the central authorities issue a stream of injunctions instructing the law enforcement agencies to put a stop to illegal activities by management and local officials. On the other hand, the representatives of the centre constantly protest that these agencies are unwilling to act vigorously; that illegal practices are condoned and often

76. Ibid., 152.
77. Barnett R. Rubin, "Russian Hegemony and State Breakdown in the Periphery: Causes and Consequences of the Civil War in Tajikistan," in *Post-Soviet Political Order: Conflict and State-Building*, ed. Barnett R. Rubin and Jack Snyder, 128–61 (New York: Routledge, 1998).
78. See William A. Clark, "Crime and Punishment in Soviet Officialdom, 1965–90," *Europe-Asia Studies* 45 (1993): 259–79.

encouraged by administrative superiors and local controllers. . . . The pursuit of personal, local and departmental interests seems to be in endemic tension, then, with the stated central ambition to defend the general societal interest against the corrosive effects of disrespect for the law . . . the relationships of patronage and protection are too strong.[79]

By many accounts, the police were enmeshed in many of the corrupt local systems of *nomenklatura* and part of the state-sponsored Mafia that dominated everyday life in Soviet Central Asia. Central Asian officials actively protected local economic managers from prosecution for economic crimes.[80] In addition, law enforcement was a key actor in facilitating private entrepreneurship, drug trafficking, and the embezzlement of state transfers and property that formed the backbone of Central Asia's massive shadow economy.[81] The real extent of the opportunism inherent in Moscow's relation with Central Asia on M-form issues is perhaps best summarized by Mikhail Gorbachev's observation that for years individuals and whole territories in Central Asia had operated "outside of government control."[82]

Rampant opportunism and the formation of republican-level patronage networks also characterized other delegated M-form functions, especially in the area of social policy. In education, for example, M-form control afforded Central Asian educational administrators great latitude in the formulation of policy, despite their nominal membership of the unionwide Communist Party. The most noteworthy of these policies was the so-called Central Asian affirmative action in higher education and technical training—admissions programs that discriminated against Slavs in favor of indigenous nationalities.[83] While Moscow had approved a certain degree of affirmative action as part of its "national equalization" program, several studies of admissions data and university entrance examinations have shown that Central Asian administrators abused the policy heavily and used it as an official pretext to strengthen their social ties and solicit bribes from applicants.[84]

79. Nick Lampert, "Law and Order in the USSR: The Case of Economic and Official Crime," *Soviet Studies* 36 (1984): 368.

80. See F. J. M. Feldbrugge, "Government and Shadow Economy," *Soviet Studies* 36 (1984): 528–43; Lampert, "Law and Order in the USSR"; and Charles A. Schwartz, "Corruption and Political Development in the USSR," *Comparative Politics* 11 (1979): 425–52.

81. For details, see Rumer, *Soviet Central Asia*, chap. 8.

82. Quoted in Gregory Gleason, "Fealty and Loyalty: Informal Authority Structures in Soviet Asia," *Soviet Studies* 43 (1991): 616.

83. See Lubin, *Labour and Nationality in Soviet Central Asia*, 155–58.

84. Lubin, *Labour and Nationality*; and Mobin Shorish, "Who Shall Be Educated: Selection and Integration in Soviet Central Asia," in *The Nationality Question in Soviet Central Asia*, ed. Edward

Combating the Central Asian Patrimonial State

Ultimately, Moscow had limited choices for mitigating the agency problems it faced with its Central Asian subordinates. The center's usual strategy was to periodically purge national parties of their corrupt personnel in favor of installing new officials, who, supposedly, would be more loyal to the Party.[85] Typically, the succession of a new republican First Secretary would initiate a comprehensive personnel turnover at the republic level, but such changes would not fundamentally alter the political incentives, constraints, and information encapsulation that characterized Soviet M-form administration. During the Brezhnev era, republican administrators were given even more autonomy and the power to construct local patronage networks in exchange for their support of the chairman.[86] For instance, the 1966 Party Congress removed provisions regarding the mandatory turnovers of personnel in certain state sectors, thereby further institutionalizing the new patrimonial bargain.[87] The agency problems, blatant abuses, and deviant patterns of state-building in Central Asia (and elsewhere) were tolerated by the center, although the exact extent of republican opportunism would not become known until the Gorbachev era. As long as political loyalty was maintained, Moscow—mistakenly, as it turns out—did not overtly concern itself with monitoring the local activities of republican cadres.

The post-Brezhnev era witnessed a major anticorruption drive by Moscow, the first systematic attempt to reign in its peripheral administrators and agricultural economic agents. In 1986, Moscow decreed an end to the use of the private farm as an accepted practice for agricultural workers. In addition, the entire array of Central Asian party leaders was swept out of office between 1982 and 1986. Some leaders died under mysterious circumstances (Tajikistan's Dzhabar Rasulov and Uzbekistan's Sharaf Rashidov) while others were visibly removed and publicly shamed (Turkmenistan's Mukhamednazar Gapurov, Kyrgyzstan's

Allworth, 86–98 (New York: Praeger, 1973). In her interviews with Central Asian immigrants on this topic, Rasma Karklins noted that 82 percent of the questioned Central Asian immigrants believed that these discriminatory social policies originated in the republics, not Moscow. One respondent explained, "Let's say Moscow had arranged it, so there would be 50 percent Kazakhs [in the universities], then they [the Kazakhs] arrange it that there are 75 percent." Rasma Karklins, *Ethnic Relations in the USSR: The Perspective from Below* (Winchester, Mass.: Unwin and Hyman, 1986): 91.

85. See Steven L. Burg, "Muslim Cadres and Soviet Political Development," *World Politics* 37 (1984): 24–47.

86. Willerton, *Patronage and Politics*.

87. Philip Roeder, *Red Sunset: The Failure of Soviet Politics* (Princeton: Princeton University Press, 1993), 107.

Turdakun Usubaliev, and Kazakhstan's Dinmukhammed Kunaev). Immediate subordinates such as oblast First Secretaries were also removed and between 1984 and 1988 over 58,000 Central Asian party officials were purged, which amounted to more than half of the *nomen-klatura*.[88] The scope of the post-Brezhnev anticorruption drive was indicative of the massive scale of corruption and opportunistic behavior that permeated regional administration.

Of course, corruption and patrimonialism, practices that were institutionalized at every rung of Central Asian agriculture and administration, did not stop as a result of these initiatives. The new "hardliner" republican leaders, such as Kyrgyzstan's Absamat Masaliev, merely plugged themselves into the same system and continued their opportunistic practices for the rest of the Soviet era. After seventy years of Soviet rule and M-form organization in key sectors, Central Asian political and economic agents had institutionalized a system of patrimonialism and informal authority. The long-standing corruption in the region was not an aberration of the system. Rather, Central Asian opportunism and the patrimonialism that it engendered logically flowed from the very organization of Central Asia's governance.

Conclusion: Two Types of Coexistent Political Institutions in One Polity

The sectoral cases in Soviet Central Asia demonstrate how the Soviet core employed both U-from and M-form types of governance and how these forms produced two distinct, and often contradictory, types of political institutions consistent with the expectations of the firm-type model. Despite official doctrines of "equalization," Soviet governance structures varied quite significantly. In U-form administered functions, governance costs were high, but Central Asian functions were deterritorialized and harmonized with the unionwide branches of the Soviet state, often with very little interaction with the republics or representation on their behalf. The unionwide coordination of the region's defense forces and industry introduced many large industries to the region; however, they were tied into the complex unionwide system of allocation and did not produce integrated industrial development within the region itself. Similarly, the Soviets directly administered matters of internal and external security within the functional divisions of its armed

---

88. Gleason, "Fealty and Loyalty," 616.

forces and internal police. Such divisions lacked institutionalized horizontal ties to republican state structures.

By contrast, in the M-form governed functions such as agriculture and policing, governance costs remained comparatively low while agency problems were rampant. Delegating the operation of certain tasks to regional administrators was considered more cost-effective than direct supervision; however, decentralization created tremendous informational asymmetries, resulting in endemic corruption. In agriculture, opportunistic behavior was rampant at both the micro and macro levels. On collective farms, managers allowed peasants to farm for commercial purposes, creating a huge informal economy and alternative system of economic allocation based on kinship and an informal market. Among regional bureaucrats, central investment flows earmarked for agricultural development were embezzled and production quotas were falsified. In some instances, local administrators used this autonomy to create their own political fiefdoms from the assets that nominally belonged to the state. As a result, M-form functions institutionalized a patrimonial form of statehood, allowing regional administrators great autonomy and room for opportunistic behavior. The periodic purges of republican titular elites did not change the structural incentives for opportunism within the administrative hierarchy.

Finally, this analysis suggests that the resolution of the long-standing debate over the degree to which the Soviets managed to transform Central Asia depends to a large extent on the types of sectors and organizational structures that are examined. In the U-form security and industrial sectors, the region was almost completely integrated into the unionwide structure and almost exclusively served the priorities of the Soviet center. The patrimonial dynamics of M-form sectors, however, drew on local distribution networks and kinship ties, despite being embedded within a set of Soviet directives and administrative institutions. Chapter 5 will explore how such different types of institutional development had important downstream consequences as well, especially after the Soviet system collapsed and the Central Asian republics became independent states with a set of acute organizational legacies.

THE LEGACIES OF HIERARCHY

DIVERGENT PATHS OF EXTRICATION

The natures of U-form and M-form governance and their effects impart varying legacies after a hierarchy collapses. Organizational forms generate different types of political institutions and downstream effects. After the original hierarchy collapses, peripheral U-form sectors will become institutional fragments, with no clear organizational ties to the new core; M-form sectors will tend to persist relatively intact (fig. 5.1) as part of a new, independent state.[1] This endogenous logic of organizational forms and posthierarchical collapse constitutes the theoretical basis for assessing the various modes of state-building in the postindependence era.

The first part of this chapter presents the organizational logic of the divergent posthierarchical paths of M-forms and U-forms and offers testable predictions about these legacies. The next section applies these arguments to the political settings of collapsed states and postimperial spaces and contrasts the predictions of the firm-type model about

---

1. While this chapter examines the legacies of these organizational forms after their collapse, one could also examine the propensity of each of these forms to disintegrate in the first place. For example, arguments about the instability of socialist ethnofederal arrangements often highlight how "M-form" type governance created institutional assets that were then used by regional elites and independence-seeking movements against the center. See especially, Rogers Brubaker, "Nationhood and the National Question in the Soviet Union and Post-Soviet Eurasia," *Theory and Society* 23 (1994): 47–78; and Yuri Slezkine, "The USSR as Communal Apartment, or How a Socialist State Promoted Ethnic Particularism," *Slavic Review* 53 (1994): 414–52; and Philip Roeder, "Soviet Federalism and Ethnic Mobilization," *World Politics* 43 (1991): 196–232. While such a discussion lies outside the parameters of this study, I examine varying modes of disintegration and hierarchical collapse later in this chapter and in the case of Yugoslavia in chapter 6.

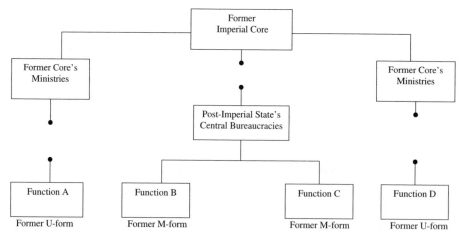

FIGURE 5.1
Organizational Legacies of U-form and M-form Governed Sectors

posthierarchical political development with ideational alternatives, notably theories of postimperial nationalism and postcolonialism. Last I revisit the sectoral cases (Central Asian defense, internal security, industry and agriculture) presented in the chapter 4 and show how M-form and U-form legacies have exerted varying effects on the state-building and consolidation of the independent post-Soviet Central Asian states.

HIERARCHICAL COLLAPSE AND PATHS OF EXTRICATION

After peripheries disengage from their former core, their extrication pathways will depend largely on whether a state sector or agency was previously organized as a U-form or an M-form in the hierarchy era.

Hierarchical Collapse and U-form Trajectories

In peripheral sectors previously governed as U-forms, their functional integration makes them dependent on a set of vertical relations and governance structures that are no longer present. After operating for a larger structure or for scale economies, U-forms will become organizational fragments of a governance structure that has contracted dramatically in scale and scope. Thus, a new state will lack the organizational capacity to support or govern that function. Second, given that U-forms were highly integrated into the core state but lacked horizontal ties to the periphery, once there is a hierarchical collapse they will lack a peripheral political constituency or support base within the bureaucracy of the nascent state. Unless the U-form can be revived or reconstituted by an external third party or other exogenous support mechanism, it will wither away or be reconfigured in the newly independent state. Of course, U-forms contained within the former core should not experience the same degree of disruption given that they will maintain the same overall organizational structure and functional divisions.

Finally, complete disengagement by a core from a former periphery might prove especially difficult if the peripheral U-form involves relationally specific assets—idiosyncratic, frequently used assets that lack readily available market substitutes.[2] In this case, their continued use or operation will be highly valued by these core functional divisions. The work of Oliver Williamson suggests a number of mixed governance forms that lie between market and hierarchy that might govern relationally specific assets, such as binding arbitration, reciprocity agreements, or joint-use agreements.[3] By disaggregating and dividing the property rights of these residual assets through mixed-governance arrangements, the former core and periphery can reconfigure the core's use of these assets without formally reconstituting the previous hierarchical order.[4]

Consequently, the presence of U-form "fragments" presents acute dilemmas for a new state. With the shift down in functional scale, U-form peripheries are severed from their functional divisions and lack an institutional base of support within the periphery. Figure 5.2 summarizes the likely posthierarchy trajectories of U-form peripheries. If the U-form contains relationally specific assets, a form of mixed governance will prevail.

> *Hypothesis 3:* After the collapse of a hierarchy, U-form sectors in the former periphery must be supported by another organization (internal or external) or they will wither away. They will exhibit "path-divergence."
>
> *Corollary 3a:* After the collapse of a hierarchy, relationally specific U-form sectors in the former periphery will be reconstituted under hybrid governance arrangements.

2. See Oliver Williamson, *The Economic Institutions of Capitalism* (New York: Free Press, 1985), 95–97.
3. Ibid., 83.
4. On the logic of mixed forms of integration in postimperial settings, see Alexander Cooley, "Imperial Wreckage: Property Rights, Sovereignty and Security in the Post-Soviet Space," *International Security* 24 (2000–2001): 100–127.

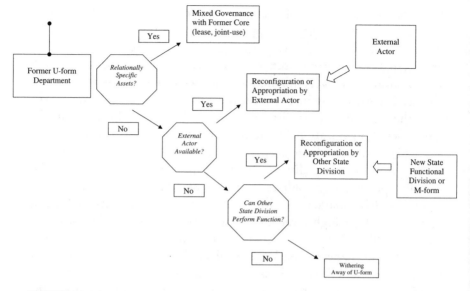

FIGURE 5.2
Potential Pathways of Peripheral U-form after Hierarchy

Hierarchical Collapse and M-form Trajectories

By contrast, M-form sectors in peripheries will survive a hierarchical collapse relatively intact. Given that M-form sectors operated as autonomous subdivisions within the original hierarchy, disengagement from the core should not adversely affect their institutional configuration. Spatially, the M-form will now correspond to the organization of the boundaries of the new unit and will be able to function independently of the former core. As a result, M-forms should be characterized by a high degree of institutional continuity or "path dependence" between their hierarchical governance and their posthierarchical governance.[5] In contrast to the "path-divergence" U-forms, these institutions should be relatively less susceptible to change or restructuring in the posthierarchy era.

> *Hypothesis 4:* After the collapse of a hierarchy, M-form sectors in the former periphery will persist while maintaining their preexisting institutional configurations. They will exhibit "path-dependence."

5. On the dynamics of path dependency, see Douglass North, *Institutions, Institutional Change and Economic Performance* (New York: Cambridge University Press, 1990), chap. 11.

Exogenous Actors, Resources, and Institutional Trajectories

Finally, resource flows from an exogenous actor or third party will have contrasting effects on U-forms and M-forms as external flows of capital or other material resources will reinforce these endogenous dynamics of posthierarchical extrication. External influences are likely to accelerate the restructuring or reconfiguration of U-form sectors. With the resources provided by an external actor or organization, U-form fragments will reconfigure themselves to serve the functional requirements of this new external organization.[6] Conversely, external resource flows will reinforce, not change, the path-dependent institutional configurations of M-forms. This dynamic should hold true, even if *external resources are actually intended to promote institutional change* or restructuring in M-forms. In sum, U-forms are much more susceptible to pressures for institutional change from exogenous sources than M-forms, regardless of the actual purpose of the external actor.

Hypothesis 5: After the collapse of a hierarchy, external flows of capital and resources will reinforce the endogenous extrication dynamics in U-forms and M-forms.

POLITICAL APPLICATIONS: PATTERNS OF STATE-BUILDING AFTER HIERARCHY

Institutional Legacies and Trajectories after Hierarchy

To date, scholars have used both ideational and institutionalist explanations to examine the relationship between imperial legacies and patterns of postimperial state-building and development. Most prevailing accounts of postcolonial trajectories emphasize ideational variables such as identity, ideology, and nationalism. Mahmoud Mamdani argues that colonialism instilled a powerful set of hegemonic racial and ethnic identities that continued to characterize authority relations and political cultures within states during the postcolonial era.[7] This line of argument also typifies most postcolonial approaches to the study of political

6. This is a variant of resource-dependency theories in the organizational literature. See Jeffrey and Gerald Salancik, *The External Control of Organizations: A Resource Dependence Perspective* (New York: Harper & Row, 1978).
7. Mahmoud Mamdani, *Citizen and Subject* (Princeton: Princeton University Press, 1996).

nationalism and other legitimizing state discourses after independence. Applying the concepts of nationalism and identity explicitly to the study of postimperial international relations, Rawi Abdelal argues that the veracity and orientation of nationalism was primarily responsible for the postimperial states' foreign-policy orientation after the collapse of the Soviet, Dutch, French, and Hapsburg empires.[8] Where national identities were strong, new states tended to orient their foreign economic policies away from former core powers while they tended to maintain closer ties where postimperial nationalisms were weak. For ideational theories, the content of peripheral identities not only derives from imperial experiences, it also influences institution building and political orientation after empire.[9] While constructivist approaches can explain broad trends in the foreign-policy orientation of postimperial states, such frameworks cannot account for the divergent paths that different sectors within these states might take. Why do some state sectors fully disengage from their imperial-era institutions while others maintain them relatively unchanged? As with the study of hierarchical governance, such theories cannot explain sectoral variance.

The critical issue of theorizing the links between the hierarchical and posthierarchical eras need not be ceded to ideational accounts. Recent institutional analyses have examined more explicitly the material origins of institutional continuities between the imperial and postimperial eras. Jeffrey Herbst has shown how patterns of authority and political geography continue to constrain the capacity of current African rulers to maintain authority within their national boundaries.[10] A study by Rafael La Porta and others has argued that a colonial legal heritage based on common law is more likely to foster productive property rights than one based on civil law.[11] More broadly, Daren Acemoglu, Simon Johnson, and James Robinson have shown that different economic institutions employed by European colonial powers—such as taxation patterns, settler protections, or property rights—explain a great deal of

8. See Rawi Abdelal, *National Purpose in the World Economy: Post-Soviet States in Comparative Perspective* (Ithaca: Cornell University Press, 2001); and Abdelal, "Purpose and Privation: Nation and Economy in Post-Habsburg Eastern Europe and Post-Soviet Eurasia," *East European Politics and Societies* 16, no. 3 (2002): 898–933.

9. Alison Brysk, Craig Parsons, and Wayne Sandholtz, "After Empire: National Identity and the Post-Colonial Family of Nations," *European Journal of International Relations* 8 (2002): 267–305.

10. Jeffrey Herbst, *States and Power in Africa: Comparative lessons in Authority and Control* (Princeton: Princeton University Press, 2000).

11. Rafael La Porta, Florencio Lopez-de-Silanes, Andrei Shleifer, and Robert Vishny, "The Quality of Government," *Journal of Law, Economics and Organization* 15 (1999): 222–82; and La Porta et al., "Law and Finance," *Journal of Political Economy* 106 (1998): 1113–55.

variation in levels of postcolonial economic development.[12] Some have even drawn on the insights of the firm-type distinction to explain the divergent patterns of economic transformation and experimentation in China and the former Soviet Union.[13]

The firm-type model builds on this institutional literature but seeks to account for variations in patterns of continuity and change within the same posthierarchical periphery. Both across different peripheries and across sectors in the same periphery, the firm-type model suggests that varying institutional legacies produced by each organizational form will shape subsequent patterns of state-building, although these legacies will be more pronounced in hierarchies that have collapsed rapidly as opposed to those that decayed over a number of years.[14] To illustrate the insights and explanatory power of this approach, I examine how the firm-type model applies to both issues of security and economy after hierarchy. A more systematic application of the model's hypotheses is then provided by the Central Asian focal case.

Security and Sectoral Trajectories after Hierarchy

It is well documented that the security institutions of developing states differ from those of their Western counterparts.[15] Across cases in Africa, Asia, and the post-Communist sphere, postimperial states lack a unitary organizational structure with clearly defined functional specializations (i.e., armed forces, police, border patrol, internal security, intelligence) and, instead, are characterized by a patchwork-type organizational structure, with various agencies, bureaucratic fragments, and informal networks all coexisting within the same new juridical unit.[16] As a result,

12. See Daren Acemoglu, Simon A. Johnson, and James A. Robinson, "The Colonial Origins of Comparative Development: An Empirical Investigation," *American Economic Review* 91 (2001): 1369–1401; and Acemoglu, Johnson, and Robinson, "Reversal of Fortune: Geography and Institutions in the Making of the Modern World Income Distribution," *Quarterly Journal of Economics* 117 (November 2002): 1231–94.

13. See Eric Maskin, Yingyi Qian, and Chenggang Xu, "Incentives, Information and Organizational Form," *Review of Economic Studies* 67 (2002): 359–78; and Qian and Xu, "Why China's Economic Reforms Differ: The M-form Hierarchy and Entry/Expansion of the Non-state Sector," *Economics of Transition* 1 (1993): 135–70.

14. On the importance of rapid collapse as opposed to protracted decline in empires, see Alexander Motyl, *Revolutions, Nations, Empires* (New York: Columbia University Press, 1999).

15. See Brian L. Job, ed., *The Insecurity Dilemma: National Security of Third World States* (Boulder, Colo.: Lynn Reinner, 1992); Steven R. David, "Explaining Third World Alignment," *World Politics* 43 (1991): 233–56; and Nicole Ball, *Security and Economy in the Third World* (Princeton: Princeton University Press, 1988).

16. Robert Jackson maintains that such states predominantly maintain juridical sovereignty, given that these various agencies lack internal control and/or a monopoly on violence. See Jackson, *Sovereignty, International Relations and the Third World* (New York: Cambridge University Press, 1993).

these multiple agencies are likely to compete aggressively over new areas of functional jurisdiction, thereby further eroding the distinctions among security-related functions.[17] For example, the armed forces of postcolonial states are more likely to step into internal policing and security roles or vice versa, depending on which M-form security organization inherited stronger institutionalized links to the new state. Indeed, Charles Tilly suggests that the military dominance in Third World societies and their lack of clear functional boundaries made postcolonial states particularly susceptible to military coups and the use of defense forces to maintain internal order.[18]

The cruel irony suggested by the firm-type model is that former peripheries that were the most directly repressed through intense U-form governance were also the ones least equipped on independence to effectively establish a monopoly of violence within their boundaries. Consider, for example, the former Portuguese colonies of Angola and Mozambique, where the Portuguese armed forces, unlike other European colonial powers in Africa (except French Algeria), actively governed these colonies as U-form extensions of their military operations. Once the Salazar-Caetano military regime collapsed within the core in 1974, so too did military colonial rule. Upon the abrupt withdrawal of the Portuguese military, both countries lacked any statewide security structures and both rapidly descended into civil war involving various paramilitary factions with external sponsors. In Mozambique, the independence war waged by the Soviet-backed Front for Liberation of Mozambique (FRELIMO) immediately gave way to a 16-year civil war with the Mozambique Resistance Movement (RENAMO), funded and supplied by South Africa. Similarly, in Angola, three distinct factions emerged after the abrupt withdrawal of Portuguese forces in 1973 and were supported during the 25-year conflict by numerous outside patrons such as the Soviet Union, Cuba, the United States, and Zaire.[19] The intense U-form security governance exerted by the Portuguese military, coupled with the lack of any preexisting national internal security forces, made the immediate Portuguese colonial legacy the most violent of any of its African counterparts.

17. See Alexander Cooley, "Globalization and National Security in the Post-Soviet Space," Paper presented to the 45th Convention of the International Studies Association, Montreal, March 17, 2004.
18. Charles Tilly, *Capital, Coercion and the Formation of European States: AD 990–1990* (Cambridge, Mass.: Blackwell, 1990), 212–13.
19. For details, see Patrick Chabal et al., *A History of Postcolonial Lusophone Africa* (Bloomington: Indiana University Press, 2002).

In the communist federations, too, the collapse of U-forms created an acute vacuum in the area of national defense that contributed to the outbreak of ethnic or secessionist conflicts. As Charles H. Fairbanks observes: "In the Soviet Union and in Yugoslavia, state institutions were much more weaker in the federal units than in the national capitals because the economy, foreign policy, the security police, ideology, and the official appointments were controlled from the center. Thus from the moment of the federal republics' secession their state structures were decisively weaker than the earlier state structure."[20] As both the focal case and the comparative case on Yugoslavia (see chap. 6) suggest, the successor postcommunist states lacked well-formed national militaries and, instead, were initially forced to fight wars of territorial consolidation with patchwork armies comprised of police forces, paramilitaries, and even mercenaries. As one analyst of postcommunist ethnic conflict observed, the very question of whether these paramilitaries and armed gangs were effectively controlled by their governments is in doubt.[21] At the same time, the former national cores—Russia and Serbia—inherited the lion's share of the communist-era armed forces.

Finally, in U-form security-related sectors containing relationally specific assets, peaceful disengagement has usually been predicated on the former core and periphery negotiating a mixed governance arrangement. In some cases, former occupying powers have retained control over strategic assets through the creation of postimperial management companies, as was the case with Great Britain and the United States in their governance of the Suez and Panama Canals. Military installations and bases also have been retained after decolonization through hybrid sovereignty arrangements with former peripheries.[22] Such was the case in the Philippines, where the United States used a variety of leasing arrangements to maintain control of Clark Air Force Base and the Subic Bay deep water harbor, and in West Africa, where the French maintained control over bases in Djibouti, Senegal, Ivory Coast, Gabon, and Chad after formally ceding sovereignty.[23] More recently, joint-use arrangements over critical naval installations facilitated South African disen-

20. Charles H. Fairbanks Jr., "Weak States and Private Armies," in *Beyond State Crisis: Postcolonial Africa and Post-Eurasia in Comparative Perspective*, ed. Mark Beissinger and Crawford Young, 146 (Baltimore: Johns Hopkins University Press).

21. John Mueller, "The Banality of 'Ethnic War,'" *International Security* 25 (2000): 42–70.

22. For an overview, see C. T. Sandars, *America's Overseas Garrisons: The Leasehold Empire* (New York: Oxford University Press, 2000).

23. On the Philippines, see William J. Berry Jr., *U.S. Bases in the Philippines: The Evolution of the Special Relationship* (Boulder, Colo.: Westview, 1989). On French bases, see Alain Rouvez, *Disconsolate Empires* (Lanham, Md.: University Press of America, 1994).

gagement from Namibia (Walvis Bay) and Russian disengagement from Ukrainian Crimea.[24] While the nature of these governance arrangements is usually temporary, with full property rights eventually reverting to former peripheries, leasing and other hybrid governance arrangements have fostered the relatively peaceful transition of relationally specific U-forms in periods of postimperial disengagement.

Conversely, the firm-type model suggests that former peripheries with strong M-form security institutions were more effective in consolidating political order than states with U-form security legacies. Perhaps the most enduring M-form security legacy left by colonial powers was the territorial police force. In former French African colonies, for example, internal security forces typically retained the colonial-era distinction between the national police, subordinated to the Ministry of Interior, and the gendarmerie, a rural force subordinated to the military.[25] The British colonial police force also gradually performed military roles in colonies, despite its legal law enforcement status, and in colonies where imperial powers created strong indigenous police forces, such as British Malaya, these often became militarized in the late colonial era and formed the backbone of postindependence national security forces.[26] Not surprisingly, settler colonies such as Kenya and Southern Rhodesia tended to be the most heavily policed, bequeathing these states a disproportionately large and coercive internal security apparatus.[27] While policing is not usually considered in studies of security, the actual security forces inherited by postcolonial states were often internal police forces concerned with maintaining internal order and squelching counterinsurgency movements during colonial rule.

In sum, the firm-type model provides a number of insights into the relationship between the hierarchical organization of security and posthierarchical state-building. Whereas M-form security-related institutions such as internal security forces or patterns of civil-military relations maintain themselves in the postimperial era, U-forms affect the

24. See Cooley, "Imperial Wreckage."
25. Otwin Marenin, "Policing African States: Towards a Critique," *Comparative Politics* 14 (1982): 385–87.
26. See, especially, Mathieu Deflem, "Law Enforcement in British Colonial Africa: A Comparative Analysis of Imperial Policing in Nyasaland, the Gold Coast, and Kenya," *Police Studies* 17 (1994): 45–68. See also D. M. Anderson and David Killingray, eds., *Policing and Decolonisation: Politics, Nationalism and the Police, 1917–1965* (Manchester: Manchester University Press, 1992); and Anderson and Killingray, eds., *Policing the Empire: Government, Authority and Control, 1830–1940* (Manchester: Manchester University Press, 1991).
27. See David Killingray, "The Maintenance of Law and Order in British Colonial Africa," *African Affairs* 85 (1986): 415–17.

internal development of security through their absence and creation of a vacuum. As a result, postimperial states are characterized by a patch-work of security forces with ill-defined functional roles and organiza-tional allegiances. Consequently, the lines separating defense, policing, and internal security were erased in the postimperial era, as these colonial-era security institutions were strengthened and often turned inward to suppress domestic political opposition and internal ethnic rebellions.

Economy and Sectoral Trajectories after Hierarchy

In the realm of economy, similar patterns of institutional continuity and change characterized the development of the posthierarchical state. In M-forms the patrimonial institutions of the imperial era continued to structure economic activity well after independence. By contrast, U-form sectors were more susceptible to institutional reconfiguration and radical change.

A major institutional feature of Africa's immediate postcolonial polit-ical economy was the state's continued governance of the agricultural sector and its control over primary commodity production through colonial-era M-form agricultural boards. As Robert Bates observed, African postcolonial states continued to use these monopoly boards to pay farmers a fraction of world market prices and to redistribute the dif-ference to the state and its bureaucratic clients.[28] Similarly, Kathryn Firmin-Sellers has shown how Ghana's independence constitution, while attempting to concentrate power in the new Convention People's Party that had fought for independence, could not fundamentally alter the insecure M-form property rights and land tenure systems that Gold Coast elites established under British rule.[29] Even after governments ini-tiated nominal acts of institutional change, such as socialist collec-tivization or, a decade later, market-oriented privatization, entrenched systems of patrimonial authority and control ensured that colonial-era M-form land-tenure patterns persisted and accommodated themselves within these new legal frameworks.[30] As Thomas Callaghy's analysis of

28. Robert Bates, *Markets and States in Tropical Africa: The Political Basis of Agricultural Policies* (Berkeley: University of California Press, 1981).
29. Kathryn Firmin-Sellers, *The Transformation of Property Rights in the Gold Coast: An Empirical Study Applying Rational Choice Theory* (New York: Cambridge University Press, 1996).
30. For example, see M. Anne Pitcher's work on the institutional durability of M-form land tenure systems in Mozambique. Pitcher, "Disruption without Transformation: Agrarian Relations and Livelihoods in Mozambique, 1975–1995," *Journal of Southern African Studies* 24 (1998): 115–40; and Pitcher, "Recreating Colonialism or Restructuring the State: Privatisation and Politics in Mozambique," *Journal of Southern African Studies* 22 (1996): 49–74.

the absolutism in the Zairian postcolonial state shows, entrenched structures of patrimonialism managed to preserve traditional and semitraditional modes of state allocation, oversight, and development well after the end of the colonial state.[31]

By contrast, U-form economic sectors typically had a very different fate. Having detached from their overall functional role within the original hierarchical polity, U-forms were far more likely to disappear or be reorganized fundamentally by the postimperial state. In general, the more integrated a peripheral economy had become through the use of the U-form, the greater the dislocation and organizational disruption it was likely to suffer after hierarchical collapse. Various paths of change and reconfiguration occurred after independence. In some cases, newly independent states immediately nationalized or expropriated U-form industries that were controlled by companies belonging to the former core, thereby providing another revenue stream for postcolonial elites to shore up their patronage networks.[32]

In other cases, hierarchical collapse also generated the near total collapse of U-form economic sectors, as the newly independent states lacked the capital, markets, managerial skills, and intermediate inputs to keep these enterprises going. Such was the case in the Japanese colonies of Taiwan and Korea, where heavy industries were tightly integrated into the Japanese production network and almost completely ground to a halt given independence.[33] Nor was this pattern confined to industry. French Algeria's two most important U-form sectors were in the agricultural sectors of wine-making and tobacco farming, the opposite structural pattern of that found in Soviet Central Asia. With the advent of Algerian independence, both sectors collapsed as tens of thousands of French settler farmers emigrated and the FLN government promoted hydrocarbon extraction and import-substitution industrialization.[34] Finally, in the cases of relationally specific assets, European imperial powers such as the Netherlands and France retained control over certain peripheral mines and site-specific extractive sectors through

31. Thomas M. Callaghy, *The State-Society Struggle: Zaire in Comparative Perspective* (New York: Columbia University Press, 1984), 3–19.

32. For an overview, see Stephen J. Kobrin, "Expropriation as an Attempt to Control Foreign Firms in LDCs: Trends from 1960 to 1979," *International Studies Quarterly* 28 (1984): 329–48.

33. See Stephen Haggard, David Kang, and Chung-In Moon, "Japanese Colonialism and Korean Development: A Critique," *World Development* 25: 870–71. For more details and an application of the firm-type model to this case, see chapter 6.

34. See Philip C. Naylor, *France and Algeria: A History of Decolonization and Transformation* (Gainesville: University Press of Florida, 2000); and Karen Farsoun, "State Capitalism in Algeria," *MERIP Reports* 35 (1975): 3–30.

the use of new production-sharing and joint-ownership agreements forged during decolonization.[35]

External Capital Flows and Institutional Trajectories

Finally, the legacies outlined by the firm-type model reformulate our understanding of the relationship between international economic integration and state-building in postimperial countries. The firm-type model suggests that these patterns of state-building are primarily *endogenously* determined and that international economic interactions will tend to accelerate these outlined dynamics of postimperial extrication.

International interactions with former U-form sectors do indeed have the potential to initiate institutional transformation. Far from encouraging liberalization, however, external flows of private capital in the 1960s and 1970s actually consolidated M-form sectors and entrenched patrimonial state-building in the developing world. Jeffry Frieden observed that 80–90 percent of all Euromarket lending to developing countries in the 1970s actually supported the growth of the public sector, thereby enhancing the state's power over independent social groups.[36] Peter Evans and Barbara Stallings have argued that transnational economic linkages in the form of investment and aid were often antithetical to domestic economic liberalization as they provided resources for states to enhance their autonomy.[37] Furthermore, one of the central findings of the "rentier state" and "resource curse" literatures is that postimperial states that are dependent on revenues from natural resources or primary commodities forgo economic and political liberalization by distributing patronage to political clients and sprawling bureaucracies.[38] Throughout the decolonized states of the developing world, external flows of capital initially promoted, not undermined, the state's M-form institutions.

These endogenous dynamics should hold even when external actors, such as international financial institutions, attempt to induce institu-

35. Hendrik Spruyt, *Ending Empire* (Ithaca: Cornell University Press, 2005).

36. Jeffry Frieden, "Third World Indebted Industrialization: International Finance and State Capitalism in Mexico, Brazil, Algeria and South Korea," *International Organization* 35 (1981): 407–31.

37. Peter Evans, "Transnational Linkages and the Economic Role of the State," in *Bringing the State Back In*, ed. Peter Evans, Dietrich Rueschmeyer, and Theda Skocpol, 192–226 (New York: Cambridge University Press, 1985); and Barbara Stallings, "International Lending and the Relative Autonomy of the State: The Case of Twentieth-Century Peru," *Politics & Society* 14 (1985): 257–88.

38. For overviews, see Alexander Cooley, "Booms and Busts: Theorizing Institutional Formation and Change in Oil States," *Review of International Political Economy* 8 (2001): 163–80; and Michael Ross, "The Political Economy of the Resource Curse," *World Politics* 51 (1999): 279–322.

tional change by imposing macroeconomic conditions on the lender. Typically, International Monetary Fund (IMF) conditionality agreements include provisions designed to combat inflation and achieve macroeconomic stability, eliminate state subsidies and free prices, privatize state-owned enterprises, and liberalize the trade and foreign exchange regimes. As a result, scholars usually view IMF conditionality as an intrusive process that undermines the sovereignty of the lender.[39] The firm-type model would predict the exact opposite, however: conditional lending by international financial institutions (IFI) to states with strong M-form sectors will merely reinforce these microlevel patrimonial dynamics and shift the burden of adjustment on nonclients or the broader public. Indeed, Nicolas van de Walle's examination of the evolution of IFI lending in Africa concludes that conditionality has not promoted real institutional change and, instead, political elites have used international aid to support their private political clients.[40]

Recent quantitative studies of conditional lending further support the hypothesis that IMF and World Bank conditionality have merely reinforced the rent-seeking and clientelist institutions that they were meant to change. A comprehensive World Bank study concluded that external aid and structural adjustment programs in developing countries lacking institutional governance failed with regularity and even promoted mismanagement and corruption.[41] More specifically, another World Bank study (quite contrary to its immediate organizational interests) found strong evidence that, over time, aid flows significantly diminished bureaucratic quality and actually alleviated pressures to reform inefficient institutions.[42] In a survey of 220 external adjustment programs, another study found that aid effectiveness dramatically decreased as a function of the tenure of a recipient country's regime.[43] Clearly, the evidence shows that not only is IFI economic conditionality insufficient for implementing institutional change in postcolonial countries, it is

39. Joseph Stiglitz, *Globalization and Its Discontents* (New York: W. W. Norton, 2002); and Stephen Krasner, *Sovereignty: Organized Hypocrisy* (Princeton: Princeton University Press, 2002), especially chap. 5. Also see Kendall Stiles, *Negotiating Debt: The IMF Lending Process* (Boulder, Colo.: Westview Press, 1991).

40. Nicolas van de Walle, *African Economies and the Politics of Permanent Crisis, 1979–1999* (New York: Cambridge University Press, 2001).

41. World Bank, *Assessing Aid: What Works, What Doesn't, and Why* (Washington, D.C.: World Bank, 1998).

42. Stephen Knack, "Aid Dependence and the Quality of Governance: A Cross-Country Empirical Analysis." *Working Paper of the World Bank* WPS 2396. (Washington, D.C.: 2000).

43. David Dollar and Jakob Svensson, "What Explains the Success or Failure of Structural Adjustment Programs?" *The Economic Journal* 110 (2000): 894–917.

actually associated with feeding some of the most negative aspects of patrimonial governance.

To summarize, the legacies of the imperial era onward had important consequences for determining economic patterns in the independence era. The patrimonial institutions that developed in M-form sectors continued to dominate state-formation after independence. M-form institutions, such as property rights, agricultural boards, and extractive institutions, maintained their institutional configurations during independence and structured economic and political activity well beyond the colonial era. U-form sectors were either appropriated and reconfigured by the patrimonial state or, if doing so proved too costly, were allowed to wither way. It is significant that a "clean break" or rapid transition to a new set of governance institutions did not happen in the vast majority of states. Despite widespread ideologies of anticolonialism or new national identities, M-form patronage institutions were well entrenched within the political structure of these former peripheries and continued to influence state-building long after independence.

SOVIET LEGACIES AND STATE-BUILDING IN POST-SOVIET CENTRAL ASIA

After the Soviet collapse, the political future of the Central Asian states seemed uncertain but potentially bright. Freed from the shackles of Soviet imperial rule and Communist ideology, observers assumed that the newly independent states of Central Asia would rapidly assert their independence and initiate substantive institutional reforms. Early analyses also stressed the potentially critical role of identity in post-Soviet state-building and speculated that the Central Asian "Muslim" states could potentially follow a secular Turkish model of development or a more religious-based "Iranian" model.[44] Central Asian elites themselves publicly emphasized the importance of adopting new identities and national role models. While President Askar Akayev proclaimed that a liberalized Kyrgyzstan would become the "Switzerland" of Central Asia, his counterpart Saparmurat Niyazov emphasized that Turkmenistan's significant natural gas reserves would turn it into the "Kuwait of the

---

44. For a discussion of these assessments, see Daniel Pipes, "The Event of Our Era: Former Soviet Muslim Republics Change the Middle East," in *Central Asia and the World*, ed. Michael Mandelbaum, 47–93 (New York: Council on Foreign Relations, 1994).

Caspian."[45] Post-Communist development, it seemed, would greatly vary as the former republics shed their Soviet affinities and adopted a new national purpose. While the states of the Central Asian region may now appear similar, in the immediate post-Soviet era they attempted to embark on varying foreign policy trajectories.

The immediate "transition" period rapidly revealed dramatic differences from these publicly adopted images.[46] Rather than the development of Western-style markets and democracy, many Soviet-era legacies and institutions continued to thrive in the independence era. Instead of promoting free and civil societies, Communist-era leaders used internal security forces to clamp down on political opposition and civil liberties. As each year passed following the Soviet collapse, the assumption that the Central Asian states were undergoing an inevitable period of "transition" appeared more untenable.[47] In fact, in many governance areas and state functions, such as a national military or the border guard, the Central Asian states seemed to lack altogether the fundamental attributes traditionally associated with state sovereignty.

As the rest of this chapter will show, patterns of Central Asian state-building have varied by sector and can be traced to whether a particular state function was governed as an M-form or U-form in the Soviet era. In both the realms of economy and security, M-form governed sectors have persisted relatively intact in the post-Soviet era, whereas U-form sectors have not. In the realm of security, the M-form governed internal police structures have emerged relatively unchanged from the Soviet era while the armed forces remain of secondary importance for maintaining both internal and external security. In the economy, Soviet-era institutions governing agriculture and land tenure survived the transition relatively unchanged whereas U-form governed heavy industries have been disrupted severely and even collapsed. Throughout the first decade of independence, external resources provided by Western actors reinforced these endogenous patterns, despite these actors' intentions or public proclamations that welcomed the prospect of enacting basic institutional reforms. This account, emphasizing sectoral variance in insti-

45. Saparmurat Niyazov, *Independence, Democracy, Prosperity* (New York: Noy, 1994), 82.

46. For analytically informed overviews of these post-Soviet regional developments, see Pauline Jones Luong, ed., *The Transformation of Central Asia: States and Societies from Soviet Rule to Independence* (Ithaca: Cornell University Press, 2004); Olivier Roy, *The New Central Asia: The Creation of Nations* (New York: New York University Press, 2000); Gregory Gleason, *Central Asia's New States: Discovering Independence* (Boulder, Colo.: Westview Press, 1997); and Boris Rumer, ed., *Central Asia in Transition: Dilemmas of Political and Economic Development* (Armonk, N.Y.: M. E. Sharpe, 1996).

47. See Alexander Cooley, "Transitioning Backwards," *The Harriman Review* II (1998): 1–11.

tutional trajectories, differs fundamentally with prevailing analyses that explain post-Soviet state-building and foreign policy trajectories in terms of unified state actions or national identities.[48]

Security Legacies and Sectoral Trends in the Post-Soviet Period

Despite their impressive strength during Soviet times, the U-form governed armed forces in the newly independent states did not survive the chaos generated by the Soviet collapse. Instead, in most Soviet successor states defense forces were an assembly of cobbled together internal security forces, paramilitaries, criminal organizations, and foreign troops (usually Russians). In contrast to the armed forces, internal security and police forces persisted in the post-Soviet period with their Soviet-era institutional structures almost completely intact. These M-form MVD and national guard units have become the most powerful sources of organized violence in the post-Soviet period.

Given that U-forms were governed exclusively by the center, the armed forces of the post-Soviet states were weak and institutionally fragmented. Having been organized along functional, deterritorialized lines, the armed forces did not establish the same set of horizontal ties, either politically or economically, with the rest of the republican state apparatus. Without Moscow's central coordination, command, and resources, the Soviet army in the post-Soviet republics degenerated into a set of isolated pockets of bases, installations, and deployments. The collapse of the Soviet military also brought its ethnic imbalances into the nation-building spotlight as new national units had very few senior officers or high-ranking officials who were indigenous nationals. For example, of the fifteen active generals in Uzbekistan in 1992, only five were Uzbeks and 85 percent of the officer corps was reported to be Slavs.[49] Similarly, Slavs constituted 95 percent of Kazakhstan's officer corps on independence.[50] Not surprisingly, the very sovereignty of these post-Soviet mil-

---

48. For examples, see Andrei Tsygankov, *Pathways after Empire: National Identity and Foreign Economic Policy in the Post-Soviet World* (Lanham, Md.: Rowman and Littlefield, 2002); and Abdelal, *National Purpose in the World Economy.* For alternate accounts of the impact of Soviet ideational and institutional legacies, see Mark Beissinger and Crawford Young, eds., *Beyond State Crisis? Postcolonial Africa and Post-Soviet Eurasia in Comparative Perspective* (Baltimore: Johns Hopkins University Press, 2002); Karen Dawisha and Bruce Parrott, eds., *The End of Empire?: The Transformation of the USSR in Comparative Perspective* (Armonk, N.Y.: M. E. Sharpe, 1996); and Mark Beissinger, "The Persisting Ambiguity of Empire," *Post-Soviet Affairs* 11 (1995): 149–84.
49. Janes On-line Defense Directory, "Uzbekistan: Armed Forces," http://www.janes.com (accessed 3/15/2004).
50. Robert V. Barylski, "The Military and State in Kazakhstan," in *Civil-Military Relations in the Soviet and Yugoslav Successor States,* ed. Constantine P. Danopoulos and Daniel Zirker, 124 (Boulder, Colo.: Westview Press, 1996).

itary "fragments" and commanding personnel became an immediate source of contention between the states of the former Soviet Union and Russia.

The exact reconfiguration of security-related U-forms in the post-Soviet era varied. In certain instances, Russia maintained specific particular security functions in the Central Asian region.[51] In the border guard, for example, Russian troops assumed sole or joint responsibility for patrolling the region's non-CIS (Commonwealth of Independent States) borders throughout the 1990s. Russia only ceded full responsibility for border patrolling to Kyrgyzstan and Turkmenistan in 1999 while in Tajikistan a 12,000 joint-force under Russian command still patrolled the 1,400 kilometer Afghanistan border through 2004.[52] In cases where security installations constituted relationally specific assets for the Russian military, Russia secured mixed governance arrangements with the Central Asian states. For example, Russia signed a twenty-year lease with the Kazakh government for the Baikonur space center and satellite launch facility and concluded a separate ten-year agreement to continue using the Emba and Saryshagan missile test sites.[53] In still other cases, the weakness of the armed forces led some Central Asian leaders and agencies to contract externally for security services. The Tajik government relied on hired fighters to defend its Afghan border throughout the 1990s while President Supramurat Niyazov of Turkmenistan employed a group of Ukrainian mercenaries to protect himself and the inner circles of his regime. The new national armed forces of the Central Asian states are small and underfunded in comparison with their Soviet predecessors and many of their functions have been taken over by other internal security agencies.

The relative decline of the armed forces becomes more apparent when compared to the relatively smooth post-Soviet transition made by M-form internal security and police forces. As M-forms, these regionally and locally controlled security organs have survived relatively intact and, in fact, have become the primary security forces in the independent Central Asian states. As table 5.1 shows, the internal security organs of the Central Asian states, most notably the renamed Soviet-era Ministries of Internal Affairs, all have a greater number of troops than the national

51. On the range of post-Soviet bilateral bargains between Russia and the former Soviet states, see Daniel W. Drezner, *The Sanctions Paradox: Economic Statecraft and International Relations* (Cambridge: Cambridge University Press, 1999), 131–247.
52. On the organization of Central Asia's border guard in comparative perspective, see George Gavrilis, "Border Guards and High States: Toward a Theory of Boundary Regimes," Ph.D. diss., Columbia University, 2003.
53. For details, see Cooley, "Imperial Wreckage," 114–18.

TABLE 5.1
Comparative Number of Internal and External Security Troops, 2003

Country or Region	National Armed Forces	Police and Internal Security	External: Internal Forces	Armed Forces per Population	Police per Population
Central Asia					
Kazakhstan	60,150	69,000[a]	.87	1:279	1:243
Kyrgyzstan	11,000	19,000	.58	1:445	1:258
Tajikistan	6,000	28,800[b]	.21	1:1144	1:238
Turkmenistan	17,500	25,500	.69	1:273	1:187
Uzbekistan	70,000	200,000	.35	1:371	1:130
Other					
Russia	860,000	700,000	1.23	1:168	1:206
Hungary	39,000[c]	37,000	1.05	1:258	1:271
New Zealand	8,750	7,100	1.23	1:452	1:557
Guatemala	32,200	9,800	3.29	1:432	1:1419
Peru	120,000	89,000	1.35	1:237	1:319
Cameroon	13,650	9,000	1.52	1:1154	1:1750
Botswana	7,800	4,695	1.66	1:202	1:335
Jordan	100,500[d]	25,000	4.02	1:54	1:218
Sri Lanka	110,000	80,000	1.38	1:179	1:247
Thailand	240,000	120,000	2.00	1:268	1:536

Source: Janes Defense Weekly On-line, *Sentinel Security Assessment;* except:
[a] International Crisis Group;
[b] Seventh United Nations Survey of Crime Trends and Operations of Criminal Justice Systems, covering the period from 1998 to 2000 (United Nations Office on Drugs and Crime, Centre for International Crime Prevention).
Notes:
[c] 2002 data.
[d] estimate.

armed forces. Comparatively speaking, such high ratios of internal to external security troops are highly unusual both for developing and developed states. Underscoring this point, a 2002 report by the International Crisis Group (ICG) on policing activities in the Central Asian states observed:

> Unlike in many developing countries, the military in Central Asian states plays a more limited role in everyday political life than the interior ministries. Police forces in the region are much more powerful than the militaries and include their own armed units designed for internal control. They have a considerable role in political life that may grow further in the future. Although the role of militaries in Central Asian societies should not be ignored, the internal security forces pose the greater threat to stability and the greater opposition to deeper economic and political reform. In Central Asia the structures of most police forces have changed little since the Soviet period.[54]

54. International Crisis Group (ICG), "Central Asia: The Politics of Police Reform," p. i, http://www.icg.org/home/index.cfm?id=1444&1=4 (accessed 3/10/05).

As a result, these internal security forces have often expanded their functional scope to discharge duties traditionally associated with armed forces and security forces. Internal security forces have been at the forefront of these countries' major post-Soviet security-preserving efforts, such as quelling Islamic movements and other armed insurgents streaming across the Afghan border.[55]

Along with MVD troops, a variety of unconventional organizations and paramilitary forces have added to the disorganized, patchwork character of the region's security forces. Many of these paramilitary units originated in the Soviet era as M-form organizations and were designed to protect certain agencies or remote regional administrators. Similarly, the national guard units actually originated in Soviet times when they were the internal security agencies responsible for maintaining political order in localities. Others have links to certain bureaucracies and are directly responsible to a particular ministry or state agency.

The patchwork nature of security forces in Central Asia also has had adverse affects on internal and external efforts to consolidate the state and rationalize the security apparatus. The nexus between security agencies and criminality often has been encouraged by the organizational legacies of these security forces. For example, in both Kyrgyzstan and Tajikistan, only 25 percent or less of the police operating budget comes from the government as the rest is raised through the conduct of unofficial activities.[56] Many Central Asian paramilitaries and government agencies sustain their operations through the regulation of the trafficking of drugs, contraband, and people.[57] In turn, just as in Soviet times, administrators within the state receive lucrative kickbacks and even play an active role in organizing these clandestine activities. For example, the Uzbek government has accused Tajikistan and a corrupt Russian border guard of allowing criminal elements to flourish unchecked while the United Nations estimates that drug-transit activity fees alone amount to about 35 percent of the country's GDP.[58]

Finally, it is worth noting that, even in the realm of internal security, the international community's efforts to reform the sector through foreign assistance have preserved these M-form configurations inadvertently. The ICG report criticizes international efforts to promote

55. See Ahmed Rashid, *Jihad: The Rise of Militant Islam in Central Asia* (New York: Penguin, 2003).
56. ICG, "Central Asia: The Politics of Police Reform," p. i.
57. Ibid. Also see Nancy Lubin, *Narcotics Interdiction in Afghanistan and Central Asia: Challenges for International Assistance* (New York: Open Society Institute, 2002).
58. See Letizia Paoli, "Illegal Drug Trade in Russia" (Vienna: UNDCCP and Max Planck Institute, 2000).

institutional reform in the police sector as ineffective and often counterproductive, accusing many of these externally funded projects by UNDP, OSCE, and USAID of inadvertently legitimizing existing practices and promoting more organizational corruption.[59] By offering material sources without addressing the institutionalized links between the police and their governmental patrons, international donors have preserved and even unintentionally strengthened Soviet-era patronage networks.

In sum, the contrasting legacies of M-forms and U-forms have created a situation whereby security agencies differ quite sharply from traditional patterns of civil-military relations and functional organization found in the West. With the collapse of U-forms and their institutional reconfiguration, M-form security agencies have expanded their functional scope. Consequently, rather than well-defined and clear functional roles, post-Soviet Central Asia security structures have been characterized by overlapping and often competing state agencies, police forces, irregular forces, and paramilitaries.

Post-Soviet Economic Organization: M-forms and U-forms

As with the security sphere, U-form and M-form sectors in the economic arena took very different paths after independence. In U-form governed heavy industries, the collapse of the Soviet Union removed the markets, supply chains, and coordinating mechanisms with which these industries operated. Since U-forms did not develop direct political ties to the republican state during the Soviet era, these industries lacked a political constituency in the post-Soviet era to lobby for their continued support. The U-forms that were not salvaged by Western investors ground to a halt in the immediate transition period. By contrast, as an M-form, the agricultural sector had long-standing ties to the state and its former republican-level administrative and planning hierarchies. These Soviet-era patrimonial institutions were maintained and even consolidated in the post-Soviet era.

A glance at more specific output data illustrates these general trends (table 5.2). With the exception of Uzbekistan, industrial output throughout the region was decimated by the transition, with Tajikistan, Kyrgyzstan, and Kazakhstan plummeting to just fractions of their late Soviet levels. The only sectoral exceptions occurred in selected extractive sectors, such as hydrocarbons (Kazakhstan, Turkmenistan) and precious metals (Uzbekistan, Kyrgyzstan), which have received the lion's

59. ICG, "Central Asia: The Politics of Police Reform," p. ii.

TABLE 5.2
Output Changes in Industry and Agriculture, 1991–99

Country	1991	1992	1993	1994	1995	1996	1997	1998	1999	% of 1990
			Changes in Industrial Output (1990 = 100)							
Kazakhstan	−0.9	−13.8	−17.0	−25.0	−15.9	−3.7	4.7	0.3	3.6	46.9
	(99.1)	(85.4)	(70.9)	(53.2)	(44.7)	(43.10)	(45.10)	(45.2)	(46.9)	
Kyrgyzstan	−7.5	−26.1	−22.9	−37.3	−12.3	2.6	19.8	−1.8	−3.8	33.7
	(92.5)	(68.4)	(52.7)	(33.1)	(29.0)	(29.7)	(35.6)	(35.0)	(33.7)	
Tajikistan	−7.3	−7.6	−28.5	−38.9	0.6	−36.8	−21.6	16.0	17.0	22.0
	(92.7)	(85.7)	(61.2)	(37.4)	(39.7)	(25.1)	(16.2)	(18.8)	(22.0)	
Turkmenistan	−9.5	−15.0	8.0	−25.0	−6.0	19.0	−20.0	4.7	19.0	69.5
	(90.5)	(76.9)	(83.1)	(62.3)	(58.6)	(69.7)	(55.7)	(58.4)	(69.5)	
Uzbekistan	1.5	−6.7	−5.3	−10.5	−5.3	1.5	2.3	3.1	1.6	82.7
	(101.5)	(94.7)	(89.7)	(80.3)	(76.0)	(77.1)	(78.9)	(81.4)	(82.7)	
			Change in Agricultural Output (1990 = 100)							
Kazakhstan	NA	NA	−6.9	−21.0	−23.9	−5.0	−0.9	−18.9	21.6	52.0[a]
			(93.1)	(73.6)	(56.0)	(53.2)	(52.7)	(42.7)	(52.0)	
Kyrgyzstan	−7.7	−2.6	−8.6	−8.6	−2.0	15.2	12.3	2.9	8.2	106.0
	(92.3)	(89.9)	(82.2)	(75.1)	(73.6)	(84.8)	(95.2)	(98.0)	(106.0)	
Tajikistan	−4.4	−26.7	−4.4	−6.5	−25.9	2.0	3.6	6.3	3.8	54.1
	(95.6)	(70.1)	(67.0)	(62.6)	(46.4)	(47.4)	(49.0)	(52.1)	(54.1)	
Turkmenistan	−9.8	−9.0	4.0	−11.0	−7.0	−49.0	14.0	24.4	25.5	64.1
	(90.2)	(82.1)	(85.4)	(76.0)	(70.7)	(36.0)	(41.1)	(51.1)	(64.1)	
Uzbekistan	−1.0	−6.0	1.5	−3.4	2.0	−5.7	4.2	4.0	6.0	100.8
	(99.0)	(93.1)	(94.5)	(91.3)	(93.1)	(87.8)	(91.5)	(95.1)	(100.8)	

Source: Compiled and calculated from Economist Intelligence Unit DataSource; World Bank.
[a] *Comparative industry total taken with* 1992 *as baseline.*

share of the region's foreign direct investment (indeed, exclude the hydrocarbon sector from the data and Turkmenistan and Kazakhstan would approach Kyrgyzstan's output losses).[60] By contrast, the output losses in agriculture have been far less severe in Kyrgyzstan, Uzbekistan, and Tajikistan, whereas they have been roughly equivalent to industrial losses in the hydrocarbon states.[61] These widespread trends document the "deindustrialization" that the area underwent during the initial transition. For example, while in 1992 Kyrgyz industry accounted for 32.2 percent of all goods produced, this figure fell to just 11.1 percent in 1996.[62]

60. These include multibillion dollar investments by Chevron and British Gas in Kazakhstan and a $250 million investment by Newmont in gold mining in Uzbekistan.
61. For a nuanced discussion, see Stanislav Zhukov, "Central Asia: Development Under Conditions of Globalization," in *Central Asia: A Gathering Storm?*, ed. Boris Rumer, 333–75 (Armonk, N.Y.: M. E. Sharpe, 2002).
62. National Statistical Committee of the Kyrgyz Republic, *Sotsialno-Ekonomikoe Razvityie Kirgizkoi Respubliki, 1992–1996* [Socioeconomic Development of the Kyrgyz Republic] (Bishkek: National Statistical Committee, 1998), 11.

TABLE 5.3
Trajectories of Selected Central Asian Industrial Sectors during the Transition, Percentage Change over the Previous Year (1991 = 100)

Country	1992	1993	1994	1995
	Chemical and Petrochemical Industry (U-form)			
Kazakhstan	−26.9 (73.1)	−44.6 (40.5)	−41.1 (23.9)	3.6 (24.8)
Kyrgyzstan	−33.4 (66.6)	−55.0 (30.0)	−45.5 (16.4)	−16.0 (13.8)
Tajikistan	−54.1 (45.9)	−42.3 (26.5)	−32.1 (18.0)	4.9 (18.9)
Turkmenistan	−35 (65)	2 (66.3)	−46 (35.8)	24 (44.4)
Uzbekistan	−26.1 (73.9)	−11.4 (65.5)	−22.3 (50.9)	12.6 (57.3)
	Ferrous and Nonferrous Metallurgy (U-form)			
Kazakhstan	−9.6 (90.4)	−24.4 (60.3)	−29.5 (40.1)	11.7 (44.8)
Kyrgyzstan	−10.6 (89.4)	−22.7 (69.1)	−0.2 (69.0)	−16.9 (57.3)
Tajikistan	−19.9 (80.1)	−21.1 (63.2)	−7.6 (58.4)	1.7 (59.4)
Turkmenistan	−30 (70.0)	−4 (67.2)	−32 (45.7)	249 (113.8)
Uzbekistan	−14.5 (85.5)	−1.2 (84.5)	−10.7 (75.5)	−0.7 (76.0)
	Machine-building and Metal Production (U-form)			
Kazakhstan	−16.3 (83.7)	−14.7 (71.4)	−37.1 (45.0)	−27.8 (32.5)
Kyrgyzstan	−35.2 (64.8)	−39.4 (39.3)	−54.3 (18.0)	−15.3 (15.2)
Tajikistan	−34.8 (65.2)	−22.0 (50.9)	−38.5 (31.3)	−25.6 (23.3)
Turkmenistan	−2 (8)	5 (93.1)	−8 (85.7)	20 (102.7)
Uzbekistan	0.2 (100.2)	7.9 (108.1)	10.3 (119.2)	19.7 (142.7)
	Electricity (M-form)			
Kazakhstan	−6.2 (93.8)	−4.4 (89.7)	−15.2 (76.1)	−1.6 (77.3)
Kyrgyzstan	−13.5 (86.5)	−9.4 (78.4)	7.5 (84.3)	1.0 (85.1)
Tajikistan	−5.6 (94.4)	6.1 (100.2)	−9.9 (90.3)	6.7 (96.4)
Turkmenistan	−1.0 (99.0)	8 (106.9)	−14 (91.9)	−3 (89.1)
Uzbekistan	−6.7 (93.3)	−1.8 (91.6)	−3.6 (88.3)	0.3 (88.6)

Source: International Monetary Fund.

Disaggregate some of the industrial data and the differences in the trajectories of the different organizational forms become even more pronounced. Table 5.3 shows industrial output data for the largest four regional industrial sectors common to all of the Central Asian states during the first four years of the transition. Three of these sectors—chemical and petrochemicals, metallurgy, and machine-building and metal production—were governed as U-forms during the Soviet era while the electricity sector operated as an M-form and serves an important baseline for comparison. With just three exceptions (metallurgy in Turkmenistan, machine-building in Turkmenistan, and machine-building in Uzbekistan) the sectors experienced tremendous output declines.[63] In some cases, certain individual U-forms withered away.[64] By contrast, output declines in the major M-form industrial sector of electricity production were more modest, ranging from 77.3 percent of 1991 levels in 1995 in Kazakhstan to 96.4 percent in Tajikistan.[65]

In the agriculture sector, by contrast, the Soviet-era M-form patrimonial institutions survived the transition relatively intact. Certain legal reforms were formally enacted in the area of land rights, such as the creation of joint-stock societies, leaseholds, agricultural cooperatives, and limited liability partnerships. These new organizational reforms have not altered existing land tenure arrangements significantly, however, and, as agricultural economist Zvi Lerman observes, "the new market-sounding names more often than not hide an internal structure which is basically unchanged since the Soviet times."[66] As table 5.4 indicates, after ten years of transition the post-Soviet Central Asian states significantly lagged behind other transitioning post-Communist states on the World Bank's Land-Policy Index of institutional reform.

Even where privatization or new property rights legislation has been passed, actual institutional change has lagged.[67] In Kyrgyzstan, a referendum was passed in 1998 allowing private land ownership, but the legislation was subsequently shelved for at least five years for political reasons. In Uzbekistan, new banks responsible for credit provision to the agricultural sector are nominally independent, but their financing and governance decisions come directly from the Central Bank.[68] As the

63. In fact, the pick-up in metallurgy occurred entirely in 1995 as the result of foreign direct investment in that sector. While all data should be treated with caution, this is especially true of Turkmenistan. The high levels of production in Uzbekistan can be accounted for entirely by foreign direct investment in the gold sector.

64. For example, in Tajikistan production of refrigerators and freezers fell from 166,900 in 1990 (its peak production) to 18,000 in 1993 to just 50 in 1995, while production in high-capacity electrical transformers dropped from 2,054 in 1990 to just 29 in 1994. Similar precipitous drops of more than 95 percent characterized U-form sectors such as machine tools, prefabricated construction materials, detergent, and roofing materials. See IMF, *Republic of Tajikistan: Selected Issues and Statistical Appendix,* Country Report No. 03/5 (Washington, D.C.: IMF, 2003), 80.

65. On output losses, coordination problems and the economic effects of the collapse of the Union-wide economy, see Mark de Broek and Kristina Kostial, "Output Decline in Transition: The Case of Kazakhstan," *IMF Working Paper* WP/98/45 (Washington, D.C.: 1998).

66. Zvi Lerman, "Land Reform and Farm Restructuring: What Has Been Accomplished to Date?" *American Economic Review* 89 (1999): 273. Also see Lerman, "Comparative Institutional Evolution: Rural Land Reform in the ECA," *World Development Report Background Paper* (Washington, D.C.: World Bank, 2001).

67. For a comprehensive survey of post-Communist land reform issues, see Katherine Verdery, *The Vanishing Hectare: Property and Value in Postsocialist Transylvania* (Ithaca: Cornell University Press, 2003).

68. A. Ilkhamov, "Shirkats, Dekhqon Farmers and Others: Farm Restructuring in Uzbekistan," *Central Asian Survey* 17 (1998): 539–60.

TABLE 5.4
Measures of Institutional Change in Agriculture and Land Policy in Central Asia and Other Transitioning Countries, 2001

Country	Legality of Private Land Ownership	Privatization Strategy	Allocation Strategy	Right of Transferability	Land-Policy Index Score*
Central Asia					
Kazakhstan	Household plots	None	Shares	Use rights only	5.4
Kyrgyzstan	All	Distribution/ Conversion	Shares	Moratorium	5.4
Tajikistan	None	None	Shares	Use rights only	2.5
Turkmenistan	All**	None; virgin land to farmers	Leasehold	None	4.0
Uzbekistan	None	None	Leasehold	None	0.6
Comparative: Eastern European or Former Soviet Union Countries					
Albania	All	Distribution	Plots	Buy/sell, lease	9.2
Bulgaria	All	Restitution	Plots	Buy/sell, lease	9.2
Estonia	All	Restitution	Plots	Buy/sell, lease	9.2
Georgia	All	Distribution	Plots	Buy/sell, lease	9.2
Hungary	All	Restitution/ Distribution	Plots	Buy/sell, lease	10.0
Russia	All	Distribution	Shares	Lease	6.7

* *Index is on scale of 0 to 10, with 10 corresponding to ideal market attributes and 0 to no market attributes.*
** *Private land ownership is officially "legal" in Turkmenistan, but this status does not seem to confer any actual property rights to owners.*
Adapted from: Zvi Lerman, Csaba Csaki, and Gershon Feder, "Land Policies and Evolving Farm Structures in Transition Countries," World Bank Policy Research Working Paper, No. WPS 2794 (Washington, D.C.: World Bank, 2002), 81, table 2.9. Available on-line at http://econ.worldbank.org.

World Bank observed, even though large Uzbek farm enterprises have been restructured, "these farms still have the same internal organizational configuration" as during the Soviet era.[69] In Turkmenistan, a leaseholding arrangement has emerged that essentially reifies the collectivized agriculture system by granting peasants one- and two-year leases to land but maintains the system of state procurement in major crops such as wheat and cotton.[70]

The lack of real institutional change in the agricultural sector is also reflected in the persistence of the patronage networks in Central Asian agricultural regions.[71] In Kyrgyzstan, the most liberalized of the Central Asian states, nepotism and corruption have become standard features in

69. World Bank, *Agriculture in Uzbekistan: Private, Dehqan, and Shirkat Farms in the Pilot Districts of the Rural Enterprise Support Project* (Washington, D.C.: IBRD: 2002), 2.
70. World Bank, *Turkmenistan: An Assessment of Leasehold-Based Farm Restructuring* Technical Paper No. 500 (Washington, D.C.: IBRD, 2001).
71. On the adoption of new electoral institutions and their interaction with these legacies, see Pauline Jones Luong, *Institutional Change and Political Continuity in Post-Soviet Central Asia: Power, Perceptions, and Pacts* (New York: Cambridge University Press, 2002).

rural administration as regional governors (Akims) continue to disperse public funds to farm directors and enterprise managers in exchange for their political loyalty.[72] In Uzbekistan, rural district governors remain responsible for coordinating the agricultural production plan with managers of large farm enterprises, a system identical to the Soviet governance system.[73] Similarly, state officials in Tajikistan deliberately have delayed restructuring so as to retain control over the production and procurement process, and local authorities are reluctant to relinquish tax revenues earned from state-owned farms.[74]

Indeed, Soviet-type agricultural embezzlement and clientelist scandals have persisted across all of the Central Asian states. According to an official report of the Kyrgyz National Bank, in 1996 over $100 million in state credits was embezzled by state officials, a staggering 13 percent of the GDP for that year.[75] In the same year, over 500 officials in the agricultural bureaucracy of Turkmenistan were officially charged with falsifying cotton and grain production figures, including the minister of agriculture, the head of the agroindustrial complex department, and the governor of an important rural province.[76] Tellingly, none of the 500 officials were prosecuted for the publicly stated reason that all officials with state ties engage in corrupt activities.

The persistence of the region's patrimonial institutions and rent-seeking state structures have fostered the widespread perception that Central Asia's informal authority networks continue to determine major decisions of economic allocation and distribution. Transparency International's 2003 index of corruption (table 5.5) confirms these perceptions, as all the Central Asian states ranked toward the very bottom of the 133 countries surveyed. Kazakhstan and Uzbekistan ranked a joint 100, Kyrgyzstan 118th, and Tajikistan a joint 124th.[77] Clearly, these

---

72. William Tordoff, "Local Government in Kyrghyzstan," *Public Administration and Development* 15 (1995): 500.

73. World Bank, *Agriculture in Uzbekistan*, 2.

74. Economist Intelligence Unit (EIU), *Tajikistan: Country Profile 2003* (London: EIU, 2004), 25–26.

75. "Kyrgyzstan: Akayev Wants to Stop Embezzlement of State Funds," Moscow ITAR-TASS News Agency, reprinted in FBIS-SOV-96-190 (September 27, 1996). For a catalog of state corruption scandals in Kyrgyzstan, see Zamira Sidikova, *Za Kulisami Demokratii Po-Kirgizskii* [Behind the Scenes of Democracy, Kyrgyz-style] (Bishkek: Respublica Newspaper Publications, 1998).

76. Naz Nazar, "Turkmenistan: Analysis of Corruption," Radio Free Europe/Radio Liberty Special Report (1997), 1.

77. Turkmenistan was not included in the survey. But in similar surveys, such as FreedomHouse's annual *Nations in Transit*, Turkmenistan ranks among the most corrupt of the post-Communist states.

TABLE 5.5
Central Asia and Comparable States in the 2003 Corruption Perceptions Index

Country	Country Rank (of 133)	CPI 2003 Score (max 10.0)	Surveys Used	High-low Range	Standard Deviation
Kazakhstan	100	2.4	7	1.6–3.8	0.9
Uzbekistan	100	2.4	6	2.0–3.3	0.5
Kyrgyzstan	118	2.1	5	1.6–2.7	0.4
Tajikistan	124	1.8	3	1.5–2.0	0.3
Guatemala	100	2.4	8	1.5–3.4	0.6
Venezuela	100	2.4	12	1.4–3.1	0.5
Ivory Coast	118	2.1	5	1.5–2.7	0.5
Libya	118	2.1	3	1.7–2.7	1.0
Georgia	124	1.8	6	0.9–2.8	0.7
Angola	124	1.8	3	1.4–2.0	0.3
Palestine	78	3.0	3	2.0–4.3	1.2
Hungary	40	4.8	13	4.0–5.6	0.6
Slovenia	29	5.9	12	4.7–8.8	1.2
Belgium	17	7.6	9	6.6–9.2	0.9

Source: Transparency International, *Corruption Perception Index, 2003,* http://www.transparency.org/cpi/2003/cpi2003.en/html (Accessed 3/10/2005).

ratings strongly indicate that the patrimonial structure of the Central Asian states continues to condition the development of its political and economic institutions well beyond the endpoint of the Soviet collapse.

Finally, the influx of Western aid, nongovernmental organizations (NGOs) and assistance into Central Asia has reinforced these patrimonial dynamics rather than unambiguously promote institutional change.[78] In areas such as democracy promotion, environmental governance and economic reform, inflows of technical assistance, NGOs, developmental aid, bilateral aid, and even humanitarian relief have served to maintain Central Asia's clientalism rather than reform it.[79] Even when dealing with actors who impose economic conditions, such

78. For a theoretical overview, see Alexander Cooley, "Western Conditions and Domestic Choices: The Role of External Actors in the Post-Communist Transition," in *Nations in Transit 2003: Democratization in East Central Europe and Eurasia,* ed. Amanda Schnetzer et al., 25–38 (Washington, D.C.: FreedomHouse, 2003).

79. On democracy-promotion NGOs, see Fiona Adamson, "International Democracy Assistance in Uzbekistan and Kyrgyzstan: Building Civil Society from the Outside?" in *The Power and Limits of NGOs: Transnational Networks and Post-Communist Societies,* ed. Sarah E. Mendelson and John K. Glenn, 177–206 (New York: Columbia University Press, 2002). On environmental NGOs, see Pauline Jones Luong and Erika Weinthal, "The NGO Paradox: Democratic Goals and Non-Democratic Outcomes in Kazakhstan," *Europe-Asia Studies* 51 (1999): 1267–84. On economic technical assistance projects, see Alexander Cooley and James Ron, "The NGO Scramble: Organizational Insecurity and the Political Economy of Transnational Action," *International Security* 27 (2002): 5–39.

as the IMF or World Bank, conditionality has been insufficient to alter the M-form and U-form trajectories.

Certainly the IMF's role in the post-Communist transition has been scrutinized and often vilified.[80] While all of the Central Asian states except Turkmenistan have received a conditionality package from the Fund, its relationship with Kyrgyzstan is particularly noteworthy. Kyrgyzstan was the first state in the region to court the IMF aggressively; it implemented a structural adjustment package in 1994 and publicly portrayed itself as the aggressive Western-style economic reformer within the region.[81] While the IMF was instrumental in helping the Kyrgyz government draft a relatively aggressive reform plan in 1994, the actual implementation of reforms has been uneven. On the one hand, certain macroeconomic targets (so-called Stage One initiatives), such as lowering the rate of inflation, stabilizing the exchange rate by adopting a new national currency, and reigning in the budget deficit, were achieved quite quickly, which led to the Fund initially lavishing praise on the overall efforts of the Kyrgyz government.[82]

On the other hand, however, the enactment of subsequent Stage 2 and 3 microlevel reforms varied according to sector and their potential threat to disrupt the patrimonial institutions of government. As Kyrgyzstan's dramatic deindustrialization suggests, initial calls for restructuring inefficient large-scale U-form industries (mostly Stage 2) did not meet with opposition within the Kyrgyz government, as few elites had vested political interests in maintaining these U-form fragments. However, Kyrgyz elites proved much less enthusiastic about implementing Stage 3 measures designed to change M-form sectors, such as agriculture, the tax code, energy, or the civil service. Instead, the evidence suggests that IMF loans, together with other forms of external capital flows, actually maintained Soviet-era institutions within these sectors rather than producing meaningful institutional change.[83]

Looking at the broader universe of post-Communist cases, there appears to be little or no positive correlation between the amount of IMF disbursements and the degree of market-oriented economic

---

80. For an overview of the literature, see Randall Stone, *Lending Credibility: The International Monetary Fund and the Post-Communist Transition* (Princeton: Princeton University Press, 2002).
81. On Kyrgyzstan's early interactions with the IMF and its reformist image, see Martha Brill Olcott, *Central Asia's New States* (Washington, D.C.: United States Institute for Peace, 1996), chap. 4.
82. Interview with Insu Kim, IMF Resident Representative, Bishkek, March 6, 1998.
83. For details and more examples, see Alexander Cooley, "International Aid to the Former Soviet States: Agent of Change or Guardian of the Status Quo?" *Problems of Post-Communism* 47 (2000): 34–44.

reforms actually enacted within a borrowing country.[84] For example, the advanced post-Communist reformers in Central Europe and the Baltic states have received about 60 SDR (Special Drawing Rights) per capita in total IMF lending during the transition, whereas the CIS states have received 78 SDR, yet the latter (including the Central Asian states) are significantly behind their Central European counterparts.[85] In fact, this excessive reliance on IMF loans is now damaging the institutional capacity of states such as Kyrgyzstan and Tajikistan as they struggle to repay these high levels of accumulated debt that now exceed their annual GDP. Contrary to the expectations of both proponents and skeptics of the Fund, the post-Soviet experiences of the Central Asian states suggest that IMF and other conditional lenders have not played a significant independent role in transforming the post-Soviet economic institutions of the Central Asian states.

These findings are also supported by a number of recent studies focusing on relations between Western "conditional" donors and the evolution of M-form issues or sectors in the post-Soviet era. Erika Weinthal has shown that Central Asian administrators in the Aral Sea region, in their desire to maintain local social and political control, used foreign aid and environmental assistance as a way of making side payments to political clients and avoiding substantive institutional change.[86] She observes that, "external sources of resources enabled national elites to placate the short-term interests of their regional clients in exchange for short-term payoffs of political and social stability during this transitional period. Outside compensation permitted the Central Asian leaders to put off sweeping economic reforms that could improve economic and environmental efficiency."[87] A World Bank background report on the institutional evolution of land reform in the agricultural sector in the CIS makes a similar point, issuing the following caution to Bank officials:

Finally, an important lesson for the World Bank. Formal claims of privatization and adoption of reform do not necessarily reflect the actual situation on the ground. If the World Bank aims to encourage improve-

---

84. Although Randall Stone argues that the degree of the Fund's lending credibility provides a more convincing explanation of the degree of economic reform enacted by borrowers. While this is an intriguing hypothesis, the Central Asian states are not examined in his study. See Stone, *Lending Credibility*.
85. See Cooley, "Western Conditions and Domestic Choices," 30–32.
86. Erica Weinthal, *State Making and Environmental Cooperation: Linking Domestic and International Politics in Central Asia* (Cambridge: MIT Press, 2002).
87. Ibid., 167.

ments in efficiency and productivity of agriculture, it should desist from lending unless there is true restructuring of the large collective farms and true changes in property rights in land. Continued financial support for the existing traditional farm enterprises is counterproductive in the context of transition to market.[88]

In fact, the presence of multiple donors promoting their own individual reform projects in each sector has served only to further dilute the implementation of institutional change. As each IFI, NGO, or development agency has sought to impose its own individual program or project, the lack of coordination between these actors and their disparate preferences allowed Central Asian governments and agencies to play one off the other as they worked at cross-purposes. The so-called multiple-principals problem delayed the reform of M-forms by several years across a wide array of sectors, including land tenure, energy, and legal codes.[89]

Across both the areas of security and economy, the post-Soviet state-building trajectories of the Central Asian states have been consistent with the predictions of the firm-type model. M-form sectors and their Soviet-era patronage networks have persisted in the post-Soviet era while U-form sectors have been reconfigured more fundamentally or changed.[90] Contrary to the expectations and intentions of the Western community, international actors have exerted very little independent influence on these trends and, instead, have encouraged the endogenous organizational dynamics of post-Soviet extrication.

This chapter has expanded on the firm-type model to develop a theory of posthierarchical legacies and patterns of state-building. In contrast to many prevailing theories that emphasize the importance of ideational variables, the firm-type model suggests that different hierarchical forms endogenously produce varying types of political legacies across security and economic sectors in their former peripheries. After the collapse of

---

88. Lerman, "Comparative Institutional Evolution," 22.
89. See Cooley and Ron, "The NGO Scramble," 16–18, and 22–23.
90. Overall, these findings also hold for the other post-Soviet states. Although some may argue that the Westernizing and aggressive proreform stances of the post-Soviet Baltic states challenge this argument, two points should be noted. First, issues of land reform, restitution, and agricultural restructuring were far more contentious in Estonia, Latvia, and Lithuania than industrial reform and housing privatization. Second, much of the comprehensive institutional change enacted by the Baltics was the fruit of another organizational pressure—the institutional conditionality imposed by the European Union in its accession talks. For a discussion of the varied transformative capacities of the EU versus the IMF and World Bank in the post-Communist states, see Cooley, "Western Conditions and Domestic Choices."

a hierarchy, peripheral U-forms will tend to be reconfigured, change, or collapse while M-forms will survive relatively intact. In the Soviet case, these types of trajectories characterized state-building across both the security and economic spheres. Having developed and illustrated the firm-type theory in the areas of organizational forms, governance, and legacies, the next chapter uses the theory's insights to explain broader puzzles and debates in the study of multinational states, colonies, and occupied states.

COMPARATIVE APPLICATIONS

YUGOSLAVIA, KOREA, AND IRAQ

The previous chapters have sketched out an organizational theory of hierarchy and advanced the plausibility that it explains some significant dynamics of transnational hierarchies and their legacies. But generating a theory and illustrating it is not sufficient. As Ronald Rogowski observes, new theories should strive to generate empirically accurate explanations but should also engage with long-standing debates and topics so as provide fresh insights and perspectives.[1] The final two chapters in this study are designed to demonstrate that the firm-type model can be applied usefully to other settings and can offer new theoretical insights into current topics and debates across different political science subfields.

This chapter applies the insights of the firm-type model to three additional cases of international hierarchy. The three comparative cases cover nominally different types of hierarchies (multinational states, empires, and occupied states) and focus on issues of political economy and security across different geographic settings. In the first case, I draw on the distinctions between organizational forms to explain the origins and dynamics of the collapse of Yugoslavia. Contrary to prevailing institutionalist theories of ethnofederalism, I chart how many M-form functions in the security and economic sphere were actually recentralized as U-forms in the late-Yugoslav period, thereby upsetting existing political equilibria and triggering the violent ethnic countermobilizations that unraveled the federation. The second case examines the debate about

1. See Ronald Rogowski, *Commerce and Coalitions* (Princeton: Princeton University Press, 1987), chap. 6.

the influence of Japanese colonial legacies on the impressive economic development of South Korea. It identifies and specifies the contrasting legacies left by M-form and U-form governed sectors after Japanese withdrawal and reconciles these trends with arguments about the types of legacies that Japanese rule bestowed. In the final case, I apply the firm-type model to the current United States occupation of Iraq. I argue that given the organization form employed by the United States—an M-form with a nested U-form of individual functional contractors—to reconstruct Iraq, its institutional transformation is likely to be slow, ineffective, and rife with both types of opportunism identified in chapter 3. Evidence from the formal American occupation supports this pessimistic assessment.

THE COLLAPSE OF YUGOSLAVIA: AN ORGANIZATIONAL APPROACH

The Debate

Theories about the origins of the Yugoslav collapse are as theoretically diverse as they are plentiful.[2] A conceptual issue at the heart of these debates is how much explanatory weight to assign structural and process-based variables. Some commentators have stressed the importance of nationalism as a mobilizing force, with scholars split on whether these identities are immutable sources of conflict or more recent social constructions.[3] Other scholars have emphasized the role of the international system, while still others have highlighted how domestic political dynamics created incentive structures for elites to manipulate nationalist symbols and myths.[4]

Opposed to these process-based variables are theories that point to certain structural attributes of the Yugoslav Federation that made it a potential "time bomb" for ethnic disintegration. The most sophisticated of these approaches emphasize the role of federalism and the evolution

2. For an overview, see Gale Stokes et al., "Instant History: Understanding the Wars of Yugoslav Succession," *Slavic Review* 55 (1996): 136–60.
3. On the long-standing ethnic animosities and the Yugoslav collapse, see Leonard J. Cohen, *Broken Bonds: The Disintegration of Yugoslavia*, 2d ed. (Boulder, Colo.: Westview Press, 1995). On the strategic use of violence in the process of identity construction, see James Ron, *Frontiers and Ghettos: State Violence in Serbia and Israel* (Berkeley: University of California Press, 2003).
4. Susanne L. Woodward, *Balkan Tragedy: Chaos and Dissolution after the Cold War* (Washington, D.C.: Brookings, 1995). See also Jack Snyder, *From Voting to Violence: Democratization and Nationalist Conflict* (New York: W. W. Norton, 2000); and V. P. Gagnon, "Ethnic Nationalism and International Conflict: The Case of Serbia," *International Security* 19 (1994–95): 130–66.

of the constitutional divisions of power within the Yugoslav federation.[5] Within an overall decentralized system of governance, the devolution of power afforded republican elites increasing resources from which to demand concessions from the center and assert political authority over republican territories. In the popular version of this narrative, the death of charismatic socialist leader Marshall Tito removed the glue that held these various factions together and made the collapse of the Yugoslav state a decade later inevitable.

How the Firm-Type Theory Might Contribute to the Debate

The firm-type theory can help advance understanding of Yugoslav dynamics in two significant ways. First, it can help to reconceptualize the types of governance patterns and hierarchies employed by the Yugoslav state with greater analytical precision than can be had with a static understanding of "federalism." The Yugoslav center employed both M-form and U-form techniques to govern its republics, and this particular mix of organizational forms varied across sector and time.

Second, the firm-type theory reveals a dynamic buildup to the Yugoslav collapse that differs from most prevailing federalist or institutional accounts. While federalist-institutionalist theories emphasize the importance of *decentralization* in the unleashing of antifederation nationalist and centrifugal forces, an explanation of late-Yugoslavia trends according to the firm-type model suggests another trend: the Yugoslav state was fatally damaged by attempts by the core to *recentralize* power in two key issue areas—the economy and the armed forces. In theoretical terms, the state that had governed important areas by M-form (the economy) or by joint M- and U-forms (the armed forces) rapidly changed these forms to almost pure U-forms. Consequently, former republican elites and stakeholders in M-form institutions countermobilized along ethnopolitical lines and proclaimed these newly adopted U-form structures as evidence of Serbian intentions to dominate the Yugoslav state. Thus, it is not the M-form organization of Yugoslav federalism that was responsible for the state's collapse but actual

---

5. For such institutionalist accounts, see Valerie Bunce, *Subversive Institutions: The Design and the Destruction of Socialism and the State* (New York: Cambridge University Press, 1999); Carol Skalnik Leff, "Democratization and the Disintegration of Multinational States: The Break-up of Communist Federations," *World Politics* 51 (1999): 205–35; Rogers Brubaker, *Nationalism Reframed: Nationhood and the National Question in the New Europe* (New York: Cambridge University Press, 1996); and Robert M. Hayden, "Constitutional Nationalism in the Formerly Yugoslav Republics," *Slavic Review* 51 (1992): 654–73.

attempts to change a set of M-form–based equilibria into a set of U-forms in critical sectors that ultimately prompted federal disintegration. Nothing in the Yugoslav national constitution or these ethnic identities made this outcome inevitable.

From M-form to U-form: External Pressures and Economic Recentralization

In the economic realm, the Yugoslav economy operated predominantly as an M-form, exhibiting decentralization over a much wider range of economic functions than its Soviet counterpart. The 1974 Constitution devolved a number of economic functions (ordinarily the responsibility of a central government) to the individual republics, including the critical issue areas of taxation, monetary policy, balance of payments recording, and banking.[6] As a result, the Yugoslav economy became decentralized and compartmentalized to the point that it resembled a miniature system of individual independent economic entities, not an integrated system of economic production and distribution.[7] Between 1976 and 1981, total money payments across republic boundaries actually declined from 14 percent of total transactions to just 10 percent and were accompanied with a stark reduction in the flow of traded goods.[8] By the 1980s, the republics themselves had imposed a number of formal and informal trade barriers on each other's goods.

Moreover, the level of economic development also varied quite starkly across these relatively compartmentalized territories, with Slovenia and Croatia exhibiting levels of per capita income almost two to three times higher than that of the other republics. For example, in 1988 Slovenian and Croatian gross national product (GNP) per capita were 203 percent and 123 percent of the Yugoslav average while Bosnia and Macedonia were just 68 percent and 63 percent, respectively.[9] The poorer republics and regions were also relatively dependent on fiscal transfers and social programs originating from the center. The M-form style delegation of economic activity, sometimes referred to as a system of "self-management," was also viewed at the time as a more dynamic and

6. Milica Zarkovic Bookman, "The Economic Basis of Regional Autarchy in Yugoslavia," *Soviet Studies* 42 (1990): 93–109.
7. Indeed, Sabrina Ramet made the point that the 1974 Constitution created a miniature international system within the boundaries of the Yugoslav Federation that was made up of six separate political actors. See Sabrina Ramet, *Nationalism and Federalism in Yugoslavia, 1963–1983* (Bloomington: Indiana University Press, 1984).
8. Bookman, "Economic Basis of Regional Autarchy," 95.
9. Egon Zizmond, "The Collapse of the Yugoslav Economy," *Soviet Studies* 44 (1992): 102.

innovative form of economic organization than the relatively centralized or U-form type governance employed by other socialist countries.

The major challenge to this M-form system of economic organization initially came not from within but from outside. Throughout the 1970s, Yugoslavia incurred a significant amount of external debt that allowed it to continue its social policies and maintain its patronage disbursals to the poorer republics and regions. As debt service grew, with total indebtedness ballooning from $4.6 billion in 1974 to $14 billion in 1979, authorities in Belgrade entered into a conditionality agreement with the IMF to restructure debt payments and impose macroeconomic austerity.[10] In addition to limiting state spending and lowering the rate of inflation, IMF experts demanded that the federal center reassert control over the statewide levers of macroeconomic authority and replace ineffective consensual decision making that gave each of the republics a veto with majority rule in economic decision making.[11] As Susanne Woodward stresses, in a rather unusual set of conditionality demands, the IMF, World Bank, and foreign creditors actually became ardent advocates of a stronger economic state that would acquire the necessary administrative capacity to subsequently implement neoliberal market reforms.[12] Such orthodox economic imperatives of imposing monetary discipline and reducing inflation could only be accomplished effectively if a single, central entity was responsible for formulating monetary and fiscal policy.

In 1985, the IMF insisted that a single, independent Central Bank recentralize and execute monetary policy, thereby dramatically increasing the capacity and power of the National Bank vis-à-vis the republics. For the better-off republics, such as Slovenia, that were more integrated into the international economic system, the recentralization of monetary policy effectively curtailed their previous practice of directly depositing foreign exchange earned from their exports into their autonomous republican banks.[13] Moreover, the individual republics that held the debts of large enterprises became increasingly squeezed by new central spending controls and their inability to spread out or roll over these debts. Under strict conditions to lower inflation and keep real interest

---

10. Susanne L. Woodward, *Socialist Unemployment: The Political Economy of Yugoslavia, 1945–1990* (Princeton: Princeton University Press, 1995), 347–52.
11. Woodward, *Balkan Tragedy*, 61. For example, see the remarkably politically numb recommendations for monetary discipline set out in Peter Knight, "Financial Discipline and Structural Adjustment in Yugoslavia," *World Bank Staff Working Papers* No. 705 (Washington, D.C.: World Bank, 1984).
12. Woodward, *Socialist Unemployment*, 350–51.
13. Ibid., 357.

rates positive, the National Bank (under pressure from the IMF) refused to bail out heavily indebted republican banks.[14] Finally, the conditionality measures led to a rapid upsurge in unemployment, thereby undermining the implicit social contract of full employment promised by the Communist League.[15] The Party and the federal system's legitimacy were bound to these social commitments.

The critical point here is that a post-1974 system of M-form economic administration did not become radically politicized until external pressures in the 1980s prompted an organizational reversion to U-form governance across many economic sectors. Commenting on the fiscal crisis in 1984, Branka Magas almost prophetically noted the possible future political implications of these externally induced organizational changes and the recentralization of hierarchical authority:

> The grip which the IMF now exercises over the country's economy needed a fulcrum and found it in the increased power of the federal state, not only over the republican and provincial centers, but also over the main levers of the economy. As the government in Belgrade becomes the main arbiter of who is going to prosper and who is going under, national intolerance has once again been placed on the country's agenda.[16]

With local and republican governments unable to meet their obligations, the less-developed republics endured enterprise closures, skyrocketing unemployment rates, and shrinking welfare payments. In Slovenia and Croatia, republican parliaments staged tax rebellions, further hollowing out the fiscal base of the federal government, as they came to associate tax payment with economic redistribution to federal institutions such as the federal army, federal administration, and less-developed republics.[17] In response, Belgrade raised money by exercising its newly obtained seigniorage, thereby further fueling the inflationary cycle. Moreover, the republics themselves perceived that the beneficiaries of the economic U-form reorganization were the Serb-dominated institutions such as the military and the federal bureaucracy as well as the less-developed republics that had become Serbian client states.

14. Woodward, *Balkan Tragedy*, 58–64.
15. Woodward, *Socialist Unemployment*, 352–54.
16. Branka Magas, *The Destruction of Yugoslavia: Tracing the Break-up 1980–92* (London: Verso, 1993), 97.
17. Woodward, *Socialist Unemployment*, 355–56.

The Growing Recentralization of Force

A variation on this pattern of recentralization and antifederalist reaction occurred in the military sphere. Traditionally, two main types of military organizations characterized the armed forces of Yugoslavia—the JNA and the Territorial Defense Forces (TOs). As with its Soviet counterpart, the JNA was intended to overcome national and ethnic differences through its pan-Yugoslav hierarchy. Throughout Tito's rule, the military functioned as the main guardian of the integrity of the federation and its institutions as well as the guarantor of Yugoslavia's external security. The military periodically intervened to quell domestic crises, including in Croatia (early 1970s), Kosovo (1981), as well as in the later crises in Slovenia (1988) and Kosovo (1989).[18]

The departmentalism normally associated with U-forms was magnified in the JNA by the institutionalized representation afforded to it. Both the 1971 and 1974 Constitutions awarded the military a political role in federal decision-making bodies equal to that enjoyed by the individual republics and autonomous regions. Even after Tito's passing, the JNA continued to function as the institutional backbone of the federation and was even given formal representation in two of the three bodies that succeeded Tito's regime—the nine-member executive bureau of the League of Communists and the Committee for Protection of the Constitutional Order. Similarly, Yugoslav authorities regarded supporting defense industries as critical, and Yugoslavia came to produce 90 percent of its military needs through a transrepublican production network that deliberately scattered vertically integrated facilities across various republics.[19]

While the JNA and the federal Defense Ministry operated as a classic U-form, the TOs mirrored the M-form institutions seen in other sectors. The TOs were irregular forces organized along republican boundaries that were established to supplement the capacity of the military. They were governed by a TO headquarters in each republic that liaisoned and coordinated with its JNA counterpart in the interests of maintaining a unified defense of the federation.[20]

18. Bunce, *Subversive Institutions*, 119.

19. James Gow, *The Serbian Project and Its Adversaries: A Strategy of War Crimes* (London: Hurst & Company, 2003), 52. On the national character of the military-industrial complex, see Gow, *Legitimacy and the Military: The Yugoslav Crisis* (New York: St. Martin's Press, 1992).

20. On the administration and role of the TOs and the political tensions these created, see David Isby, "Yugoslavia 1991—Armed Forces in Conflict," *Jane's Intelligence Review* (September 1991): 395–97.

In reality, the organizational tension between the U-form JNA and the M-form TOs was never fully resolved. A prestigious political actor during Tito's rule, the JNA was guaranteed a central role in political planning.[21] Attempts to decentralize the JNA hierarchy were implemented and 25 percent of the troop contingent from each republic was required to be based within each home territory.[22] In addition, the regional/republican TOs were strengthened and placed under co-equal joint command structures with JNA. This "mixed-form" approach to the military (similar to the structure of the Soviet MVD) was enshrined in the 1974 Constitution.

In a key organizational reshuffling in late 1988, the JNA, without public discussion, replaced the old Army districts that were contiguous with republican and TO boundaries with new Military Districts that overlapped republican boundaries. Included in this reorganization was the merging of Slovenia and Croatia into a single regional headquarters.[23] The new districts also aided the interests of Serbian populations within their jurisdiction, such as the Serbs in Krajina. Whether these organizational changes were made in anticipation of a looming internal conflict or as a purely political maneuvering by the JNA, they signaled a sinister ethnic dimension that conflated the consolidation of JNA power with the promotion of Serbian ethnic interests.[24]

The JNA treated the 1990 republican elections with distrust and outright hostility, using them as an opportunity to further monopolize its control over instruments of collective violence. On the day after elections, JNA troops confiscated the weapons caches held by the Territorial Defense units in Slovenia and Croatia (and later in Bosnia), thereby denying them a previously held Constitutional guarantee to constitute an autonomous territorial defense.[25] In addition to launching a sustained operation to disarm the TOs, JNA authorities also halted shipments of weapons from domestic suppliers, effectively forcing the republican governments and their paramilitary units to acquire arms from overseas. For its part, the JNA had come to associate the TOs with the undermining of the federation and justified these actions in the interests of preserving the integrity of the state. A JNA report from 1991, informally known as the Generals' Manifesto, included the following

21. Gow, *Legitimacy and the Military.*
22. Gow, *The Serbian Project and Its Adversaries,* 53.
23. Ibid., 54.
24. See Bunce, *Subversive Institutions,* 198–99 nn. 6 and 7 (173).
25. For a detailed account, see Laura Silber and Allan Little, *Yugoslavia: Death of a Nation* (New York: Penguin, 1997), chap. 5. Also see Marcus Tanner, "Yugoslav Troops Occupy Slovene Defence Force HQ," *The Independent (UK),* October 6, 1990, 11.

statement of purpose that responded to domestic and foreign political developments:

> Our basic task must be the creation of conditions for the functioning of the Federal state. This means, first of all, the liquidation of all breaches made in the field of unity of the armed forces: i.e. disarming and liquidating all paramilitary organizations in Yugoslavia. Implementation of this task will create the basic conditions for a peaceful resolution of the crisis and a democratic transformation of Yugoslavia. At the same time, it will inflict a powerful defeat upon nationalist-separatist politics and practice, while encouraging forces working for the preservation and development of Yugoslavia on socialist foundations.[26]

As the JNA was reorganized, its recentralization took on an increasingly ethnopolitical character. Serbian forces asserted control over the air, ground, and navy elements of the old JNA in addition to the existing Territorial Defense Force. The core of the Yugoslav U-form in defense was rapidly emerging as the de facto Serbian national army and guardian of the federation. By 1991, the ethnic imbalance in the composition of the officer core of the JNA further fueled Slovenian and Croatian perceptions that the institution no longer represented the political interests of the member republics. For example, in 1991 Serbs accounted for a full 60 percent of the officer core (40 percent of the population) of the JNA compared to just 14 percent by Croatians (23 percent of the population), 2 percent by Slovenians (7 percent), and 2.5 percent by Muslims (8 percent).[27] Moreover, given the overall budgetary situation and economic crisis, the very financing of JNA operations by the center acquired a political and threatening dimension for the republics. As overall republican contributions to the federal budget declined, the JNA retained a high level of spending, thereby absorbing an ever-increasing proportion of federal revenues.[28]

For other republics, such official proclamations of juridical and constitutional purpose became code words for establishing Serbian hegemony throughout the Yugoslav space. JNA demands for exclusive authority increasingly were viewed as acts of warmongering. In a key standoff in January 1991, the JNA was placed on full alert in Croatia

---

26. Magas, *The Destruction of Yugoslavia*, 267; quote from p. 273.
27. Robin Alison Remington, "The Yugoslav Army: Trauma and Transition," in *Civil-Military Relations in the Soviet and Yugoslav Successor States*, ed. Constantine P. Danopoulos and Daniel Zirker, 167 (Boulder, Colo.: Westview Press, 1996).
28. See Woodward, *Balkan Tragedy*, 66–67.

(mobilizing tanks and troops) and it demanded that Croatian authorities hand over the Croatian Ministers of Defense and the Interior for refusing to comply with a previous army order to disband the republic's self-defense forces, which it termed "illegal paramilitary" organizations. In the same month, both the Croatian and Slovenian TOs defied JNA deadlines to disarm their "illegal paramilitary forces," with Slovenia's minister of militia affairs Janez Jansa insisting that "our defense forces are not illegal by any means."[29]

Obviously, ethnic tensions in Yugoslavia had been mounting throughout the late 1980s, but nationalist actions and intentions became threatening precisely when they disrupted previous institutional balances and organizational hierarchies. Whereas the JNA retained much of its legitimacy until the late 1980s, the center's attempts to weaken the republican TOs and recentralize command structures undermined the organization's credibility as a pan-Yugoslav guardian. The growing Serbian-JNA alliance effectively turned the institution into a tool for a dominant ethnic faction and became a threat that mobilized peripheral republican elites for war. At the same time, republican opposition forces were formed from preexisting M-form institutions, such as the police (which formed the core of the Croat army), TOs, and paramilitary groups.

Conclusions

The bloody collapse of the Yugoslav federation remains one of the critical events for scholars of international relations and comparative politics. Although numerous plausible explanations have been advanced, including institutional accounts that stress the instability of Yugoslavia's national federalist system, the firm-type model provides important insights into both the unusual governance forms of Yugoslavia and the origins of the state's disintegration. The relatively unified Communist system of the 1950s and 1960s gave way to an M-form system with six separate republics and two autonomous territories whose political elites used their access to the center to pursue their respective parochial political interests.[30] However, these agency problems only turned into demands for actual secession and violent conflict when the Serbian-

29. "Disarming of Yugoslav Militias Delayed," *Los Angeles Times*, January 20, 1991, 39.
30. Gojko Vuckovic, "Failure of Socialist Self-Management to Create a Viable Nation-State, and Disintegration of the Yugoslav Administrative State and State Institutions," *East European Quarterly* 32 (1998): 372.

dominated center disrupted existing M-form-based political equilibria by demanding the reorganization of M-form functions along U-form lines. In the area of macroeconomic policy, the IMF and the World Bank insisted that monetary and fiscal policy be brought under the exclusive control of the center while, in the military, the JNA dissolved all M-form autonomous territorial forces within the individual republics. In addition, during the 1980s the presidency attempted to amend the federal constitution to recentralize control over certain symbolic and national functions, such as the legal system, railroad, and the national postal and telephone systems. As Valerie Bunce observes, these attempts at recentralization served the political and economic interests of the Serbs, who sought to use the establishment of a strong state as a solution to the federation's crises but signaled a level of nationalist intent that afforded republican elites the justification for demanding outright secession.[31] On the other hand, areas where the recentralization of organizational form actually might have helped to foster interethnic dialogue and communication, especially the acutely segmented media sector, were not undertaken by the center in time to have any significant impact on political developments.[32] Overall, while national identities and the Yugoslav constitution contributed to the collapse of the federation, preceding changes in organizational forms throughout the 1980s were immediately responsible for their politicization.

JAPANESE COLONIALISM AND KOREAN DEVELOPMENT

The Debate

Among the more remarkable developmental success stories is the spectacular economic growth of South Korea and its transformation from a devastated, impoverished country in 1960 to one of the most economically advanced countries in the world. Observers of the South Korean "miracle" have underscored the critical role played by state intervention in Korea's economic policy and the types of "developmental institutions" that facilitated this planning.[33] More recently, this focus has evolved into

---

31. Bunce, *Subversive Institutions*, 93.
32. Snyder, *From Voting to Violence*, 213–20.
33. For an overview, see Meredith Woo Cumings, ed., *The Developmental State* (Ithaca: Cornell University Press, 1999). Also see Alice Amsden, *Asia's Next Giant: South Korea and Late Industrialization* (New York: Oxford University Press, 1992); and Robert Wade, *Governing the Market: Economic Theory and the Role of Government in East Asian Industrialization* (Princeton: Princeton University Press, 1990).

a debate about the impact of Japanese colonialism on the origins and formation of the Korean developmental state.

Proponents of the "Japanese colonialism" thesis argue that, while socially brutal and politically repressive, Japanese rule in Korea (1904–45) bequeathed an institutional legacy that facilitated economic development decades later. Advocates of this position identify three such legacies. First, they argue that Japanese-led industrialization fundamentally reorganized state-society relations, turning a precolonial society that was ruled by aristocratic landholders into a modernized, industrial state with great capacity and involvement in economic affairs, that is, a developmental state.[34] Second, proponents of the thesis point to certain continuities in specific economic sectors—in the form of both enterprises and technical knowledge—between the colonial and postwar eras.[35] Finally, some argue that the Japanese colonial rule enacted fundamental social changes not directly related to economic policy, such as reforming the educational and law enforcement systems, which later provided the social and institutional context in which rapid economic development could take place. According to these advocates, omitting the Japanese origins of the rise of the Korean developmental state neglects a key source of these post-1960 institutional developments.[36]

Opponents of the thesis maintain that any Japanese contribution to Korean development was temporary and did not endure through intervening events such as World War II, the U.S. occupation, the Korean War, and the corrupt patrimonial regime of Syngman Rhee.[37] Second, the bureaucratic ties established by the post–World War II Korean state and then developmental state are not necessarily comparable in form or political purpose to those established by the Japanese. Finally, the critics maintain that far from being favorable, Japanese social legacies retarded economic development until they were rolled back through measures of labor and land reform undertaken in Korea after the peninsular war.

34. Atul Kohli, "Where Do High-Growth Political Economies Come From? The Japanese Lineage of South Korea's 'Development State,'" *World Development* 22 (1994): 1269–93; and Kohli, "Japanese Colonialism and Korean Development: A Reply," *World Development* 25 (1997): 883–88.
35. Timothy C. Lim, "The Origins of Societal Power in South Korea: Understanding the Physical and Human Legacies of Japanese Colonialism," *Modern Asian Studies* 33 (1999): 603–33; Carter Eckert, *Offspring of Empire: The Koch'ang Kims and the Colonial Origins of Korean Capitalism, 1876–1945* (Seattle: University of Washington Press, 1991); and Dennis L. McNamara, *The Colonial Origins of Korean Enterprise, 1910–1945* (New York: Cambridge University Press, 1990).
36. Also see Bruce Cumings, "The Origins and Development of the Northeast Asian Political Economy: Industrial Sectors, Product Cycles, and Political Consequences," *International Organization* 38 (1984): 1–40.
37. Stephan Haggard, David Kang, and Chung-In Moon, "Japanese Colonialism and Korean Development: A Critique," *World Development* 25 (1997): 867–81.

How the Firm-Type Theory Might Contribute to the Debate

The debate is highly charged, given that it involves emotionally laden issues relating to possible Korean collaboration and the implicit acceptance of Japanese colonial rule as a modernizing force.[38] Even proponents of the thesis go to great lengths to emphasize the repressive nature of Japanese rule, taking care to limit their analytical focus to the impact of Japanese institutional legacies on economic development and not the impact of Japanese rule as a whole. Evaluating the causal impact of these colonial legacies is rendered more difficult by the fact that most theorists of postcolonial legacies and economic development ignore the Japanese case altogether and concentrate on European colonial powers.

For this reason, it is critical to disentangle the various causal claims on both sides before attempting to theoretically recast the various processes at issue. Specifically, the firm-type model suggests that the two sides of the Japanese colonialism debate are actually discussing different types of colonial legacies. These legacies stem from the varying governance forms employed by the Japanese in Korea. By specifying which sectors were governed as U-forms and which as M-forms, we can hypothesize more precisely as to which colonial-era institutions endured after the collapse of Japanese rule.

M-forms and U-forms in Japanese-Governed Korea

The question of how to organize and integrate newly acquired imperial territories was extensively debated within the Japanese Imperial Diet. In fact, the Japanese government drew on extensive counseling from external advisors—including both British and French advisors—to explore the relative merits of various types of legal integration. This uncertainty itself reflects one of the central themes outlined in this study—whether to treat the new imperial acquisitions as distinct colonies or as an integral part of metropolitan Japan.[39] As it turned out, the new territories achieved varying degrees of integration to the metropole. The Korean case featured many elements found in a classical M-form but also exhibited some U-form characteristics.

---

38. For historiographical studies, see Andre Schmid, "Colonialism and the 'Korea Problem' in the Historiography of Modern Japan: A Review Article," *The Journal of Asian Studies* 59 (2000): 951–76; and Koen de Ceuster, "The Nation Exorcised: The Historiography of Collaboration in South Korea," *Korean Studies* 25 (2002): 207–42.

39. Edward I-te Chen, "The Attempt to Integrate the Empire: Legal Perspectives," in *The Japanese Colonial Empire, 1895–1945,* ed. Ramon H. Myers and Mark R. Peattie, 261–62 (Princeton: Princeton University Press, 1984).

Several important sectors in Korea were governed as U-forms. As with all overseas territories, the areas of national security, aviation, and shipping were completely harmonized according to Diet law in Tokyo, as were banking and trade regulations.[40] In terms of economic control of various sectors, the Japanese introduced several new industries and restructured agricultural production so as to serve its own consumption patterns. In the area of rice milling, for example, Japan concentrated production in a handful of large plants that owned 54 percent of all rice mills in Korea by 1939. Estimates of the total formal Japanese control of Korean agricultural land as exercised by land-management companies range from 6 percent to 20 percent.[41]

Aside from rice-milling, Japanese ownership of enterprises in Korea tended to employ the U-form in heavy and capital-intensive industries. In an organizational pattern that was similar to the Soviet case, Tokyo established large-scale industrial enterprises throughout Korea and its imperial holdings, taking advantage of cheap labor and proximities to regional markets. For instance, in 1941 Japanese firms accounted for 98 percent of paid-in capital in the metal industry and 99 percent in the chemical industry, as output in these sectors were highly concentrated in a small number of vertically integrated facilities.[42] In 1934 the Japanese mainland companies owned 62.8 percent of textile factories, 68.0 percent of wood-processing firms, and 76.8 percent of machinery-producing enterprises. In terms of size, Japanese firms in 1934 owned 87.2 percent of all factories in Korea with more than 200 employees, 66.7 percent of factories with 100–199 employees, and 39.1 percent of factories with 5–49 employees.[43]

In other areas, Korea was governed as an M-form. The governor general was subordinate only to the Emperor, on whose behalf he yielded administrative power, and his accompanying rule was absolute. Under the jurisdiction of the governor came the various subordinate functions, which were exercised by mainlanders. At the local level, and consistent with other M-form cases, the Japanese maintained the preexisting system of institutions such as landlords, village-heads, and household groups.[44]

40. Ibid., 254–55.
41. Samuel Pao-San Ho, "Colonialism and Development: Korea, Taiwan, and Kwantung," in *The Japanese Colonial Empire, 1895–1945*, ed. Ramon H. Myers and Mark R. Peattie, 371–72 (Princeton: Princeton University Press, 1984).
42. Haggard, Kang, and Moon, "Japanese Colonialism and Korean Development," 871.
43. Data on ownership patterns are from Mizoguchi Toshiyuki and Yamamato Yuzo, "Capital Formation in Taiwan and Korea," in *The Japanese Colonial Empire, 1895–1945*, ed. Ramon H. Myers and Mark R. Peattie, 419 (Princeton: Princeton University Press, 1984).
44. W. G. Beasley, *Japanese Imperialism, 1894–1945* (New York: Oxford University Press, 1987), 145.

Formally, the autonomy of Korean colonial institutions in a process of "delegated legislation" extended to law courts, local autonomy systems, government monopolies, customs and taxation, and—as in Taiwan—the criminal code, criminal procedure, civil procedure, commercial and maritime law, and real estate.[45]

As with other cases of M-form rule, this great autonomy also created significant control problems as Tokyo authorities consistently struggled with the political power afforded to the Korean governor. As one commentator observes, "the governor-general of Korea was thus given enormous power and prestige to advance his views in the central government. This made it difficult for the civil authorities of the central government to bring the governor-general of Korea under civil supervision."[46] In fact, the creation of a centralized Ministry of Colonial Affairs in 1942 prompted ruling governor-general Yamanshi Hanzo to threaten to resign rather than accept the supervision of the new Tokyo minister, and he reportedly ordered his administration to ignore all communications from Tokyo signed by the minister.[47]

In sum, the Japanese employed both U-form and M-form organization. Japanese enterprises in agroindustry and heavy industry were vertically integrated into the operations of mainland firms, and accompanying economic laws were harmonized with economic regulations in Tokyo. Conversely, the governor of Korea exercised a great deal of discretion and autonomy from Tokyo and most social, judicial, and political functions were administered as M-forms.

U-forms Tend to Collapse

Critics of the Japanese colonialism thesis are persuasive when they discuss the legacies of the large U-form enterprises left in Korea. They point out that the vast majority of industrial enterprises that dominated whole economic sectors within the Korean colonial state collapsed after World War II, the subsequent peninsular war, and American occupation. Consequently, these events severed any meaningful links between the organizational forms established by the Japanese and the Korean developmental state of the 1960s. In this area, the data is compelling. In 1948, Korean industrial output was just 20 percent of its peak 1941 level, with textiles dropping 74 percent, foodstuffs 93 percent, and machinery

45. I-te Chen, "Attempt to Integrate the Empire," 261–62.
46. Ibid., 245.
47. Ibid., 264.

84 percent. In manufacturing, the number of firms between 1945 and 1949 was more than halved (falling from 300,520 to 122,159) while employment dropped by 60 percent. As a result, the departure of the Japanese and their system of vertical integration also contributed to the postwar economic chaos in Korea while creating a significant vacuum in external economic relations. Furthermore, critics convincingly argue that many of these vertically integrated sectors—especially metals and machinery—by the late 1930s had become overwhelmingly concentrated in North Korea, thus further ensuring discontinuity on partition.[48] The political form of Japanese industry, then, seemingly did not endure beyond the Japanese occupation.

Moreover, other exogenous shocks further cut the links between Japanese-established industries and the Korean developmental state. The subsequent Korean War was the final external event that severed any existing Japanese legacies, with some 45 percent of all nationwide industrial enterprises suffering damage and over 80 percent of Seoul's industry and public utilities reportedly being damaged or destroyed. Leroy Jones and Il Sakong estimate that the economic costs to the South totaled $3 billion or twice its GNP, and therefore conclude that the legacies of the peninsular war swept away any enduring physical legacies of the Japanese colonial era.[49] Finally, critics of the colonial legacy thesis argue that, even after the ravaging effects of two damaging wars, the attempts to enact a rational developmental state along the Japanese model were themselves severely undermined by the endemic corruption and patrimonialism that characterized Syngman Rhee's regime.

M-forms Persist

Conversely, the types of colonial legacies highlighted by proponents of the thesis typically stem from M-form sectors. In the area of land tenure, for instance, Atul Kohli argues that the social power of precolonial aristocratic landlords was broken by the rationalized and penetrative bureaucracies of the colonial state.[50] In particular, the colonial state was able to extract significant taxes from the landowning elite and curtailed their influence in state affairs. Over time, it institutionalized a new

48. Haggard, Kang, and Moon, "Japanese Colonialism and Korean Development," 871–72.
49. Leroy P. Jones and Il Sakong, *Government, Business, and Entrepreneurship in Economic Development: The Korean Case* (Cambridge: Harvard University Press, 1980), 35.
50. Atul Kohli, "Where Do High-Growth Political Economies Come From? The Japanese Lineages of Korea's Development State," in *The Developmental State*, ed. Meredith Woo Cumings, 97–100 (Ithaca: Cornell University Press, 1999).

pattern of state-society interactions that emphasized the power of the bureaucracy and civil service.[51]

Supporters of the colonial legacies thesis also contend that the very void left by collapsed large-scale Japanese enterprises allowed Korean entrepreneurs with some experience during the colonial era to mimic these large organizational forms and reintroduce monopolistic industries across various sectors of the Korean economy.[52] As Kohli suggests, "even if most factories were destroyed during the Korean War, the knowledge of industrial technology and management, as well as experience of urban living, a modern educational system survived, leaving a positive legacy for postwar industrialization."[53] For instance, Carter Eckert has shown how the Kim-yon Su textile company, a joint Korean-Japanese enterprise in the late colonial era, was formed through the collaboration of Korean business capital with Japanese administration, creating the first chaebol or state-business partnership in textiles.[54] By another estimate, 60 percent of the founders of Korea's leading 50 chaebols had some business experience in the colonial era.[55]

Finally, proponents of the colonialism thesis point to the social legacies bequeathed by the colonial state. The M-form governance and transformation of sectors such as education, law enforcement, and social policy all provided political order and public goods that supported the subsequent growth of the developmental state. For instance, in the area of policing, Japanese authorities made concerted efforts to incorporate Korean police, as Koreans accounted for 57 percent of the police force in 1919 and 40 percent in 1930.[56] Moreover, the Japanese conveniently exploited the traditional Korean system of village elders in organizing their penetrating surveillance systems. In education, Japanese educational policy propagandized the virtues of Japanese rule but also dramatically increased the rates of literacy in the Korean population and consciously prepared Koreans to staff positions within the colonial bureaucracy.[57] By the time Japanese rule collapsed, the institutional basis for Korea's state capacity was positioned across a range of sectors.

51. Ibid., 103.

52. Lim, "Origins of Societal Power in South Korea," 603–33.

53. Kohli, "Japanese Colonialism and Korean Development: A Reply," 884.

54. Eckert, *Offspring of Empire*.

55. Ibid., 254.

56. Ching-Chih Chen, "Police and Community Control Systems in the Empire," in *The Japanese Colonial Empire, 1895–1945*, ed. Ramon H. Myers and Mark R. Peattie, 225 (Princeton: Princeton University Press, 1984).

57. E. Patricia Tsurumi, "Colonial Education in Korea and Taiwan," in *The Japanese Colonial Empire, 1895–1945*, ed. Ramon H. Myers and Mark R. Peattie, 275–311 (Princeton: Princeton University Press, 1984).

Conclusions

The firm-type model suggests that each side in the debate over Japanese colonialism and Korean development is addressing the legacies of different organizational forms. Critics of the colonialism thesis point to the stark discontinuities created by the postcolonial collapse of U-form-governed large-scale Japanese heavy industries. However, proponents of the thesis make strong arguments about the institutional legacies, especially in the realm of state capacity and social policy that Japanese M-form rule engendered. Thus, although an application of the firm-type model to the debate about Japanese colonialism and Korean development does not the resolve the debate, it recasts the analytics of the argument by pointing to how each side addresses different organizational legacies of the colonial era. Moreover, both the collapse of U-form sectors and the endurance of M-form institutions are consistent with the broader overall predictions of the firm-type model as outlined in the previous chapters.

THE AMERICAN OCCUPATION OF IRAQ: PROBLEMS AND PROSPECTS

Finally, the American-led occupation of Iraq, from March 2003 to June 2004, offers a contemporary case of hierarchy for applying the insights of the firm-type model. The exact causes of the Iraqi war remain debated, but among the reasons cited by supporters of Operation Iraqi Freedom (OIF) were for the United States to liberate the country from authoritarian rule and transform its basic institutions of governance. By purging the country of the Baathist governing apparatus and creating new institutions for a sustainable democracy, Iraq could potentially become a successful model of institutional transformation to be emulated by the rest of the Middle East.[58] However, the end of the military campaign was followed by an occupation and reconstruction effort plagued by problems, mismanagement, and dysfunctions, leading critics to argue that the U.S. Pentagon failed to adequately prepare for postwar occupation and reconstruction.[59] The current prevailing wisdom on the

58. See Joseph Braude, *The New Iraq: Rebuilding the Country for Its People, the Middle East, and the World* (New York: Basic Books, 2003); and Kenneth Pollack, *The Gathering Storm: The Case for Invading Iraq* (New York: Random House, 2002).
59. See, especially, International Crisis Group, "Reconstructing Iraq," ICG Middle East Report No. 30 (Baghdad and Brussels: September 2, 2004). Also see the earlier account in David Rieff, "Blueprint for a Mess: How the Bush Administration's Prewar Planners Bungled Postwar Iraq," *New York Times Magazine*, November 2, 2003.

American occupation is that the United States underestimated both the degree of insurgent attacks and the internal obstacles it would face in rebuilding the country's institutions and infrastructure. The lack of a reconstruction plan, however, should not imply that the formal U.S. occupation was not "organized." In fact, both supporters and critics of the occupation usually neglect a key organizational feature of the occupation: that most of the administrative and reconstruction efforts were undertaken by a plethora of private contractors assigned by overlapping and competing U.S. agencies. The firm-type model explains the coordination problems, mismanagement, bureaucratic struggles, and rebuilding failures in Iraq as a function of the incentives structures and opportunism that this particular type organization engendered.

The Organizational Forms of Occupation and Reconstruction

Of course, the attempt to transform domestic institutions of another country through the use of military force and occupation is not new. Attempts by the great powers to coercively transform the domestic institutions of target states have been a recurring feature of international politics.[60] Indeed, many proponents of OIF pointed to the post–World War II allied occupations of Japan and Germany as important models. They suggested that externally imposed democratization and domestic institutional change could be successfully achieved, especially if the United States exhibited a strong political will, a long-term commitment to democratization, and provided adequate financial resources to complete the task.[61]

An application of the firm-type model suggests that beyond some superficial similarities, the organization of the Iraqi occupation and reconstruction differed sharply from that of previous nation-building attempts in Japan, Korea, or Germany. These differences cut against, not for, the expectation that institutional transformation in Iraq will be successful, even in the medium and long terms.

As in previous American occupations, an administrative authority—the Coalitional Provisional Authority—working in close consultation with the U.S. military, administered Iraq. Under the leadership of Ambassador Paul Bremer, the CPA was directly answerable to the U.S.

---

60. For a five-century catalog and theoretically informed discussion, see John M. Owen, IV, "The Foreign Imposition of Domestic Institutions," *International Organization* 56 (2002): 375–410.
61. See especially James Dobbins et al., *America's Role in Nation-Building: From Germany to Iraq* (Santa Monica, Calif.: RAND, 2003). On the dangers of the analogy, see Douglas Porch, "Occupational Hazards: Myths of 1945 and U.S. Iraq Policy," *The National Interest* 72 (2003): 35–45.

Defense Department and was responsible for overseeing the activities of the Iraqi Governance Council and supervising the Iraqi bureaucracy. In Japan, the allied occupation was organized by the General Headquarters Supreme Commander for the Allied Powers (SCAP) and headed by General Douglass MacArthur.[62] SCAP commanded several functional divisions (such as Economics, Welfare, Medical, and Utilities) and ruled "indirectly" in the mainland islands by directing its functional counterparts within the Japanese bureaucracy. The Korean occupation featured a similar system of control, with the United States Army Military Government in Korea (USAMGIK) governing the American zone with complete authority.[63] The postwar German occupation differed somewhat in its division among four separate powers and its more intense purging of domestic institutions through denazification.[64] As a result, a fragmented and weakened West Germany emerged that could be integrated more easily into Western international institutions.[65] Nevertheless, in all these cases the main American administrative body operated as an M-form under the auspices of the U.S. military and/or Defense Department.

What distinguished the American governance of Iraq from these previous administrations was its reliance on a wide array of private, for-profit contractors to accomplish these various functional tasks. Three distinct governmental organizations—United States Agency for International Development (USAID), the Department of Defense (DoD), and the State Department—assumed some role (in addition to the everyday decisions made by the CPA) in managing and hiring contractors to execute the various functional tasks associated with governance and reconstruction. In organizational terms, these functional contractors created a nested U-form structure within the overall M-form managed by the CPA. These individual functional contractors were technically subordinated to the CPA, even though the USAID-funded groups actually were appointed through the development agency's tender process and retained responsibility for managing their projects. Unlike a classical M-form, however, where functional divisions are merely extensions of the M-form subdivision, these contractors were distinct

62. See Takemae Eiji, *The Allied Occupation of Japan* (New York: Continuum, 2003), especially the organizational chart on p. 104. Also see John W. Dower, *Embracing Defeat: Japan in the Wake of World War II* (New York: W. W. Norton, 1999).

63. On the occupation of Korea, see Bruce Cumings, *The Origins of the Korean War: The Roaring of the Cataract, 1947–1950* (Princeton: Princeton University Press, 1990).

64. See Edward Peterson, *The American Occupation of Germany: Retreat to Victory* (Detroit: Wayne State University Press, 1977).

65. See Marc Trachtenberg, *A Constructed Peace: The Making of a European Settlement 1945–1963* (Princeton: Princeton University Press, 1999).

organizational entities that operated on temporary contracts to provide these various functions.

Of course, the use of contractors is itself not a new organizational feature of international hierarchy as charter companies originally governed many overseas European imperial peripheries. What was different in American-governed Iraq was the striking number of contractors employed—about 125 during the formal occupation. Table 6.1 lists the leading 50 project contractors by value of contract working on Iraqi governance and reconstruction. Strikingly, each of the major state functions typically associated with state governance was contracted to a different private corporation.[66] For example, American authorities contracted Kellogg, Brown and Root (Halliburton, 1) to repair and operate the oil sector, Bechtel (5) to repair infrastructure and public works, Bearing Point (21) to oversee economic restructuring, Creative Associates (20) to reform the educational sector, Dyncorp (30) to organize law enforcement, and Abt Associates (32) to support the Health Ministry. This use of for-profit contractors for individual functions is a critical organizational difference between the administration of Iraq and that of previous occupations.

Organizational Form and Opportunism during Iraqi Reconstruction

Accordingly, this distinct organizational structure (nested U-form contractors within the CPA M-form) would predict that U.S. reconstruction efforts were complicated by two distinct types of opportunism. On the one hand, reconstruction suffered from departmentalism as various government agencies vied for authority and influence. Such classic interagency competition was mirrored in intercontractor departmentalism as individual contractors working on separate functional tasks competed to guard their jurisdictional turf and conflated their contractual interests with those of the overall reconstruction effort. At the same time, their embedding within the M-form structure predicts that contractors' relationships with both the CPA and Washington would be characterized by acute agency problems, particularly given the widespread political uncertainty, poor central monitoring capacities, and lack of information about their activities. Moreover, the use of short-term renewable contracting, particularly the "cost-plus" contract, exacerbated

---

66. There is a growing literature on the market for security services and the U.S. use of contractors. See P. W. Singer, *Corporate Warriors* (Ithaca: Cornell University Press, 2003), and Deborah Avant, *The Market for Force* (New York: Cambridge University Press, 2005).

TABLE 6.1

Reconstruction Contractors in Occupied Iraq Ranked (1–50) by Dollar Value of Contract, March 2003–July 1, 2004

Rank	Contractor	Value ($ mil)	Agency	Function/Purpose
1	Kellogg, Brown & Root (Halliburton)	10,832	DoD	Repair oil industry and provide oil supplies
2	Parsons Corp.	5,286	DoD	Logistical support for the clearing of ordnance and explosives; provide design-build and construction-related services for education and health sector
3	Flour Corp.	3,755	DoD	Provide design-build and construction-related services for US CENTCOM area
4	Shaw Group/Shaw E&I	3,051	DoD	Renovate Al Kasik Army Base and provide design-build and construction-related services for US CENTCOM area
5	Bechtel Group, Inc.	2,830	USAID	Rehabilitate Iraqi infrastructure and public works
6	Perini Corp.	2,525	DoD	Field support for CENTCOM
7	Contrack International, Inc.	2,325	DoD	Provide design-build and construction-related services for US CENTCOM area
8	Tetra Tech, Inc.	1,542	DoD	Capture and destroy enemy ammunition
8	USA Environmental, Inc.	1,542	DoD	Capture and destroy enemy ammunition
10	CH2M Hill	1,528	DoD	Support CPA Public Works and Water Management Sector program office
11	American International Contractors, Inc.	1,500	DoD	Provide design-build and construction-related services for US CENTCOM area
11	Odebrect-Austin	1,500	DoD	Provide design-build and construction-related services for US CENTCOM area
13	Zapata Engineering	1,478	DoD	Manage ordnance and explosives
14	Environmental Chemical Corporation	1,475	DoD	Manage munitions disposal
14	Explosive Ordnance Technologies, Inc.	1,475	DoD	Provide conventional and recovered chemical warfare munitions response services at U.S. sites
16	Stanley Baker Hill, L.L.C	1,200	DoD	Provide construction management and engineering services
17	International American Products, Inc.	628.4	DoD	Rebuild electrical infrastructure and Ministry of Electricity
18	Research Triangle Institute	466.1	USAID	Help create local and provincial governments and promote Iraqi civic participation in the political process
19	Titan Corp.	402.0	DoD	Provide linguists and translation services for reconstruction and counterinsurgency efforts
20	Creative Associates International, Inc.	273.5	USAID	Provide educational supplies and training
21	Bearing Point, Inc.	240.2	USAID	Manage economic recovery and restructuring
22	Readiness Management Support LC	174.0	USAID	Provide logistical support services to USAID and reconstruction contractors
23	Harris Corp.	165.0	DoD	Develop the Iraqi Media Network (television and radio)
24	Science Applications International, Corp.	159.3	DoD	Charge the Iraqi Reconstruction and Development Council to rebuild twenty-three Iraqi ministries and mass media
25	Lucent Technologies World Services, Inc.	75.0	DoD	Repair and modernize existing Iraqi communications systems
26	EOD Technology, Inc.	71.9	DoD	Help clear ordnance and explosives
27	NANA Pacific	70.0	DoD	Upgrade Iraqi seaports
28	CACI International, Inc.	66.2	Interior	Provide professional interrogation and analyst support services

TABLE 6.1 — cont.

Rank	Contractor	Value ($ mil)	Agency	Function/Purpose
29	Earth Tech, Inc.	65.4	DoD	Renovate the An Numaniyah military base
30	Dyncorp	50.0	State	Support law enforcement
31	Vinell Corporation (Northrup Gruman)	48.1	DoD	Train the new Iraqi Army
32	Abt Associates, Inc.	43.8	USAID	Support for the Health Ministry and health equipment
33	Parsons Energy and Chemical Group	43.3	DoD	Provide program support for the rebuilding and modernization of Iraq's electric power system
34	Development Alternatives Inc.	39.5	USAID	Undertake reconstruction activities, social welfare initiatives, and restore marshlands in southern Iraq
35	International Resources Group	38.0	USAID	Provide expertise on technical reconstruction
36	Skylink Air and Logistic Support (USA), Inc.	27.3	USAID	Administer airport and transport to Kuwait
37	AECOM	21.6	DoD	Provide support, coordination, and standardization for the CPA's six sector program management offices
38	Blackwater Security Consulting, L.L.C.	21.3	DoD	Provide security guards and helicopters for the CPA administrator, Ambassador L. Paul Bremer
39	Laguna Construction Company, Inc.	19.5	DoD	Upgrade Iraqi Ministry of Defense Building
40	Weston Solutions, Inc.	16.3	DoD	Construct and renovate Umm Qasr Naval Base
41	Motorola, Inc.	15.6	DoD	Provide electronic and communication facilities for the Army
42	Management Systems International	15.1	USAID	Evaluate and monitor USAID's projects
43	Global Risk Strategies, Ltd.	14.7	DoD	Manage personal and facility security for U.S. Defense Contract Management Agency
44	Stevedoring Services of America	14.3	USAID	Operate and manage port at Umm Qasr
45	Raytheon Technical Services	12.4	DoD	Provide engineering technical services
46	Kropp Holdings	11.9	DoD	Provide liquid propellants, fuel, and fuel expense management software
47	General Electric Company	8.53	DoD	Provide emergency electrical generators to U.S. military
48	Foster Wheeler Co.	8.42	DoD	Support the CPA's oil sector program management office
49	Stanley Consultants	7.71	DoD	Provide consulting services to the U.S. Army
50	Liberty Shipping Group, Ltd.	7.3	USAID	Provide emergency ocean freight services to USAID

Sources: All contract values are compiled from The Center for Public Integrity's "Windfalls of War" project. Available at http://www.publicintegrity.org/wow.

Project descriptions are also adapted from U.S. Department of Commerce, "U.S. Government Reconstruction FY 2004 Prime Contracts and Subcontracts Awarded." Available at www.export.gov/iraq/pdf/contracts04_print.pdf.

Note:
16 Contractors > $1 billion
24 Contractors > $100 mil
46 Contractors > $10 mil
85 Contractors > $1 mil
Total Contractors = 125

these agency problems and further distorted incentive structures. Accordingly, many of the publicized difficulties of Iraqi reconstruction were not just the products of inadequate planning and a continuing lack of security but were the predictable results of these organizational imperatives.[67]

U-form Opportunism: Coordination Problems and Departmentalism

Perceptions that various U.S. governmental agencies were not "on the same page" characterized the entire formal occupation. Immediately following the war, the Pentagon and the State Department sparred over a number of important governance issues, such as the composition and staffing of the CPA, the future official role of Iraq expatriates who had worked with the Pentagon, and the future role of the United Nations in the rebuilding effort.[68] With both the DoD and the State Department, in addition to USAID (technically a State Department appendage) and the CPA itself, able to hold contract tenders, American reconstruction efforts suffered from a lack of overall coordination and weak planning. An exhaustive six-month assessment of the reconstruction effort by the Center of Public Integrity (CPI) described the contracting process as beset by "almost incomprehensible confusion" with agencies themselves lacking information about their own as well as each other's activities and project goals.[69] Typifying the "turf wars" involved, one contractor of a USAID project observed that, "CPA is run by a bunch of political hacks and incompetents who have no idea what they are doing. Every time we turn around there's a new order coming from CPA, 'Do it this way—no, do it that way instead!' It's just unbelievable."[70] CPA officials also were criticized widely by international officials as lacking in the most basic understanding of development work while Iraqis themselves leveled devastating judgments on the poor quality of the Pentagon-dominated CPA staff.[71] In May 2004, the Bush adminis-

---

67. In its devastating critique of the reconstruction, the ICG report made a similar observation. See ICG, "Reconstructing Iraq," i–ii.
68. Karen DeYoung and Peter Slevin, "Pentagon, State Spar on Team to Run Iraq: Rumsfeld Rejects State Dept. Choices," *Washington Post,* April 1, 2003, A25.
69. See Center for Public Integrity, "Winning Contractors: U.S. Contractors Reap the Windfalls of Post-war Reconstruction," Washington, D.C. (October 30, 2003). For reactions to the report, see Peter Slevin, "Postwar Contracting Called Uncoordinated," *Washington Post,* October 31, 2003, A23.
70. Rod Nordland and Michael Hirsh, "The $87 Billion Money Pit," *Newsweek,* November 3, 2003, 30–32.
71. See ICG, "Reconstructing Iraq," 9–10.

tration announced that it would transfer the oversight of the reconstruction effort to the State Department after the formal transfer of Iraqi sovereignty in June 2004. Along with the State Department's subsequent decision in September 2004 to shift $3.4 billion in funds away from large reconstruction projects to improving security, economic, and social conditions, these organizational shifts were widely interpreted as a partial repudiation of the CPA's competence and reconstruction strategy.[72]

Coordination problems and turf wars also plagued the actual field operations of major contractors throughout the occupation. In many cases, the functional division of responsibilities created logistical problems related to integrating multiple functions and their separate contractors. For example, the much-maligned failure of CPA officials to restore power-generation during the fall of 2003 was partially the result of an ongoing "chicken-and-egg problem" between Bechtel and Halliburton. Bechtel, which was responsible for electricity, and Halliburton, which was responsible for securing fuel, could not coordinate their efforts to supply each other components needed as intermediary inputs.[73] While Bechtel needed natural gas and fuel to operate Iraqi power stations, Halliburton required electricity to restart Iraqi refineries so that it could provide fuel. As a result, the necessary project integration was delayed by months and the power crisis in the country was unnecessarily exacerbated. Similarly, Bechtel failed to meet every major deadline for rebuilding Iraq's water system specified in its April 2003 contract and left several major sewage plants and water-treatment plants out of commission even after the handover of sovereignty, although it did paint most of the actual buildings.[74] In interviews, Bechtel officials blamed their lack of progress on their inability to obtain the necessary equipment (for which they are indemnified contractually) and an overall lack of security.[75]

Beyond these jurisdiction conflicts and coordination difficulties, the contracting process also was criticized as beholden to cronyism and insider influences. The work of Halliburton was particularly singled out given that Vice President Dick Cheney was the former CEO of Hal-

---

72. See, especially, Jonathan Weisman, "U.S. Plans to Divert Iraq Money," *Washington Post*, September 15, 2004, A23; and Peter Grier and Faye Bowers, "What's Behind US Strategy Shift in Iraq War," *Christian Science Monitor*, September 17, 2004, 2.

73. Nordland and Hirsh, "The $87 Billion Money Pit," 30–32. On problems of the power sector, also see T. Christian Miller, "Iraq Power Grid Shows U.S. Flaws," *Los Angeles Times*, September 12, 2004, A1.

74. See Christian Parenti, "Fables of the Reconstruction: The Effort to Rebuild Iraq Looks Less Like an Aid Mission than a Criminal Racket," *The Nation* 276 (Aug 30–Sept. 6, 2004): 16–20.

75. Parenti, "Fables of the Reconstruction," 17.

liburton and KBR was granted an open-ended, no-bid contract during OIF to extinguish oil fires and repair the oil sector. However, the evidence suggests that Washington lobbying influences and insider ties had a broad influence on the initial selection of contractors. According to the CPI, eighteen of the top thirty contractors in Iraq in March 2004 had given campaign contributions in excess of $100,000 from 1990 to 2002 while fifteen of these companies donated in excess of $1 million during the same period. Furthermore, 60 percent of these contractors had high-ranking employees or board members who had served in or maintained close ties with both the Republican and previous Democratic administrations.[76]

Allegations of cronyism and departmentalism were further fueled by the failure of many foreign competitors, even ones permitted to bid, to secure contracts. In February 2004, the Polish state-owned arms company Bumar Group accused the CPA of willfully ignoring key bidding documents while reaching its decision to award an Army contract to the Virginia-based company Nour USA.[77] Bumar also accused Nour of misrepresenting its costs while using well-known political lobbyists and donors to secure approval. In addition, critics of the award pointed to Nour's President A. Huda Farouki being a close friend of Ahmed Chalabi, a member of the Iraqi Governing Council and political ally of the CPA and Pentagon.[78]

M-form Opportunism: Principal-Agent Problems and Collusion

On the other hand, one would also expect to find principal-agent problems in the conduct of CPA contractors and their relation to overseeing governmental bodies. In fact, the typical M-form agency problems seem only to be intensified by the incentives generated by the contracting process.[79] Specifically, both DoD and USAID have employed Iraqi contractors under the "cost-plus" model. Under this type of contract, fees and bonuses are calculated as a percentage of the overall contract.[80] Since profits grow as a percentage of the overall contract,

76. Center for Public Integrity, "Winning Contractors."

77. T. Christian Miller and Ela Kasprzycka, "Polish Firm Protests Loss of Iraq Bid," *Los Angeles Times,* February 19, 2004, A4.

78. See Knut Royce, "Start-up Company with Connections: U.S. Gives $400m in Work to Contractor with Ties to Pentagon Favorite on Iraqi Governing Council," *Newsday,* February 15, 2004, A07.

79. On various agency problems that plague the operations of security contractors, see Singer, *Corporate Warriors.*

80. For a discussion of various types of contracts and USAID's procurement process, see Ruben Berrios, *Contracting for Development: The Role of For-Profit Contractors in U.S. Foreign Development Assistance* (Boulder, Colo.: Praeger, 2000).

there are few incentives to economize, improve efficiency, or cut waste within the overall project. In addition, start-up costs are fixed costs but are also calculated as percentages of the total project's value. Thus, as the project gets extended and/or is renewed, the category of "administrative overhead" becomes a rent of increasing return that can be appropriated by contractors.[81] Thus, the "cost-plus" contract is itself laden with incentives for contractors to conceal negative project information and provide overly optimistic progress reports. Furthermore, USAID aggressively shielded, under a federal trade secrets law, Iraqi contractors from disclosing categorized expenses such as fees, bonuses, profits, administrative expenses, and operating costs. While a very few contractors, most notably the U.S. Army Corps of Engineers, disclosed information on their cost structure, most refused to do so.[82]

The extent of the agency problems and abuse by U.S. contractors was highlighted by a number of scathing reports and audits citing multiple cases of fraud, kickbacks, and abuse. A July 2004 report to Congress by the CPA's own Inspector General Stuart W. Bowen Jr. stated that the American occupying force had been involved in sixty-nine criminal investigations (a remarkably high figure for a contract audit), of which twenty-seven were still open after the transfer of sovereignty.[83] Among its multiple examples of abuses, the IG found that a senior U.S. advisor "manipulated the contracting system" to award a $7.2 million security contract and that an American contractor performed phantom billing for $3.3 million for nonexistent personnel.[84] The audit also showed that CPA agencies often preferred to use Iraqi funds instead of U.S. funds in order to circumvent U.S. federal contracting oversight procedures and that the CPA regularly had violated its own procedural rules for authorizing Iraqi funds, such as ensuring Iraqi representation at planning meetings.[85] Indeed, of the $1.5 billion in discretionary Iraqi funds allocated to contractors by the CPA, about 85 percent went to U.S. and

81. On rent-seeking and contractual incentive structures, see Alexander Cooley and James Ron, "The NGO Scramble: Organizational Insecurity and the Political Economy of Transnational Action," *International Security* 27 (2002): 5–38.

82. See David Wood, "Profits Kept Secret in Iraq Reconstruction Contracts," *Newhouse News Service,* October 17, 2003, http://www.newhousenews.com/archive/wood101703.html (accessed 3/10/05).

83. T. Christian Miller, "Iraq Funds Are Focus of 27 Criminal Inquiries," *Los Angeles Times,* July 30, 2004, A1.

84. Ibid.

85. Ariana Eunjung Cha, "$1.9 Billion of Iraq's Money Goes to U.S. Contractors," *Washington Post,* August 4, 2004, A1.

U.K. firms while only 2 percent went to Iraqi entities.[86] In the same month, a report by the International Advisory and Monitoring Board on Iraq (IMMBI)—the United Nations oversight body—criticized the CPA for "lax accounting," its failure to provide detailed information about contracts, and an overall lack of accountability.[87] Clearly, the incentive structures, lax oversight, and disclosure requirements generated rampant opportunism among contractors.[88]

In fact, multiple allegations of overspending and deliberate overcharging have surfaced regarding the activities and billing practices of KBR (a subsidiary of Halliburton), the largest contractor in Iraq.[89] In the fall of 2003, stories first emerged that KBR gouged prices on imported fuel from Kuwait by $1 a gallon on 57 million gallons, forcing the Pentagon to initiate a criminal investigation into the matter after a wave of media scrutiny and congressional hearings.[90] At roughly the same time, KBR was also implicated in a "meals not served" scandal that alleges the company billed the Army for three times more meals than it actually produced, an overcharge of $27 million across five facilities.[91] On January 13, 2004, the company fired two executives accused of taking $6.3 million in kickbacks from a Kuwaiti-based company providing support services to U.S. troops under yet another contract.[92] Finally, a Defense Department auditor in a August 16, 2004, report stated that KBR had not provided adequate data to support its expenses and identified "significant unsupported costs" totaling about $1.8 billion or 42

86. Open Society Institute, "Disorder, Negligence and Mismanagement: How the CPA Handled Iraq Reconstruction Funds," Iraq Revenue Watch Project, Report 4 (September 2004), 1. Available on-line at http://www.iraqrevenuewatch.org. Earlier reports (pre-May 2004) are at http://www.iraqrevenuewatch.org/reports/.
87. Erik Eckholm, "Financial Controls in Iraq Are Criticized by Overseers," New York Times, July 16, 2004, A10.
88. For more details on abuses by individual contractors, see OSI, "Disorder, Negligence and Mismanagement"; ICG, "Reconstructing Iraq," 20–24; and The Center for Public Integrity's "Windfalls of War" project. Available on-line at http://www.publicintegrity.org/wow.
89. For an overview, see Andre Verlov and Daniel Politi, "Halliburton Contracts Balloon," Center for Public Integrity, Windfalls of War Project, http://www.publicintergrity.org/wow/reports.aspx?aid=366 (accessed 3/10/05).
90. Douglas Jehl, "U.S. Sees Evidence of Overcharging in Iraq Contract," New York Times, December 12, 2003, A1; and Michael Hedges and David Ivanovich, "Audit: Halliburton Overbilled Millions," Houston Chronicle, December 12, 2004, 1.
91. See William Hartung, Testimony before the Senate Democratic Policy Committee Oversight Hearing on Iraq Contracting Practices, Washington, D.C., February 14, 2004. Available on-line http://democrats.senate.gov/dpc (accessed 3/10/2005). Also see Eric Schmitt, "Halliburton Stops Billing U.S. for Meals Served to Troops," New York Times, February 17, 2004, A8.
92. David Teather, "Halliburton Staff Sacked 'for Taking Bribes,'" The Guardian (Manchester), January 24, 2004, 16.

percent of the $4.3 billion in bills that were reviewed.[93] As William Hartung observed of the incentives underlying KBR's behavior in his prepared testimony before the U.S. Senate:

> If there are kickbacks, that means there has to be enough "padding" in the contract to allow for the kickback, plus profit for all concerned. And if there's a kickback on open contract, plus an overcharge on another, plus a systematic overbilling on a third, we have to ask ourselves when we stop treating these as isolated instances and acknowledge that there is a systematic problem of waste, fraud, abuse, and possible criminality involved in Halliburton's operations in Iraq.[94]

After months of negative coverage, scathing audits, and Congressional hearings into the activities of KBR, the Army announced in summer of 2004 that it would rebid portions of the giant logistical KBR contract in a competitive process. Nevertheless, despite vague threats by the Army to withhold certain future payments, KBR easily remained the largest single contractor in Iraq well after the transfer of sovereignty.

Finally, as with other M-form relations, one would expect a significant degree of collusion and collaboration between contractors and clients. For example, critics maintain that U.S. contractors Halliburton and Bechtel subcontracted various projects to businessmen with close ties to Iraq's Governing Council.[95] The ICG, drawing on interviews and the Iraqi media, found that corruption was "widespread " and Iraqi politicians (especially ministers and Interim Governing Council members), bureaucrats, and customs officials had benefited enormously from subcontracting kickbacks.[96] Perceptions of favoritism and cronyism in the subcontracting process became commonplace early on in the reconstruction as major contractors looked to curry favor with Iraqi authorities that might be formally charged with the process after the future transfer of sovereignty. Future collusion between contractors and local officials is only likely to increase under the contracting system and, over the long run, will work to the detriment of overall efforts to reconstruct and develop Iraq's domestic institutions.[97] As the previous chap-

---

93. Robert O'Harrow Jr., "Auditor Criticizes Iraq Contract Oversight: Halliburton Unit Failed to Justify Expenses, Memo Says," *Washington Post*, August 25, 2004, E1.
94. William Hartung, "Testimony before the Senate Democratic Policy Committee," 7.
95. For example, see Paul Richter and Edmund Sanders, "Contracts Go to Allies of Iraq's Chalabi," *Los Angeles Times*, November 7, 2003, A1.
96. See ICG, "Reconstructing Iraq," 20–28.
97. For a cautionary account of collusion between Western contractors and politicians in Russia, see Janine Wedel, *Collision and Collusion: The Strange Case of Western Aid to Eastern Europe* (New York: St. Martin's Press, 1998).

ters underscored, international assistance for reform and external revenue windfalls are unlikely to promote institutional change in Iraq, especially when funneled through its existing patronage networks and bureaucratic structures.

Conclusion: The Politics of a Privatized Occupation

The American occupation and reconstruction of Iraq reconstruction was organized as a nested U-form of numerous contractors with an overall M-form structure. The firm-type theory suggests that both departmentalism and agency problems would plague reconstruction efforts and the governance of the occupation and overwhelming evidence has emerged to support such an account. Although American officials were accused of lacking in an overall plan and/or demonstrating ideologically driven optimism about their capacity to transform Iraq, the actual organization of CPA activities was a peculiar organizational form that actually managed to combine the most negative attributes of both U-form and M-form governance.

Moreover, the poor incentive structures and lack of monitoring raised significant questions about the political accountability of these multiple contractors. Under the laws of war and occupation, an occupying power bears the responsibility for providing security and basic human services. However, with the use of contractors, it was not exactly clear which party exactly should bear responsibility or be assigned blame for a project's success or failure.[98] The issue was driven home most dramatically during the Abu Ghraib prison abuse scandal of spring of 2004 when it was discovered that several Americans implicated in the explosive scandal were employees of CACI, the contractor (table 6.1, no. 28) hired to provide "professional interrogation services" to the Department of Defense. Moreover, in a strategic sense, the use of contractors also allowed American officials to disavow formal responsibility for those incidents. Questions of legal accountability, immunity, and grievance procedures will continue to surround the actions and work of foreign-based contractors well into the future.

From this perspective, the closest analogy to the reconstruction efforts of Iraqi contractors is not the postwar reconstruction of Germany or Japan but the more recent problems encountered by Western contractors in their efforts to reconstruct war-ravaged Bosnia and Kosovo. In

---

98. On problems of authority and accountability with military contractors, see Deborah Avant, *The Market for Force* (New York: Cambridge University Press, 2005).

both Balkan territories, perceptions that reconstruction efforts were primarily geared to funding Western companies and NGOs, as opposed to dealing with the needs of local people, are widespread and the contracting process has been severely criticized for its rigidity, cronyism, and waste.[99] The firm-type model suggests that the successful promotion of institutional change, even under conditions of hierarchy, is a difficult task. Under the types of organizational forms deployed by the United States in Iraq, it will be highly unlikely for the foreseeable future, regardless of future American commitment, resolve, or spending in the country.

New theories and analytical constructs need to be evaluated not only by their internal coherence and empirical accuracy but also by their potential to offer new explanations and fresh perspectives on long-standing debates. This chapter has applied the firm-type model of hierarchy to two widely contested political issues in different geographical settings—the origins of the collapse of Yugoslavia and the impact of Japanese colonialism on Korean development. The final case in this chapter has shown the model's utility for explaining the systematic difficulties and problems that plagued U.S. reconstruction efforts in Iraq. I return to the issue of hierarchy and international politics in chapter 7 and outline what the concepts developed in this book might tell us about globalization and contemporary organizational trends in international politics.

99. For example, see Ian Smilie and Goran Todorovic, "Reconstructing Bosnia, Constructing Civil Society," in *Patronage or Partnership: Local Capacity Building in Humanitarian Crises*, ed. Ian Smilie, 25–50 (Bloomfield, Conn.: Kumarian, 2001).

HIERARCHY IN A GLOBALIZED WORLD

This book has developed a theory of hierarchy and applied it to various political settings and theoretical issues in international politics. It has laid out a unifying theory for the study of political hierarchy across traditional subfields, used it to generate new explanations for certain empirical processes, and provided new explanations and insights into existing debates. This final chapter examines how the firm-type model might increase understanding of the contemporary international system and political trends in globalization, a phenomenon that has increasingly occupied the attention of social scientists with its bewildering array of issues, processes, and outcomes.

Two theoretical trends have emerged in the study of globalization in the realm of international politics. The first explicitly has stressed the links between globalization and hierarchy. A broad array of theorists, including historical institutionalists, post-Marxists, Gramscians, political geographers, and critical theorists, have explored how various hierarchical processes and their ideologies underpin the development of contemporary global governance. Some scholars have revived the concept of hegemony to show how the United States exerts ideological dominance within global economic institutions such as the IMF, World Bank, and the World Trade Organization (WTO).[1] Other theorists have concentrated on the normative underpinnings of the global economy

---

1. See Joseph Stiglitz, *Globalization and Its Discontents* (New York: W. W. Norton, 2002); and Robert Wade, "US Hegemony and the World Bank: The Fight over People and Ideas," *Review of International Political Economy* 9 (2002): 215–43.

and its propensity to create new divisions and flows of international labor.[2] Still others have explicitly equated globalization with imperialism, arguing that the promotion of economic liberalization, globalization, and democracy by the United States is no different than imperial orders of the past.[3] In perhaps the most widely acclaimed neo-Marxist account of globalization, Michael Hardt and Antonio Negri claim that the present global system constitutes a deterritorialized system of "empire" that operates under a "single logic of rule."[4] Finally, as a partial response to real-world events and the U.S. military campaigns in Afghanistan and Iraq, accusations of a new "global" imperialism have been leveled against the United States.[5]

Globalization also has spawned a new wave of constructivist scholarship that seeks to identify and explain a broad array of new nonstate actors, processes, and normative understandings that challenge the traditional nation-state system. Many scholars have focused on the growing role of international nongovernmental actors (NGOs) in the international system, their normative underpinnings, and their capacity to foster change in the practices of states.[6] Constructivist scholars of international political economy have drawn attention to new nonstate actors in the global economy such as offshore tax havens and private credit rating agencies and their growing influence in regulating global economic activity.[7] Global economic actors and processes, such as the new international division of labor, deterritorialized monetary arrangements, and international economic organizations, have all been critically examined from normative and ideational perspectives.[8] In so doing, these new

2. James Mittelman, *The Globalization Syndrome: Transformation and Resistance* (Princeton: Princeton University Press, 2000).

3. See James Petras and Henry Veltmeyer, *Globalization Unmasked: Imperialism in the 21st Century* (New York: ZED, 2001); and Mark Laffey and Tarak Barkawi, "The Imperial Peace: Democracy, Force and Globalisation," *European Journal of International Relations* 5 (1999): 403–34.

4. Michael Hardt and Antonio Negri, *Empire* (Cambridge: Harvard University Press, 2001).

5. On the United States as a new empire, especially in the post–Cold War era, see Chalmers Johnson, *The Sorrows of Empire: Militarism, Secrecy and the End of the Republic* (New York: Metropolitan, 2004); and Andrew J. Bacevich, *American Empire* (Cambridge: Harvard University, 2002). Bacevich argues that both globalization and empire have been actively pursued by the United States through its unilateral policies.

6. Margaret Keck and Katherine Sikkink, *Activists Beyond Borders: Advocacy Networks in International Politics* (Ithaca: Cornell University Press, 1998).

7. See Ronen Palan, *The Offshore World: Sovereign Markets, Virtual Places, and Nomad Millionaires* (Ithaca: Cornell University Press, 2003); and Timothy Sinclair, "Passing Judgment: Credit Rating Processes as Regulatory Mechanisms of Governance in the Emerging World Order," *Review of International Political Economy* 1 (1994): 133–59.

8. For a representative overview, see David Held et al., *Global Transformations: Politics, Economics and Cultures* (Palo Alto: Stanford University Press, 1999).

constructivist theories of globalization criticize prevailing rationalist, state-centric theories for failing to explain the political dynamics of these new global actors and processes.[9]

Much is at stake in the study of globalization. If, indeed, globalization includes elements of hierarchical governance, then the organizational theory developed in this book should be able to distinguish and apply the logics of the U-form and M-form on a global scale. If contemporary global governance structures represent a new set of institutions and processes that can be explained only through normative or ideational approaches, as constructivist theorists claim, then rationalist theories will become increasingly inadequate for explaining current and future trends in world politics. However, if rationalist concepts can satisfactorily explain the structural dynamics of globalization and its hierarchical tendencies, as well as offer credible alternative explanations for the political behavior of global nonstate actors, then the antirationalist arguments will be dealt a significant blow.[10]

This chapter revisits a basic point of this book. As with the study of international hierarchical forms in general, the new theories of globalization conflate an ontological critique of international relations theory with a methodological one. The claim that prevailing state-centered paradigms such as neorealism and neoliberalism cannot account for the rise of global actors and processes does not logically precipitate the conclusion that rationalist theories cannot explain their organizational dynamics, incentive structures, and political consequences. Globalization does, indeed, exhibit many structural features of hierarchy, but its organizational dynamics do not necessarily follow a particular ideational order or set of normative imperatives.

In this concluding chapter, I apply the firm-type model to some major aspects of contemporary globalization in both state and nonstate spheres of international governance that have been studied predominantly by critical theorists and constructivist theory. The discussion is not intended to be exhaustive but, rather, illustrative of the very different theoretical focus and alternative explanations that the rationalist firm-type theory can bring to the study of globalization and nonstate actors. Accordingly, as a plausibility probe, this final chapter will address global

9. For a representative critique, see Susan Strange, *The Retreat of the State* (Cambridge: Cambridge University Press, 1996).
10. Such a theoretical critique of the globalization literature differs from Stephen Krasner's argument that rational state rulers have consistently violated state sovereignty throughout history when pressured by international and global actors. See Stephen Krasner, *Sovereignty: Organized Hypocrisy* (Princeton: Princeton University Press, 2000).

actors and processes that have been specifically flagged by constructivists as challenging or disconfirming rationalist approaches to the study of international politics and governance.

The chapter contains four small case studies, two examining global processes linked to state actors and two linked to nonstate actors. First, I demonstrate how the firm-type model specifies with greater analytical precision the institutional features of varying types of global monetary integration such as currency unions, dollarization, and currency boards. The next case examines how contemporary colonies and dependencies have strategically taken advantage of their M-form status in order to profit from the provision of offshore services while simultaneously avoiding international regimes and their initiatives to curtail the operations of tax havens. The subsequent section explores how private international credit rating agencies are increasingly performing global U-form functions in their dissemination of information about global bond issuers. The final case challenges conventional notions about international NGOs, the current academic and global activist symbol of the importance of nonhierarchical "networks," by showing how many international nongovernmental organizations (INGOs) actually exhibit many structural features and behaviors that resemble those of a hierarchical M-form organization. As a result, I expect the behavior of these INGOs to be much more strategic, competitive, and opportunistic than the benign normative assumptions made by scholars of INGOs and transnational networks. I conclude the chapter, and the book, by reprising the major themes developed in this study of hierarchical forms and governance in the international system.

The Organization of Global Processes: Forms of Monetary Integration

Globalization refers to the increased movement of goods, capital, and labor across national borders, the accompanying rise of stateless forces, and the transformative effects of these processes. Traditional functions and processes once associated almost exclusively with nation-states are rapidly now becoming "deterritorialized" and performed on a more global scale.[11] Accordingly, globalization is reconfiguring political authority within the international system, but the precise nature of these transformations follows varying organizational forms and their logics.

---

11. Philip Cerny, "Globalization and the Changing Logic of Collective Action," *International Organization* 49 (1996): 595–625.

Those who view "globalization as hierarchy" are not necessarily wrong, but they ignore the varying organizational logics that global governance can assume. Applying the firm-type model to trends in contemporary international monetary integration and governance illustrates some of these differences.

As scholars of international monetary affairs have argued, the contiguity of national territories with national currencies is a relatively bounded historical phenomenon.[12] In the post–Bretton Woods era, national sovereignty over monetary flows is diminishing again. Prevailing political analyses of contemporary monetary orders emphasize the ideational and ideological underpinnings of monetary integration. For example, Ilene Grabel has described the global rise of monetary institutions such as currency boards and dollarization as functions of the rise of neo-orthodox ideas about financial liberalization.[13] Similarly Kate McNamara has observed that European monetary integration was predicated on the adoption of common neoliberal ideas among key European central bankers.[14] While the rise of neoliberalism and orthodox monetary ideas may explain the origins of certain forms of monetary integration, these ideas themselves cannot account for the organizational differences among these different monetary institutions and the varying political consequences that these varying forms engender. The movement away from territorial currencies is taking several forms, some organizationally hierarchical and others not. Table 7.1 offers a breakdown of contemporary forms of monetary union, divided into three categories—currency unions, dollarized countries, and countries with currency boards. While all three arrangements require the participating country to cede elements of its monetary sovereignty, their organizational forms vary significantly. While the currency union is a nonhierarchical or H-form type of sovereign monetary pooling, dollarization (U-form) and currency boards (M-form) are distinct hierarchical forms with accompanying political consequences.[15]

12. See Benjamin Cohen, *The Future of Money* (Princeton: Princeton University Press, 2004); and Eric Helleiner, *The Making of National Money: Territorial Currencies in Historical Perspective* (Ithaca: Cornell University Press, 2003).

13. Ilene Grabel, "Ideology, Power, and the Rise of Independent Monetary Institutions in Emerging Economies," in *Monetary Orders: Ambiguous Politics, Ubiquitous Economics*, ed. Jonathan Kirshner, 25–52 (Ithaca: Cornell University Press, 2003).

14. Kathleen R. McNamara, *The Currency of Ideas: Monetary Politics in the European Union* (Ithaca: Cornell University Press, 1998).

15. For a comparative theoretical assessment, see Benjamin Cohen, *The Future of Money* (Princeton: Princeton University Press, 2004), especially 33–66. Also see John Williamson, "Dollarization Does not Make Sense Everywhere," in *The Dollarization Debate*, ed. Dominick Salvatore, James W. Dean, and Thomas D. Willett, 172–76 (New York: Oxford: 2003).

TABLE 7.1
Deterritorialized Forms of Monetary Governance, 2004 (Unless Other Year Specified)

A. Monetary Unions (H-forms, nonhierarchical)

Union (date adopted)	Member States	Institutional Arrangements
East Caribbean Currency Union (1965)	Antigua and Barbuda, Dominica, Grenada, St. Kitts and Nevis, St. Lucia, St. Vincent and Grenadines	Single currency (East Caribbean Dollar), single Central Bank
European Economic and Monetary Union (1999)	Austria, Belgium, Finland, France, Germany, Greece, Ireland, Italy, Luxembourg, Netherlands, Portugal, Spain	Single currency (Euro), single Central Bank (European Central Bank)
CFA Franc Zone (1963–64)	Benin, Burkina Faso, Cameroon, Central African Republic, Chad, Comoros, Congo-Brazzaville, Ivory Coast, Equatorial Guinea, Gabon, Guinea-Bissau, Mali, Niger, Senegal, Togo	Two regional currencies (CFA Franc) and Comorian national Franc; two regional central banks and Comoros National Bank
Common Monetary Area	Lesotho, Namibia, South Africa, Swaziland	Three currencies pegged to South African Rand, four Central Banks

B. Dollarized and Near-Dollarized* Countries (U-forms)

Country	Currency Used	Since
Andorra	Euro	2002
East Timor	U.S. Dollar	2000
Ecuador*	U.S. Dollar	2000
El Salvador*	U.S. Dollar	2001
Kiribati	Australian Dollar	1943
Kosovo	Euro	1999
Liechtenstein	Swiss Franc	1921
Marshall Islands	U.S. Dollar	1944
Micronesia	U.S. Dollar	1944
Monaco	Euro	1865
Montenegro	Euro	1999
Nauru	Australian Dollar	1914
Palau	U.S. Dollar	1944
Panama*	U.S. Dollar	1904
San Marino	Euro	2002
Tuvalu*	Australian Dollar	1892
Vatican City	Euro	2002

C. Countries/Territories Employing a Currency Board (M-forms)

Country	Anchor Currency	Since	Local Currency
Argentina	U.S. Dollar	(1991–2002)	Argentinian Peso
Bosnia and Herzegovina	Euro	1998	Bosnian Marka
Brunei Darussalam	Singapore Dollar	1967	Brunei Dollar
Bulgaria	Euro	1997	Lev
Djibouti	U.S. Dollar	1949	Djibouti Franc
Estonia	Euro	1992	Kroon
Hong Kong	U.S. Dollar	1983	Hong Kong Dollar
Lithuania	Euro	1994	Litas

Source: Adapted from Benjamin Cohen, *The Future of Money* (Princeton: Princeton University Press, 2003), 62–64, Tables 1–3, 5.
* States that rely on foreign currency but also issue a token local currency.

Monetary H-forms: The Organization of Currency Unions

Typically, the pooling of national currencies into monetary unions involves the surrendering of monetary autonomy by a country's central bank and the delegation of this authority to a set of common governing institutions. The most important contemporary monetary union is the Eurozone, established in 1999 by ten countries of the European Union. Politically, members of the Eurozone delegate their monetary authority to the European Central Bank. While the control of the ECB undermines the sovereign autonomy of member countries, the ECB itself is governed by a mutually agreed upon set of institutions and procedures established by the Eurozone members, rendering such integration similar to the idealized type of federalism or H-form organization discussed in chapter 1.[16] In addition to the Eurozone, other contemporary monetary unions include the East Caribbean Currency Union and the CFA France Zone. Recently, members of the ASEAN and MERCOSUR regional economic blocs have also discussed the possibility of unifying their currencies in the future.

Monetary U-forms: The Organization of Dollarization

Conversely, some countries are deterritorializing monetary governance by adopting a foreign currency, a process referred to as dollarization (regardless of whether or not the adopted currency is the U.S. dollar). As a specifically U-form type of hierarchy, dollarization replaces a country's monetary policy and governance with the institutions of the country whose currency it adopts. As Benjamin Cohen maintains, despite the fact that states relinquish autonomy under both types of integration, currency integration and dollarization entail politically significant organizational differences:

> ... there is a loss of monetary autonomy, since the dollarizing country can no longer exercise unilateral control over its money supply or exchange rate. That is true with a common currency too, of course. But as compared with currency unification, the degree of loss is greater since dollarization as such implies no direct part in the making of monetary policy. With currency unification, each country presumably has a seat at the table where joint policy is made. With dollarization, unless based on

16. For a critique, see Sheri Berman and Kathleen McNamara, "Bank on Democracy," *Foreign Affairs* 78 (May/June 1999): 2–8.

agreement with explicit provision for power sharing, all authority is simply ceded to the partner country's central bank. The relationship is not one of parity but of hierarchy, with no promise at all that a dollarizing country's specific circumstances or needs would be taken into account when monetary decisions are made.[17]

Many economists view dollarization as economically beneficial to states in that it allows them to lower rates of inflation and instill a high degree of investor confidence by reducing uncertainty about domestic monetary policy.[18] However, the hierarchical nature of dollarization, as Cohen and others point out, also potentially imposes important political costs on an adopting country in addition to its loss of monetary autonomy and the symbolic loss of national identity.[19] First, dollarized countries must forgo revenues from seigniorage—the excess sum of the nominal value of money over its cost of production—as the revenue stream is redirected to and controlled by the issuing central bank.[20] Indeed, the ability to derive income from issuing money, while not a significant part of GDP, can be an important source of revenue for financing the operations of a national bank or government. Historically, the turn to seigniorage has been a state's domestic revenue source of last resort.[21]

Second, from an organizational perspective, policy decisions by an issuing country's monetary agency are likely to be based on the needs, trade-offs, and perceptions of economic conditions solely within the issuing country. In the case of the United States, the U.S. Treasury executes policy based on its domestic needs and political pressures and would be unlikely to modify policy based on the differing conditions in a dollarized country. Thus, not only do dollarized countries effectively cede policy autonomy, they will also be affected by the particular decisions made by a monetary authority based on prevailing economic conditions outside the dollarized country.

Third, dollarization, and the harmonization of monetary policy, endows the issuing country's monetary institution with the ability to

17. Benjamin Cohen, "Monetary Union: The Political Dimension," in *The Dollarization Debate*, ed. Dominick Salvatore, James W. Dean, and Thomas D. Willett (New York: Oxford: 2003), 228.
18. For representative works by some of the leading proponents, see Kurt Schuler, *Should Developing Countries Have Central Banks? Currency Quality and Monetary Systems in 155 Developing Countries* (London: Institute for Economic Affairs, 1996).
19. On identity and monetary policy, see Helleiner, *Making of National Money*; and Rawi Abdelal, *National Purpose and the World Economy* (Ithaca: Cornell University Press, 2001).
20. This is Benjamin Cohen's definition. See Cohen, *The Future of Money*, 18.
21. See Charles Goodhart, "The Political Economy of Monetary Union," in *Understanding Interdependence: The Politics of the Open Economy*, ed. Peter B. Kenan (Princeton: Princeton University Press, 1995), 455–56.

exert pressure and diplomatic leverage.[22] What Jonathan Kirshner refers to as the exercise of "monetary power" is greatly enhanced and facilitated when a more powerful country commands the monetary institutions of the peripheral country in a U-form fashion.[23] For example, prior to its military intervention in 1989, the United States was able to impose economic sanctions on Panama by curtailing the flow of official money transfers to and from the practically dollarized Central American country. The U.S. Treasury sanctions effectively halted the banking and monetary operations of Manuel Noriega's government, initiated a liquidity crisis and demonetized the economy, weakened Noriega's political standing by blocking his ability to pay civil servants and the military, and resulted in a contraction of national output of nearly 20 percent that year.[24] Tellingly, even these harsh monetary sanctions had been watered down by an act of departmentalism. Given the U.S. Treasury's reluctance to completely destroy the activities of U.S. investors and businesses operating in Panama, the formal enactment of the sanctions was delayed by a few months and contained loopholes for foreign companies, thereby tempering their effects.[25]

Monetary M-forms: The Organization of Currency Boards

Finally, international monetary integration also has taken the form of a currency board, which can be fruitfully distinguished as an M-form type of hierarchy. In a currency board, a country effectively agrees to give up an autonomous national bank and pegs its circulating territorial currency to the value of an external currency. Adopting a board typically requires that a country maintain 100 percent foreign currency reserves of all circulating money while the domestic and anchor currencies remain freely exchangeable. As with dollarization, these arrangements bind the decision-making authority of national politicians and tie monetary policy to developments in the reserve currency. Originally developed as a way of ensuring monetary stability in colonies, without formally circulating a home currency in the periphery, the currency board was once again adopted by a number of countries in the 1990s

22. See Benjamin Cohen, "US Policy on Dollarization: A Political Analysis," *Geopolitics* 7 (2002): 5–26. Also see Eric Helleiner, "Dollarization Diplomacy: US Policy towards Latin America Coming Full Circle?" *Review of International Political Economy* 19 (2003): 406–29.
23. Jonathan Kirshner, *Currency and Coercion: The Politics of Monetary Power* (Princeton: Princeton University Press, 1995).
24. Cohen, "US Policy on Dollarization." Also see the discussion of the episode in Kirshner, *Currency and Coercion*, 159–66.
25. Margaret Scranton, *The Noriega Years* (Boulder, Colo.: Lynne Reinner, 1991), 307–8.

(including Argentina, Bulgaria, Estonia, and Lithuania) in attempts to stabilize their economies and secure international confidence in their monetary conditions.

As with other M-forms, the possibility of defection in this organizational arrangement is much stronger than that of dedollarization in its U-form counterpart.[26] Monetary authorities can and have reneged on their basic commitments to the rules of the board in order to alleviate financial crises and pressures. In perhaps the most dramatic instance of monetary "opportunism," Argentina abolished its currency board in 2001 after it could no longer sustain confidence in the full convertibility of the peso and quell capital flight.[27] Prior to its abolition, Argentinian officials "tinkered" with policies that violated the strict rules of the board, including allowing the Central Bank to lend to government agencies and commercial banks at multiple interest rates, introducing a system of multiple exchange rates in June 2001, and maintaining insufficient reserves of foreign exchange.[28] The abolition of the board and subsequent Argentinian devaluation exacerbated the ongoing financial crisis, thereby decimating the Argentinian economy and saddling the country with new levels of extraordinary debt.[29] Despite being hierarchical, currency boards leave some room for agency and, ultimately, disengagement by domestic monetary authorities in a way that U-form dollarization does not.

Given the diverse contemporary trends in monetary internationalization, the firm-type model suggests that important analytical distinctions should be drawn among these arrangements. Distinguishing monetary arrangements as different organizational forms allows us to specify the varying governance dynamics and divergent political consequences of these organizational forms. Some forms of monetary integration are indeed examples of hierarchical trends within the globalization of money, but there are different logics associated with U-form and M-form types of monetary governance.

26. I am thankful to Mark Blyth for his insights on this point.

27. On the origins of the Argentinian crisis, see Javier Corrales, "The Politics of Argentina's Meltdown," *World Policy Journal* 19 (2002): 29–42; and Manuel Pastor and Carol Wise, "From Poster Child to Basket Case," *Foreign Affairs* 80 (July/August 2001): 60–72.

28. See Kurt Schuler, "Fixing Argentina," *CATO Policy Analysis* 445 (July 2002). Available online at http://www.cato.org/pubs/pas/pa445.pdf (accessed 3/10/2005).

29. Martin Feldstein, "Argentina's Fall: Lessons from the Latest Financial Crisis," *Foreign Affairs* 81 (March/April 2002): 8–14.

Contemporary M-forms and the Rise of Tax Havens

The rise of tax havens and microstates as key actors in the global economy is yet another area in which the relationship between globalization and international hierarchy is quite strong, although not in the way usually acknowledged by globalization theorists. Microstates offer sites where global economic actors (including firms, states, organizations, and individuals) can bypass traditional sovereign demands for disclosure, regulation, and oversight. Ronen Palan has argued that such actors have found a niche in the international economy by selling various facets of their sovereignty.[30] By offering services related to finance and banking, tax avoidance, incorporation, e-commerce, and illicit sectors forbidden by many states (drug-financing, gambling, and/or pornography), such locales offer "virtual places" that designate certain sectors or legal spheres as "offshore."[31] For Palan, the very creation of an offshore realm by contemporary tax havens is a social construction or legal fiction that cannot be properly understood by rationalist theories of international relations.[32]

While the rise of tax havens is a rapidly growing dimension of the global economic system, the proliferation of tax havens does not necessarily vindicate critiques of rationalist approaches to the international political economy. In fact, the firm-type model suggests two important organizational links between the governance of tax havens and their operations within the contemporary system. While some tax havens in the international economy are bona fide sovereign states, a high proportion are nonsovereign actors, such as colonies, dependencies, and principalities.[33] These include British colonies and dependencies such as the Cayman Islands, Bermuda, Gibraltar, and the Channel Islands, which offer the advantages of well-established British financial practices.[34] The Pacific island jurisdictions of the Cook Islands and Norfolk Island, the U.S. Virgin Islands, and a rim of semisovereign microstates in Europe, such as Andorra, Liechtenstein, and Monaco, round out this

30. Ronen Palan, "Tax Havens and State Sovereignty," *International Organization* 56 (2002): 151–57.
31. Palan, *The Offshore World.*
32. Ash Amin and Rolen Palan, "Towards a Non-Rationalist International Political Economy," *Review of International Political Economy* 8 (2001): 559–77.
33. For an overview of the politics of contemporary colonies and dependencies, see Robert Aldrich and John Connell, *The Last Colonies* (New York: Cambridge University Press, 1998).
34. See R. T. Naylor, *Wages of Crime: Black Markets, Illegal Finance, and the Underworld Economy* (Ithaca: Cornell University Press, 2002), 162–72.

list of contemporary tax haven dependencies. Furthermore, a number of the sovereign entities that are tax havens, such as Vanuatu and Nauru, have only been independent for a short period of time. Why are a disproportionately high number of tax havens nonsovereign or partially sovereign political units?

The answer may lie in the fact that the M-form type of governance and its organizational structure enable tax havens to provide these commercialized "sovereign" functions without interference from the international community and the regimes of sovereign states. First, the informational structure of the M-form enables many of these territories to encapsulate information about their financial practices and to operate in relative secrecy and isolation. Bank secrecy laws in tax havens prevent home banks from legally divulging information about their clients and accounts to any third parties, including states, international organizations, firms, and individuals. As a result, economic actors have flooded to these territories to take advantage of the secrecy laws that govern financial services and related sectors, such as registry and incorporation services. For example, despite a tiny 40,000-person population, the Cayman Islands remain the world's fifth largest financial center, hosting forty-seven of the world's largest fifty banks and offering incorporation services to 60,000 registered companies.[35] Tellingly, a main operating strategy of the Enron Corporation was to take advantage of nondisclosure laws in the Caymans and other dependencies by creating dummy subsidiary corporations. Prior to its demise, the company had created 900 subsidiaries in tax havens, including 692 in the Cayman Islands, and 119 in the Turks and Caicos, thereby helping the company avoid paying United States income taxes in four of its last five years.[36]

Second, to ensure confidentiality in their practices, tax havens use their M-form status to avoid the regulatory initiatives of the international community and to bypass the jurisdiction of international regimes. Unlike nation-states that are increasingly subject to a dense network of international institutions and treaty obligations, dependencies can simply use their nonsovereign status to avoid the directives of international governance altogether. For example, the territories of Gibraltar and Jersey, both British dependencies on the European periphery, are neither parts of the United Kingdom nor the European Union

---

35. James Canute, "Caribbean Tax Haven Offers Assistance," *Financial Times*, February 13, 2002, 27. For comparative data and a comprehensive table, see Palan, *The Offshore World*, 35–38.
36. David Cay Johnston, "Enron Avoided Income Taxes in 4 of 5 Years," *New York Times*, January 17, 2002, A1.

and are therefore not required to harmonize their financial practices and oversight procedures with those of the European Union.[37] Conversely, the sovereign state of Cyprus, a nation-state that had been engaging in offshore banking and money laundering, was forced to curtail its activity in the sector as a precondition for entering the European Union.[38] Of the thirty-five tax havens identified by a 2000 OECD report as engaged in harmful tax practices and deemed to be uncooperative with the OECD and the international community, fifteen were contemporary dependencies or nonsovereign principalities or territories (table 7.2).[39] Furthermore, nineteen of these thirty-five tax havens governed their monetary systems according to some hierarchical arrangement.

In sum, while the number of M-forms in the international system has dwindled as a result of decolonization, a number of contemporary colonies and dependencies manage to survive, and in some cases prosper, by becoming tax havens in order to attract revenues from international sources. In turn, the M-form status of these tax havens subjects them to minimal oversight from their core polity or the international community while allowing them to preserve the informational secrecy necessary for maintaining these offshore practices. Certainly, constructivists such as Palan are justified in drawing attention to the socially constructed nature of "offshore" and "onshore" as legal categories. Nonetheless, important organizational features that are better explained by rationalist theories also characterize contemporary tax havens.

GLOBALIZATION AND PRIVATE GOVERNANCE: U-FORMS AND M-FORMS

While both U-form and M-form types of integration within globalization in the public sphere can be distinguished, the operations of private actors that contribute to global governance also take different hierarchical forms. Unlike prevailing accounts of private authority that stress the ideational, normative, and legal foundations of private governance, I suggest that private actors face similar trade-offs and engage in

---

37. For more on secret financial practices, sovereign status, and lax British oversight, see Austin Mitchell et al., "No Accounting for Tax Havens," report prepared by the Association for Accountancy & Business Affairs (London, 2002). Available on-line at http://visar.csustan.edu/aaba/aabajourVol2-No1.html (accessed on 3/10/2005).

38. See Jeremy Page, "Russians Seek New Tax Havens as Cyprus Cleans Up," *Reuters*, June 23, 2003.

39. OECD, "Towards Global Tax Co-operation: Progress in Identifying and Eliminating Harmful Tax Practices," Report to the 2000 Ministerial Council Meeting (Paris: OECD 2000), 17.

TABLE 7.2
OCED-Classified Tax Havens and Hierarchical Status

Country/Polity	Sovereign Status (state, M-form)	Monetary Hierarchy?
Andorra	State	Yes, U-form (Euro)
Anguilla	M-form, overseas territory of United Kingdom	Yes, U-form (East Caribbean Dollar)
Antigua and Barbuda	State	No, East Caribbean Common Currency
Aruba	Mixed form, Kingdom of the Netherlands	No (central bank with currency peg)
Bahamas	State	Yes, Mixed form (Bahamian dollar, and U.S. Dollar)
Bahrain	State	No
Barbados	State	No
Belize	State	No
British Virgin Islands	M-form, overseas territory of United Kingdom	Yes, U-form (U.S. Dollar)
Cook Islands	Mixed form, in association with New Zealand	Yes, U-form (New Zealand Dollar)
Dominica	State	No, East Caribbean Common Currency
Gibraltar	M-form, overseas territory of United Kingdom	Yes, U-form (U.K. Pound)
Guernsey/Sark/Aldeney	M-form, Dependency of the British Crown	Yes, Mixed form (U.K. Pound and Guernsey Pound)
Isle of Man	M-form, Dependency of the British Crown	Yes, Mixed form (U.K. Pound and Manx Pound)
Jersey	M-form, Dependency of the British Crown	Yes, Mixed form (U.K. Pound and Jersey Pound)
Liberia	State	Yes, Mixed form (Liberian Dollar and U.S. Dollar); dollarized from 1944–82 (U.S. Dollar)
Lechtenstein	Principality	Yes, U-form (Swiss Franc)
Maldives	State	No
Marshall Islands	State	Yes, U-form (U.S. Dollar)
Monaco	Principality	Yes, U-form (Euro)
Montserrat	M-form, overseas territory of United Kingdom	Yes, U-form (East Caribbean Dollar)
Nauru	State	Yes, U-form (Australian Dollar)
Netherlands Antilles	Mixed form, Kingdom of the Netherlands	No (central bank with currency peg)
Niue	Mixed form, in association with New Zealand	Yes, U-form New Zealand Dollar
Panama	State	Yes, U-form (U.S. Dollar)
Samoa	State	No
Seychelles	State	No
St. Lucia	State	No
St. Kitts and Nevis	State	No, East Caribbean Common Currency
St. Vincent and the Grenadines	State	No, East Caribbean Common Currency
Tonga	State	No
Turks and Caicos	M-form, overseas territory of United Kingdom	Yes, U-form (U.S. Dollar)
U.S. Virgin Islands	M-form, external territory of the United States	Yes, U-form (U.S. Dollar)
Vanuatu	State	No

similar types of opportunism as their U-form and M-form political counterparts. The exclusive functional roles played by credit rating agencies in global financial markets and the M-form organizational structure of international NGOs are instructive in this regard.

New Private Functions: The Example of Credit-Rating Agencies

One of the most overlooked areas of private functional governance is the role played by credit rating agencies in international financial markets. In his popular book on globalization, Thomas Friedman, the chief foreign affairs correspondent of the *New York Times*, characterizes the credit agency Moodys as a new global superpower.[40] Along with Fitch and Standard and Poors, the so-called big three credit-rating agencies retain unprecedented power in the international financial system through their ability to reward and punish both international corporations and states. Although the ratings agencies publicly maintain that they are merely in the business of providing information to investors, their role has significantly expanded in the post–Bretton Woods era as sovereign countries and private corporations have turned to private capital markets for their borrowing needs.

The big three not only provide information but also function practically as exclusive issuers of global regulatory licenses.[41] Since the ratings process itself has become so deeply embedded within the operation of financial markets, to the point that both countries and corporations must secure a rating before they issue debt, credit-rating agencies effectively regulate access to the bond market. While an investment grade rating allows a country or corporation to issue bonds, a downgrade raises the interest rates that these parties must offer bondholders, or, in extreme cases, entirely inhibits their access to private markets. Thus, an unrated state faces de facto exclusion from international financial markets.

Moreover, these private actor ratings are becoming embedded in international regulatory practices, treaties, and regimes. For example, the Basel II International Banking Accords established that, by January 2007, the national bank regulators of signatory parties must use the big-three ratings as a standard measure of bank portfolio risk.[42] As a result

---

40. Thomas Friedman, *The Lexus and the Olive Tree: Understanding Globalization* (New York: Anchor Books, 2000).
41. See Sinclair, "Passing Judgment."
42. For details, see Michael R. King and Timothy J. Sinclair, "Private Actors and Public Policy: A Requiem for the New Basel Capital Accord," *International Political Science Review* 24 (2003): 345–62.

of this regulatory power, and as with other forms of U-form governance, states and companies must harmonize their financial and macroeconomic practices with the expectations of the big three. Consequently, states are increasingly engaging in ratings-agency diplomacy, as government representatives almost continuously coordinate expectations, manage relations with the agencies, and even lobby them for improvements in their rating. In short, credit-rating agencies are spurring the harmonization of economic governance in the countries that they rate.

Of course, many critics of the big three argue that their ratings criteria are not neutral and their role in the operation of financial markets often has exacerbated market volatility and instability. Analysts of the ratings process correctly point out that the big three have helped to institutionalize "neoliberal orthodoxy." For example, the big three endured heavy criticism for their role in exacerbating the East Asian financial crisis. As Thailand and, later, South Korea fended off currency speculators, downgrades by the credit-rating agencies contributed to investor panic and prompted institutions to call in short-term loans.[43] In turn, this experience led the agencies themselves to revise their ratings criteria. Indeed, broader surveys indicate that, overall, the rating agencies have done a poor job in predicting crises and have downgraded countries only in reaction to developments in the financial markets.[44] Similarly, the failure of the agencies to predict the rapid demise of WorldCom and Enron initiated calls for a reexamination of their role. That the agencies collect paid subscriptions and consulting fees from the states and companies that they actually rate has led to accusations that the agencies face a significant conflict of interest when assessing their clients.[45]

Just as functional agencies within polities engage in departmentalist behavior and vie for organizational and jurisdictional influence, one should expect similar types of organizational imperatives to drive the behavior of private actors playing global functional roles. In fact, the big-three rating agencies have zealously guarded their turf, mainly through their close ties to the United States Security and Exchange Commission (SEC). The most significant barrier to entry for other potential ratings agencies is the SEC's decision to recognize only the big three as Nationally Recognized Statistical Rating Organizations or

43. See Robert Wade, "The Asian Debt-and-Development Crisis of 1997–? Causes and Consequences," *World Development* 26 (1998): 1535–63.
44. See Morris Goldstein, Graciela L. Kaminsky, and Carol Reinhart, *Assessing Financial Vulnerability: An Early Warning System for Emerging Markets* (Washington, D.C.: Institute for International Economics, 2000).
45. See Janice Revell, "Ratings Ruckus," *Fortune* 147 (May 26, 2003): 44.

NRSROs, even though other bureaus have applied for this status periodically and have been rejected every time.[46] Some commentators have even suggested that the exclusion of other institutions from NRSRO status has made the industry inefficient and unadaptive to changing financial conditions.[47]

In organizational terms, the functions and consequences of the big three conform to many of the expectations for U-form governance. Such a perspective is not necessarily mutually exclusive with a more ideational account that draws attention to the "neoliberal" orthodoxy that informs the methodology of their ratings. While constructivist accounts can explain the origins of the ratings criteria and their evolution, a more organizational account focuses on the organizational interests, incentives, and political actions of the big three. One important area where a constructivist explanation would differ from this organizational theory would be in accounting for the mechanisms of diffusion of these economic "norms." While constructivist approaches would argue that states and firms have internalized these agencies' ideas about economic governance, an organizational account would emphasize that the process of harmonization is less costly to states and firms than openly defying the big three, whether policymakers actually believe these ideas or not. As private actors increasingly execute other regulatory functions within the international economy, one would expect to observe similar organizational logics to emerge.

New Private Territorial Actors: Are MNCs and NGOs Organized Differently?

An application of the firm-type model to globalized private actors usually not studied in terms of their hierarchical form and incentive structures may explain certain aspects of their behavior that ideational theories cannot. Obviously, many multinational corporations (MNCs) embody the M-form structure. However, as an empirical matter, are not-for-profit transnational actors organizationally dissimilar from their for-profit counterparts?

Consider, for example, the organizational structure and operations of certain prominent international nongovernmental organizations. The

---

46. See *The Economist*, "Rating Agencies; Exclusion Zone," February 8, 2003, 65; and Jason Kirby, "Members Only," *Canadian Business* 75 (April 15, 2002): 53–59.
47. Howard Stock, "Are Rating Agencies Hobbled by Conflicts?" *Investor Relations Business*, December 16, 2002, 1.

prevailing wisdom among international relations scholars is that NGOs are part of emerging transnational governance networks that oppose hierarchical forms of authority. In an influential article, Jessica Mathews maintains that NGOs have initiated a radical reorganization or "power shift" in the forms of global governance by "disrupt[ing] hierarchies" and by spreading, "power among more people and groups."[48] Similarly, in their standard-setting account of NGOs and transnational networks, Margaret Keck and Katherine Sikkink maintain that transnational networks constitute a distinct form within international governance by linking different types of actors, such as local activists, international NGOs, international organizations, and states.[49] Many scholars of NGOs explicitly maintain that what differentiates these NGO networks from other political actors is their commitment to similar normative principles and universal values.[50]

While NGOs perform important work and their study should be included in the study of international relations and global governance, one should be cautious about conflating an actor's "normative motivations" with either its immediate strategic goals or actual organizational incentives. After all, members of many different types of political organizations—political parties, governmental agencies, unions, and lobbies—may hold deep normative beliefs about the importance of their political purpose, but such values can be separated from the overall strategies and organizational interests that their political bodies pursue. As Aseem Prakesh and Susanne Sell suggest, ideas can just as easily be invoked strategically by NGOs as by for-profit corporations and there is no analytical reason to assume that one type of organization is anymore normatively motivated than the other.[51]

In fact, many NGOs exhibit an international organizational structure that is quite similar to the M-form (table 7.3). For example, major international humanitarian organizations and aid groups such as CARE or Save the Children are divided into multiple national-level organizations, much like the territorial divisions of the M-form. Like M-forms, these national-level organizations tend to operate autonomously, maintain fiscal self-sufficiency, and only consult with central offices on matters relating to broad strategy and organizational goals. Moreover, national-

48. Jessica Mathews, "Power Shift," *Foreign Affairs* 76 (January/February 1997): 52–53.
49. Keck and Sikkink, *Activists Beyond Borders.*
50. See Richard Price, "Transnational Civil Society and Advocacy in World Politics," *World Politics* 55 (2003): 579–606.
51. Aseem Prakesh and Susanne K. Sell, "Using Ideas Strategically," *International Studies Quarterly* 48 (2004): 143–75.

TABLE 7.3
Selected International Nongovernmental Organizations: Organizational Structure and Subsidiary
Fundraising Divisions

INGO	Autonomous Divisions/Branches in Different Countries	Executive Headquarters, Location
Amnesty International	57	International Secretariat, London, U.K.
CARE International	11	International Secretariat, Geneva, Switzerland
Greenpeace	38 national and regional offices	Greenpeace International, Amsterdam, Netherlands
International Committee for the Red Cross	74 delegations	International Secretariat, Geneva, Switzerland
Medecins Sans Frontieres	19	International Office, Brussels, Belgium
Oxfam International	12	International Secretariat, Oxford, U.K.
Save the Children International Alliance	29	International Alliance, London, U.K.
World Wildlife Fund	40	International Secretariat, Gland, Switzerland

Source: Official internet websites of respective INGOs.

level offices from the same organization often compete over the same
contracts and projects, especially in situations of complex emergencies
and relief efforts.[52] Such behavior resembles less the transnational networks outlined by NGO theorists and more the hierarchical M-form
described by the firm-type model.

Furthermore, just as states and companies are outsourcing functions
and projects to the private sector, international actors are increasingly
delegating projects to INGOs. Far from being a mere funding source or
"technical issue," the subcontracting process has observable causal effects
on the organizational activities and behavior of NGOs. When faced with
a competitive market in which they must outbid competitors and maintain existing contracts, NGOs will behave in a similarly competitive
manner as multinational corporations that bid on international tenders.
In turn, competitive subcontracting encourages a permanent scramble
among NGOs, driving them to outbid and compete against each other
for their organizational survival. Tellingly, in certain complex emergencies and postconflict reconstruction, both MNCs and NGOs are increas-

52. See Alexander Cooley and James Ron, "The NGO Scramble: Organizational Insecurity and
the Political Economy of Transnational Action," *International Security* 25 (2002): 10–11.

ingly being treated as equals in the tender process as both bid for projects and contracts.

Finally, treating NGOs as M-form organizations leads to the prediction that agency problems and opportunism are also likely to characterize the behavior of NGO subdivisions. Like their corporate counterparts, NGOs are likely to encapsulate information, especially negative project information that might threaten their immediate funding source and organizational survival. The contracting frenzies, competitive environments, and uncertainty generated by the humanitarian emergencies and reconstruction efforts in settings such as Rwanda, the Balkans, and Afghanistan suggest that, when faced with similar contracting processes and environments as for-profit MNCs, NGOs are likely to behave in a similar fashion.[53] When project monitoring is weak, NGO contractors are likely to use the resources of the donor to pursue their more narrow organizational interests and not necessarily the donor's preferences. Moreover, such organizational structures and contractual incentives are likely to inhibit broad-based collective action among NGOs in response to a common challenge, regardless of their common normative values and motivating beliefs. Such was the case in Goma (ex-Zaire), where a competitive contracting environment prevented humanitarian NGOs from jointly drawing attention to and preventing the rearmament of Hutu militias within the confines of these refugee camps.[54]

In sum, when one examines the actual organizational behavior, structure, and incentives that confront NGOs, their organization and behavior increasingly resembles that of their for-profit M-form counterparts. The common assumption that NGOs are part of antihierarchical global networks that are bound by common norms and principles must be questioned. At best, it fails to address the evolving incentives and organizational characteristics found in the NGO world while, at worst, the assumption generates inaccurate predictions about the actual behavior of NGOs in market-type settings.

53. This point is underscored in Cooley and Ron, "The NGO Scramble." On similar types of competitive dynamics in Kosovo and Afghanistan, see David Rieff, *A Bed for the Night* (New York: Simon & Schuster, 2002). On Bosnia, see Ian Smilie, ed., *Patronage or Partnership: Local Capacity-Building in Humanitarian Crises* (Bloomfield, Conn.: Kumarian Press, 2001).
54. See Cooley and Ron, "NGO Scramble," 28–31. Also see Sarah Kenyon Lischer, "Collateral Damage: Humanitarian Assistance as a Cause of Conflict," *International Security* 28 (2003): 79–109.

ORDER, GOVERNANCE, AND HIERARCHY IN
INTERNATIONAL POLITICS

Overall, this chapter has argued that globalization poses a broader theoretical challenge to constructivist theory than is normally acknowledged. Nonstate actors and deterritorializing processes may embody new norms and identities spawned by globalization, but their organizational dynamics can and should be subjected to rationalist analysis. In many cases, such explanations seem to be relatively straightforward: states prefer high credit ratings because it saves them money, NGOs prefer to obtain contracts in order to fund their operations, and microstates prefer to maintain secrecy over their banking practices in order to retain customers and attract offshore revenue streams away from more regulated nation-states. Such organizational behaviors are not predicated on any particular form of identity.

There is an irony here. At a time when ideational approaches are increasingly challenging rationalist paradigms, various modes of public and private authority in the international system are integrating global functions and organizing political governance in a manner that is highly systematic, differentiated, and, yes, rationalized. Accordingly, the constructivist analytical challenge to rationalist theory is occurring precisely at a time when rationalism's analytical assumptions increasingly reflect the organizational environment facing major political actors in the international system. Of course, there is some room for reconciling these approaches. While more sociological approaches can explain the origins of the various ideologies, normative assumptions, identities, and legal categories that underpin many contemporary institutions of global governance, rationalist theories such as the firm-type model are better suited to explaining their organizational dynamics and the immediate incentive structures that drive their behavior.

Certainly, the firm-type model presented in this study is one of many possible theories. It is not a comprehensive guide to the study of states, occupied peripheries, or empires, nor does it address the origins of these polities or even offer explanations for much of the dynamics observable in them. But it does suggest that constructivist theory can no longer rest on identifying nonstate forms of political organization in the international system and then assigning to these phenomena a distinct type of ideational order or normative character. Just as realist theories and their attention to international power distribution fail to explain many important issues and questions in the study of international politics, so, too, the constructivist fixation on the ideational distinctness of different political actors prevents us from making connections among empirical trends and puzzles (old and new) in the international system. Empires, states, and military occupations of various historical eras and identities have faced common dilemmas of organization and governance that are not always reducible to identity-based variables.

Constructivists will surely respond that the formulation presented here is stylized and that identity, legitimacy, purpose, and ideology are all elements essential to understanding the dynamics of hierarchy and international politics. They are not alone. Political leaders and decision makers with ideational purposes continue to be seduced by the perceived transformative power of hierarchy while they ignore the organizational challenges and political consequences that hierarchical governance necessarily brings. From finance ministers who believe that imposing a currency board will cure their ailing economy to policymakers in hegemonic states who believe that promoting institutional change in distant peripheries is simply a function of projecting superior military power and introducing liberal values, the inevitable organizational difficulties of hierarchy are overlooked too often in the interest of pursuing grand ideas, dogged ideological assumptions, and plain old wishful thinking.

The dual organizational logics of hierarchy cannot be overcome easily. However, they can be clarified and understood more broadly. Indeed, many of these lessons seem to be intuitively internalized by states and organizations although they are rarely articulated publicly. For example, when the United States needs to accomplish a sensitive low-intensity military operation, it relies on the functional skill and expertise of Special Forces that report almost directly to the executive. It would seem very odd indeed, if the United States were to contract out such critical security operations rather than rely on in-house capacity and U-form organization. Yet, the M-form contracting model is precisely the way that the United States has chosen to reconstruct Iraq and Afghanistan, states whose future successful transformation—as repeatedly admitted by America's own policymakers—have become the centerpieces of current American foreign policy and security strategy. Such important tasks should not be organized so poorly.

More broadly, this book suggests that both scholars of international politics and policymakers need to devote as much attention to the study of hierarchy and its nuances as they do the systemic condition of anarchy. Both groups tend to use hierarchy-related terms such as "empire" and "hegemony" rather loosely when they really wish to refer to the overseas exercise of power by a dominant state. Yet, the mere exercise of power or authority by a state does not necessarily make that action "imperial." These distinctions do matter. If we do not adequately understand the various manners in which these power projections are organized, delegated, and administered, we will surely lack the analytical capacity to properly understand their practical problems and their political consequences. Focusing more centrally on the politics of hierarchy also has the potential to identify the actors, processes, and institutions that are common across a broad range of regions and cultures, thus further allowing regional studies to integrate its nuanced insights and descriptions with the broader, comparative analytical objectives of the social sciences. Finally, the organizational theory of hierarchy presented here suggests that common analytical frameworks for hierarchical administration can be developed across the fields of management scholarship, institutional economics, organizational sociology, and political science. Surely, there are many additional insights that these fields can provide for each other.

The good news is that scholars have an increasingly formidable array of conceptual tools, methods, and techniques to understand the dynamics and diverse manifestations of hierarchy. Developing a common set of issues, approaches, and research agendas should remain a principal challenge for those interested not only in promoting global governance but also in improving its study.

INDEX

Note: Page numbers with an *f* indicate figures; those with a *t* indicate tables; those with an *n* indicate footnotes.